John Bickford Heard

National Christianity

Caesarism and Clericalism

John Bickford Heard

National Christianity
Caesarism and Clericalism

ISBN/EAN: 9783337026448

Printed in Europe, USA, Canada, Australia, Japan

Cover: Foto ©Lupo / pixelio.de

More available books at **www.hansebooks.com**

NATIONAL CHRISTIANITY
OR
CÆSARISM AND CLERICALISM

A

PRINTED BY W. SPEAIGHT AND SONS,
FETTER LANE, LONDON.

NATIONAL CHRISTIANITY

OR

CÆSARISM AND CLERICALISM

BY THE

REV. J. B. HEARD, M.A.

*Of Caius College, Cambridge, and late Vicar of Bilton, Harrogate.
Author of " The Tripartite Nature," &c., &c., &c.*

LONDON
LONGMANS, GREEN, AND CO.
1877

TO THE READER.

As this Work has not been written in support of any special Sectarian views, nor with any animus against what is good in the Church of England, it is hoped it will be read without prejudice by the supporters of pure religion in the Established as well as the Free Churches.

PREFACE.

In dealing with the question of National Churches, one is struck with the difficulty of approaching such a subject with a perfectly unprejudiced mind. If ever there was need of attending to Dr. Johnson's advice, and "clearing the mind of cant," it is on a topic like this. The Christian world is divided into two camps on this subject. There are those who are opposed to any relation of the Church to the State, and who see in this connection only another form of "worldliness." Again, there are those who desire to maintain this connection, and who, while admitting the worldliness resulting from it, refer it to other causes, or to certain local peculiarities not inseparable from the institution itself. As long as men reason in this way, setting out with certain prepossessions for or against the connection of Church and State, and drawing conclusions perfectly logical from these arbitrary prepossessions, it is impossible to advance the cause of truth and charity. Logic, in fact, is a lever so irresistible, that it only wants a fulcrum of self-interest with which to move the world. This explains why it is that dogmatic statements on either side have such little weight. Either we admit the premises, and the conclusion then becomes the veriest truism ; or we deny them, and then there is no common ground on which to join issue.

Discarding, then, the dogmatic method, which leaves us exactly where it finds us, we propose to look at the question in the light of history and experience. The growth of National Churches took its rise from the desire felt from the first to develop Christianity into a dogmatic and organised system of religion such as the world could understand, and which the governing classes could make use of as an instrument for holding society together. As the new religion began to spread at the time when the Roman Empire was falling to pieces, it opportunely offered itself for such a purpose. But it could not have been made use of as an instrument of government unless it had first developed into a sacerdotal system. The history of that first corruption is instructive. It had not long taken root in Imperial Rome before it renounced the primitive type of the Church. Instead of the autonomy of the Churches, those little religious republics federated more or less loosely together like the Greek Commonwealths ; it adopted the Roman and imperial idea of unity under a form of diocesan monarchy. It was at this stage of its development that Christianity offered itself to a crafty usurper, Constantine, as an instrument for cementing his ill-gotten political power ; and, by declaring himself the *patronus Ecclesiæ*, and the *malleus hæreticorum*, he secured a fresh lease of existence to the declining Roman Empire. At what a cost to Christianity and the world this Byzantine union of Church and State was effected, history has very imperfectly described. Nothing, it is said, succeeds like success; and hence it is that Constantine's assumption of a certain primacy over the Church was condoned. But we must not forget the important fact that unless it had been already corrupt it could not have been adopted by Constantine at all. But the fact is, that one form of corruption led on to another. Clericalism, which took its rise when Cyprian asserted the monarchical theory of Church government, culminated in Cæsarism as soon as the Emperor Constantine had discovered that Christianity could be employed as an engine of State. Thus it is that since that fatal time, as Dante described the *funesta dote*, its funeral dower of State dignity, Erastianism and Ecclesiasticism have been the two poles between which all National Churches have ever since oscillated. During the Middle Ages we find the Church claiming a supremacy over the State; and since the Reformation, generally speaking, the State has retaliated, and has asserted its supremacy over the Church.

Thus it is that the struggle of these two principles of Cæsarism and Clericalism is the true key to Church history, and we may trace the various corruptions of Christianity to the way in which these two opposing tendencies have held their ground in the Church. There is no prospect of either of these evils expelling the other, nor should we even desire it. It appears, on the contrary, that the one evil is permitted by God to counteract and hold the other in check. Certain it is that as the first decline of Christianity from the primitive standard of purity was marked by the rise and extension of these two tendencies, so its recovery will depend on our being able to deal simultaneously, if possible, a death blow at these twin evils. Together they grew and together they must perish if the Church is ever to recover her primitive purity and return to the simplicity of the truth as it is in Jesus.

In confirmation of these views, we remark that a Free Church in a Free State is a dream and a delusion unless we can put down and abolish the hierarchical as well as the Erastian principle. As M. de Laveleye remarks, in a recent article on the subject, "Such a system as the Cavour principle is only good for Protestant countries. In a Catholic country it conducts directly to the enslavement of the State and the absolute domination of the Pope, as is to be seen in Belgium. The State professes to ignore the Church and not to concern itself with it. But the Church only admits the system provisionally, and with a view of drawing from it the means of establishing its own power." Statesmen are coming to see that a Free Church and a Free State are incompatible if the so-called "Free Church," as soon as it is let loose from the bonds of State, is worked as a sacerdotal system, resting on a basis of dogmatic and traditional authority solely, and opposing liberty of conscience and private judgment. How a Free State is to deal with those Churches which are sacerdotally organised, and are, therefore, intolerant of all others not so organised, is a problem which we need not discuss in this place. But we notice it here in order to point out that the question of Disestablishment is not so simple as some suppose. To set the Church free from State control and patronage is only one-half of our task. We must also endeavour to free the laity from the bondage of subjection to clerical authority. But it may be said that the people will free themselves as soon as the Church is disestablished. This may be so, and in a Protestant country such as ours is, this would probably be the case in the long run. Still we adhere to the opinion that the two stages of liberation must go on together. Disestablishment will liberate the Church from Cæsarism only; disendowment, or, which comes to the same thing, the rigid application in every case of the voluntary principle, must follow, in order to liberate the laity as well from Clericalism.

It is not difficult to show from history that as these two corruptions of Christianity arose at the same time and from similar causes, so they must decline together and in the same way. We shall point out in the first place what the Church was intended to be—her primitive and ideal state, as seen in the Acts of the Apostles and in the visions of the Apocalypse. We shall then go on to describe what she has fallen to; and, in the third place, go on to trace the stages by which she has declined from her primitive and ideal to her present and actual state. In dealing with this question, it is only fair, however, to the other side to show that there was much to be said in excuse for those who, at the time of the Reformation, still clung to the theory of National Churches, or, in other words, to the Old Testament plan of a theocratic community, in which Church and State are only the same society in its two aspects as a civil and religious community. It is only a noble delusion that can captivate and fascinate a noble mind. A theory such as that, on which Calvin and Hooker, Luther and Knox, were substantially agreed, must have had much to commend it. It is mere prejudice not to admit this. We know that this theory of the union, or rather fusion, of Church and State was not so much as questioned till the middle of the seventeenth century, and then only timidly and tentatively by a few sectaries who were regarded as fanatics and visionaries for disputing it. But the paradoxes of one age become the commonplaces of another, and so in our day the counter theory of the entire separation of Church and State is slowly but surely gaining ground. It is admitted on all sides that it is the theory of the future. But how to deal with existing institutions, how to lift society off from the one plane of theocratic ideas, and to set it on the new plane of religious neutrality on the part of the State, this is the problem which is now exercising thoughtful minds in all directions.

The aim, then, of this essay will be to point out that we have at last reached a state of things in this country in which continued compromise is impossible. We have come to the conclusion that in England at present the evils of a State Church largely outweigh any compensating advantages. We shall accordingly devote a chapter or two to this branch of the subject. We shall cast up as fairly as we can the *pros* and *cons* of State connection, and then strike the balance simply from a utilitarian point of view. If, as may be shown, the evils on the whole preponderate over the benefits, if the result of the connection is felt to be that instead of making the State spiritual it rather tends to make the Church worldly, then the conclusion must follow that the time has gone by for leaving the Establishment intact under the hope that it will reform itself. It will become the duty of Christian men in our day not merely to content themselves with withdrawing from the State Church into little spiritual societies of their own, as they did two centuries ago. We are bound to carry the question one step farther than our Puritan forefathers, and to consummate the triumph of religious liberty by obtaining religious equality as well. We must labour to remove those invidious preferences which the State still shows to one sect of Christians over another in this country.

We have thus laid down the outlines of the argument. It must be left to others to say whether such an argument commends itself to their judgment, and will help to advance those foundation truths of the Gospel which are dearer to all real Christians than any sect or party, theory or system, of Church government. We may say of ourselves that, though theoretically opposed to Establishments, we submitted to the bonds of the Act of Uniformity and the Royal supremacy, those two pillars on which our English Establishment rests, so long as we conscientiously could. But when we found that this so-called National Church has been for years past rapidly degenerating into a sacerdotal sect, we felt convinced that the time to protest had come. We find that the National Church is honeycombed with unbelief through the action of Erastianism and Ecclesiasticism; and, seeing no remedy for these evils but one, we take this opportunity of laying before the public a dispassionate statement of our reasons for desiring Disestablishment. This book, in a word, is an answer to Mr. Gladstone's ominous query, "Is the Church of England worth preserving?"

TABLE OF CONTENTS.

                                                            PAGE

PREFACE v

INTRODUCTION.

The decline of the Church from the primitive standard of purity traced to its source xvii

CHAPTER I.

THE CHURCH AS IT WAS INTENDED TO BE.

The Church was founded as an embodiment of the "Kingdom of Heaven." When it lost this idea of the "Kingdom," and was transformed into a hierarchy, it rapidly declined 1

CHAPTER II.

THE MYTH-MAKING AGE OF CHURCH HISTORY.

Myth and legend contrasted. No legendary distortion of facts possible, unless a mythical corruption of its idea has already prevailed 20

CHAPTER III.

THE THREE TEMPTATIONS OF THE CHURCH.

A comparison between the three temptations of Christ and those by which the Church has been assailed—Bread, or Endowment; the kingdoms of this world, or Establishment; and the pinnacle of the temple, or the Papal supremacy 40

CHAPTER IV.
CLERICALISM LEADS TO CÆSARISM.

The connection between a Church State and a State Church—the constant tendency of the one form to pass into the other 63

CHAPTER V.
ENDOWMENT AND ESTABLISHMENT.

Churches, as they decline in purity, fall back on endowments as a machinery to keep up the original momentum. This leads in the course of time to their establishment, and so to their subjection to the State 82

CHAPTER VI.
THE FREE CHURCH IN A FREE STATE THEORY.

Count Cavour's principle criticised. It is a question-begging phrase, and must fail unless the sacerdotal principle be first broken down 97

CHAPTER VII.
THE THREE EVILS OF THE ENGLISH ESTABLISHMENT.

Prelacy, Patronage, Purchase: its three great corruptions . 109

CHAPTER VIII.
SCEPTICISM AND SUPERSTITION.

These two developments of Ritualism invariably go together 132

CHAPTER IX.
TOLERATION.

History of the rise and growth of ideas of toleration . . 150

CHAPTER X.

CHURCH DEFENCE—ITS ARGUMENTS.

The strength of the attack measured by that of the defence. The argument stated that since the Church was never formally established and endowed by the State it cannot be disestablished and disendowed . . . 173

CHAPTER XI.

THE CHURCH IN DANGER.

This cry and its meaning dissected. It is the temporalities which are attacked, hence the alarm 205

CHAPTER XII.

REFORM, NOT REVOLUTION.

The argument of the Evangelical party, that we should "stand by the ship" and "put down Ritualism," considered 221

CHAPTER XIII.

THE CONSERVATIVE ARGUMENT.

No one would think now-a-days of setting up an Establishment; but finding one in existence we are bound to preserve it 242

CHAPTER XIV.

CONCLUDING REFLECTIONS.

Summary of arguments. The true road to the ultimate reunion of Christendom lies in the return to primitive simplicity as well of doctrine as of discipline . . . 256

INTRODUCTION.

It is impossible to consider the condition of the Church in general, or of any of the Churches in particular, without feeling that it is little less than chaotic. It may be the chaos which precedes a new cosmos, but of the fact of this fallen and disordered state there cannot be a second opinion. To apply the remedy we must first know the disease. To know what the Church has fallen from, we must first ascertain what she was intended to be. If she has failed in her mission, it must be on account of some leaven of worldliness, some secret principle of evil, hidden in her constitution from the very first, and which led to an early falling away from the primitive standard. We propose, therefore, to deal with the question in hand under the three following heads :—

 I. What the Church was intended to be.

 II. What she has actually become.

 III. The stages by which she descended from her ideal to her present actual state.

The method which we purpose to follow is thus seen to be that on which medical science has made such advances in modern times. It took a long time before it was understood that the laws of disease can only be determined by first knowing the laws of health, and for this reason medicine was an unprogressive science almost down to our day. It was torn between contending sects of dogmatists and empirics, between those who had a Catholicon or universal remedy for all ailments, and the compounding chemists who had as many drugs as there were symptoms of the disease. Now, at least, we know better than to attack the symptoms in this way, and waste time on the outworks of the fortress. We ascertain, in the first place, the laws of health, and from the normal proceed to the abnormal. It is in the same order that we should trace the corruptions of the Church to their source. We should determine, in the first place, what the Church was intended to be, and then consider what she has actually become. The result of this comparison between the ideal and the actual—in other words, from her healthy and unhealthy condition—will suggest to us what the disease is in itself, and where its seat lies.

I. With regard to the first question, the Church of Christ was intended to become the manifestation of the kingdom of God among men. In the words of the Lord's Prayer, God's will was to be done on earth as in heaven. The Church was to be the manifestation of those principles in their operation among men, a spectacle which, according to the apostle (Eph. iii. 10), would display even to the principalities and powers in heavenly places, by the Church, the manifold wisdom of God. Thus the kingdom of God and the Church of Christ are related to each other as a force and its embodiment; or as a motive power and the machine by which it acts. It is instructive here to remark that

Christ, during His ministry on earth, dwelt almost exclusively on the kingdom of God. All His parables are illustrations of this; His preaching was that the kingdom of heaven was at hand. The apostles, on the other hand, after the Holy Ghost had been given, and a society formed to embody and set forth these principles, go on to describe the Church and assume its existence. When Christ was on earth the Church was not yet formed,—it was taken, as we may so say, as Eve was, from the pierced side of the sleeping Adam. It has been thus bought by His blood that He might present it to Himself, a glorious Church, not having spot, or wrinkle, or any such thing. The Church is thus constituted as a society to set forth the hidden Saviour to men. In this sense it is His Body, the fulness of Him, that filleth all in all. It embodies His hidden spirit, and manifests the mind of Christ among men in the same way that Christ, the Eternal Word, embodies and manifests the will of God in the worlds above.

II. We have only to glance at this, her ideal state, to see how far short her actual state is from it. So far from the kingdom of God having been set up on earth, the Church, as a society, has become one of the kingdoms of this world. She has been regulated by its principles, and has submitted to its rules of action. In defiance (Luke xxii. 25) of her Master's expressed command, she has organised herself as a hierarchy with gradations of rank, forgetting that he who would be chief, must first be servant of all. It is almost a profane parody of this great truth, that the head of the most despotic hierarchy in the world should call himself *servus servorum Dei*. It is thus with a sort of pride which apes humility he assumes by implication one of the titles of Him who came not to be ministered to but to minister, and who, in proof of this, took a towel and girded Himself, and washed His disciples' feet. Even this function of Christ has been turned into a sort of ostentatious badge of kingship on the part of Popes and Emperors, the most Christian King of Spain and His Apostolic Majesty of Austria vieing with the Pope in thus assuming to do the works of Christ, without having caught any of the spirit in which those works were done.

III. This leads us, in the third place, to ascertain what the cause of corruption is, by comparing the ideal with the actual state of the Church. The corruption entered, as we have seen, with the hierarchical principle —in other words, from forgetting that the kingdom of heaven is not governed by gradations of rank, as in the kingdoms of this world. Passing out of the stage of little religious republics or commonwealths, such as the apostles founded in Athens, Corinth, Ephesus, and elsewhere, the Gospel, when it reached Rome, soon fell under the influence of the Roman idea of a great centralised Monarchy. It thus soon lost its simplicity, and by the age of Cyprian the Monarchical principle had overshadowed the Republican; organisation took the place of life, uniformity of unity, and thus the way was prepared for its being converted into a national cult by Constantine, and treated as a department of State. Its bishops became prelates—a term of office borrowed from the Byzantine Empire—their dioceses corresponded to the civil divisions of the Empire, and so it entered on that stage of subjection of the ecclesiastical to the civil supremacy which Döllinger has aptly described as Byzantinism.

Its history ever since is little else than the conflict between the two opposite tyrannies of Clericalism and Cæsarism. During the Middle Ages, the Pope and the Emperor were the respective champions of these two principles; nor did the Reformation put an end to this long conflict, as some Protestants fondly imagine. It only asserted the royal supremacy over the sacerdotal, which was a clear gain on the whole for the liberties of the Church and the world, but a gain which was obtained by setting up one tyranny to check another. Ever since, and in the majority of cases, as far as Europe is concerned, the Church has been locked in the fatal embrace of the State. The two tendencies known as Erastianism and Ecclesiasticism have been struggling ever since in the womb of modern society, like the twins Esau and Jacob, and the only remedy for this unnatural conflict is the birth of a State which shall be purely secular, and of a Church which shall be purely spiritual. The so-called National Churches of the Reformation have, without an exception, failed to reach this standard of a purely spiritual society. It was impossible, from the nature of the case, that they should do so. Their temporalities as such dragged them down into a fatal alliance with the Civil Power. The best and purest of these reformed Churches, that of Scotland, for instance, however faithful her protest against Erastianism, has had to admit, by the secession of 1843, that she was in a false position. Her nationalism was little else than the Protestant counterpart of Ultramontanism, the position, namely, that while it was the duty of the Civil Power to cherish and protect her, she, on the other hand, had no reciprocal duties to that Civil Power. The Free Church of Scotland is thus unlearning, under Voluntaryism, the mistaken theories of the seventeenth century. She is slowly reaching the truth that all endowed Churches are Establishments in the germ, and partake of the nature of Establishments. Thus Clericalism and Cæsarism are departures from the simplicity of the Gospel which exist as the counterpart the one of the other. They stand or fall together, and the road to a true and final reform lies in abandoning both principles alike.

Our purpose, then, is to point out the evil, under the conviction that the remedy will suggest itself. Thus a mere separation of Church and State by Act of Parliament, though a step in the right direction, is not enough. It is conceivable, indeed, that the first result of such a separation might be, as we see is the case with Ultramontanism on the Continent, to set up a hierarchical society more arrogant and intolerant than ever. Cavour's maxim of a "Free Church in a Free State" is thus only a plausible sophism, unless we are careful to define what we mean by a Free Church and a Free State. If we mean a Church like the Roman hierarchy in Italy, or such as the Disestablished Church in England might become, then we can understand why some thoughtful men hesitate to consent to this arrangement. To use the argument of Sir John Lubbock, they say that of two evils the present is the least; they prefer, in other words, Cæsarism to Clericalism. But this need not be so. Let a Free Church only be understood in the sense of a spiritual society as the kingdom of God, which "is not meat and drink but righteousness and joy and peace in the Holy Ghost;" let this society have the minimum of organisation and the maximum of free individual life; let its only law be love to Christ, and its only bond be that of "charity, which is the bond of perfectness" (Col. iii. 14); and then such a Free Church never can come into collision with the powers that be. It will owe no man anything but to love one another. We are aware that we are speaking parables to those whose ideas of religion are only legal, and who take a regulative view of religion. But for those who have risen beyond these Old Testament conceptions, and who have caught a glimpse of the true idea of the kingdom of God among men, such a conception of a Free Church in a Free State will not seem a mere chimera. They will see in the Church of Christ an embodiment of the ideal or millennial state of society—an ideal, it is true, which we have never reached as yet, but which one of the seven angels which had the seven vials full of the seven last plagues showed to St. John, when he said, " Come hither, and I will show thee the bride, the Lamb's wife." As yet that Church is invisible. The new and holy Jerusalem has not yet descended from heaven as a bride adorned for her bridegroom. Like her Lord, at present, she is within the veil, and will not be fully manifested till His appearing. But all questions of Church reform must lead up to this consummation, or they are worse than useless. Then, and then only, will the Hooker ideal of a Church and State, which are only different names for the same thing, become actual and possible. For the present it is better, because truer to fact, that we should recognise the contrast between the Church and the world—a contrast which we can no more bridge over by any theory of alliance or concomitance than we can reconcile the contrast between flesh and spirit. At present, these are contrary the one to the other, and he is the best Christian as well as the wisest statesman who accepts the facts as they are, and works on towards the day of the restitution of all things, when the great cry shall be heard, " the kingdoms of this world have become the kingdoms of our Lord and of His Christ."

I propose, then, to trace the degeneracy of the Church to its source, in the fact of its failing to uphold this contrast between the kingdom of heaven and the kingdoms of this world. The only organisation which should have been recognised by the Church was that suggested by the text, " Neither be ye called masters, for one is your Master, even Christ." Instead of that, it fell under the hierarchical principle as soon as it reached Rome, and the Church, even before it was established under Constantine, became a weak copy of the monarchical forms of the Empire. Can we wonder that it soon degenerated into a centralised despotism? From Cyprian to Hildebrand there is but one step, and Constantine helped it to take that step. That was a splendid sophism which misled so holy and pure a nature as that of Richard Hooker, the author of the " Ecclesiastical Polity." Relying on an analogy from the heavenly hierarchy, for which there is nothing whatever in Scripture, but a good deal in the writings of the pseudo-Dionysius, the Areopagite, he conceived of the Church as a polity, with orders and gradations of rank and office corresponding, each to each, to the ranks and degrees of men in civil life. The Church was thus supposed to be the double of the State—the one being the nation in its relation to man, and the other in its relation Godward. It is a noble theory as wrought out in his eloquent pages, and prefaced by one of the sublimest impersonations of law which ever came from an uninspired pen. But the illusions of genius are dangerous in proportion, as they can be so easily twisted into chains for fettering free thought and enforcing a spiritual despotism. But for Hooker a Laud would have been impossible. It is another illustration of the old maxim, *corruptio optimi pessima.* On this account, if we would guard truth, we must jealously watch the first approaches of error. It is too late to strike at the hierarchical principle when it has developed into some monstrous form of arrogance or impiety in a Hildebrand or a Borgia; we must look for the beginnings of the evil when the mystery of iniquity is already to be seen in the germ. The danger of dallying with Church principles, as they are commonly called, and drawing the line at some arbitrary point somewhere between the fourth and the fourteenth century, has been often pointed out. It reminds us of the story of a man who kept some tiger's whelps, whom he treated as playmates, until one day, when he was asleep, one of the cubs licked his hand till it had drawn blood, on which the man awoke, saw his danger, and at once killed his former playmate. The Anglican and Old Catholic theory of religion both labour under this fatal weakness, and there is something in it which falls in with and flatters one of our national defects—namely, our love of compromise and dislike of a rigorous logical theory, whether on politics or religion.

But surely Christianity can be either nothing at all, or it is something more than an improved type of Judaism, with its hierocracy (to use Ewald's term, which is more expressive than theocracy) modernised and developed. The rule of Christ, that a tree is known by its fruits, is applicable to this as to other things. How can we expect spiritual fruits from a carnal Judaical institution? Men do not gather grapes of thorns, or figs of thistles. No reform, then, of the Church is worth much which does not go down to this root-principle of the hierarchy. Here was the germ of all the apostacy, which began long before Constantine, and which has lasted down long after the Reformation. It is this which has infected the Reformed Churches and made their testimony to the truth as it is in Jesus almost as feeble and powerless as that of the pre-Reformation Church itself. It is, moreover, our failure to see this which makes the separation of Church and State on the Cavour maxim of a Free Church in a Free State a mockery, a delusion, and a snare. Disestablishment will only be another name for re-Establishment, if the Church is to set up for itself again as an organised hierarchy. If disendowed to-day, it will be re-endowed to-morrow, if the roots of sacerdotalism are left in the soil. Like Nebuchadnezzar's tree cut down to a stump, and with a band of iron and brass round it, it will spring up again if its roots are to be left in the ground, and to be wet with the dews of heaven. Cæsarism, indeed, and Clericalism go together. The one evil calls out the other into existence, and perhaps in the providence of God it is intended that Cæsarism should act as a check to Clericalism. The mere political Nonconformist, then, who can see only the evils of Cæsarism, and calls out for Disestablishment, pure and simple, as the panacea for all the corruptions of the Church, might find himself mistaken if he had his wishes, and could carry his point at one sweep. The right plan is to seek to abate both forms of corruption simultaneously. We must go back on the work of our Protestant reformers of the sixteenth century more thoroughly, and carry out their principles still more trenchantly than they were willing or able to do. They could not see, as we now do, that the spiritual Babylon is a tree like that of Nebuchadnezzar's dream. It is not enough to "hew down the tree, cut off his branches, shake off his leaves, and scatter his fruit," if the "stump of his roots is left in the earth." On this account we are of opinion that no half reforms, and no mere political *coup d'église*, like that which disestablished the Irish Church, is enough. It may be that the loss of a political status—in other words, the decline of Cæsarism—may lead to the decline of Clericalism. But it is quite possible, as we see in the case of modern Ultramontanism, that Clericalism may revive on the ruins of Cæsarism, and in that case it is better to leave Erastianism untouched for the present as the natural check to Ecclesiasticism. The two counteracting forces having grown up together may be left to decline together. On this question of detail men may differ; but the point at present is to see where the root of the evil lies, so that we may act on the safe Baconian rule, that we cannot apply the remedy till we have first explored the seat of the disease. It is within these limits, therefore, that our inquiry proceeds, and to this point our argument leads up.

CÆSARISM AND CLERICALISM.

CHAPTER I.

THE CHURCH AS IT WAS INTENDED TO BE.

OUR first inquiry is, what the Church was intended to be; and to understand this we must have some conception of the meaning of the expression, "the kingdom of God." If we turn to the New Testament we find that our Lord's teaching was almost entirely concerning the kingdom of heaven. Only once or twice, and that incidentally, with reference to that kingdom, does He refer to an *ecclesia* or society which was to exhibit and embody these inward principles. The difference between the preaching of John and of Jesus was this—that the one proclaimed that the kingdom of heaven was at hand, the other that the kingdom of heaven was already among them, that it was suffering violence, and that the violent took it by force. At the same time He added, as a warning against carnal conceptions and Judaising ideas of the Messiah, that this kingdom came not with observation or outward pomp. It was not, Lo here, or, Lo there, but it was an internal and spiritual kingdom; as the Apostle Paul elsewhere explains, it was not meat and drink—*i.e.*, a repetition of Jewish ritual and ceremonial observances—

but righteousness and joy, and peace in the Holy Ghost.

Christ came, then, to set up the true kingdom of God upon earth. By this we mean, that He came to inculcate certain principles, and to form a society of which these principles were to become the animating motive. In the true order of thought, the idea of the kingdom of God comes before that of the Church; whereas in our popular teaching, and even among devout people, who ought to know better, it is precisely the reverse. They hold that, in some sense, Christ has planted a Church on earth—a body of believers, that is, in the doctrines which He taught, and in the miracles which He wrought. They also hold that this Church, which is militant now on earth, will be by-and-by triumphant, and that Christ's kingdom will only then have come when the kingdoms of this world shall have become the kingdoms of our Lord and of His Christ. They thus reason, so to speak, preposterously. They put the last first, and the first last. They begin with the Church, whereas the inspired writer of the book which is called the Acts of the Apostles, strikes a different note in the opening verses of that narrative, which is a continuation of the Gospel history. He regards it as the evangel of the Lord Christ from heaven, as the former treatise was the evangel of the Son of Man on earth. To the question of the disciples still under bondage to Jewish ideas, "Lord, wilt Thou at this time restore the kingdom to Israel?" Christ distinctly tells them that it is not a question of times and seasons at all. The kingdom of God was to begin as soon as they were endued with power from on high, and then they should see that kingdom take shape in a new and spiritual society, utterly unlike any which they had before either seen or looked for. Not more than ten days after this the kingdom of God began. It was set up in the hearts of a few disciples—a hundred and twenty in all—who were assembled together in one place, and who were of one heart. There was first *unum cor*, and only afterwards *una via*. Unity produced uniformity, not in the reverse order, as we too often look for the blessing. The internal led to the external, not the reverse. The Church had no other meaning than this as the embodiment of those spiritual principles which the apostle sums up as " Christ in you the hope of glory." There would be no need for any such society at all if the principles of that kingdom had been already understood among men.* But they were not. The Jewish Church had utterly failed to embody the true idea of the kingdom of God among men. Instead of a kingdom of priests—*i.e.*, a race of men dedicated to the service of God—Israel was, at best, nothing more than a race of religionists, holding Monotheism, it is true, as other races clung to Polytheism, but in little else contrasted with the nations around them. The Jewish Church had failed because it was a theocracy in name, while, in reality, it was only a hierocracy. They had fallen more or less under the caste system, common to Egypt, India, and other Oriental nations. There was a warrior caste and a priestly caste, and underneath these a degraded mass of the common people, to whom no particular

* For some truly suggestive thoughts as to the inner meaning of the Book of the Acts of the Apostles, see Baumgarten on the Acts—by far the most suggestive Commentary on this subject which we can refer to.

functions were assigned, and whose only duty it was to obey their superiors in Church and State. As has been often remarked (by no one better than the late J. S. Mill, in his treatise on Liberty), if it had not been for the prophets, who were of no caste at all, but were extraordinary men, raised up to fulfil an extraordinary mission, the light would have died out altogether in Israel. As it was, God kept the sacred fire alight by a succession of prophets, irregular and informal, and whose only mark of distinction was that they wandered about in sheep skins and goat skins, being destitute, afflicted, tormented,—

> "Unasked their toil, ungrateful their advice,
> Starving their gains, and martyrdom their price."

The Jewish Church thus failed to see that the Church was intended to embody the kingdom. Let us turn now to the Gentiles, and see how far they, too, have failed. There is no doubt as to what the early Church was designed to be. To a great extent, in the apostles' day, at least, it came up to this glorious ideal. We find in the earliest times of all, little communities of believers planted out in the world, in it but not of it. These societies were in no sense called out from the world to form a new institution, which we describe as the Church. This is the mistake of ecclesiastical historians. It came to this, as a matter of fact. As early as Cyprian's and Tertullian's days, the Church became a visible community, already in dangerous rivalry with the Empire—a secret society, which the Empire could neither disband nor mould to its purposes. Hence the persecutions of the early Church arose from this suspicion—not in every case ill-founded

—that the Church was a conspiracy against the Empire. This explains the fact that it was not the most careless, but the most politic and conscientious of the Cæsars— a Trajan, a Decius, and a Diocletian—that were the bitterest persecutors. But who was to blame for this? Church historians, taking the most rhetorical of the apologists, Tertullian, for their authority, throw the blame of this entirely on the Emperors. It was a case, they say, of Herod troubled at the birth of the child King, and slaying the infants, that so he might get rid of a possible rival. Herod's conduct was of a piece with his general character—it was only one more wanton act of a tyrant, of whom it was said, better be Herod's sow than his wife. But wanton cruelty was not the motive in the case, at least, of the later persecutions. Christians had begun to menace the tranquillity of the Empire. There is no disguising the fact, that besides the contrast which their lives presented to that of the Pagans, there was about them the air of a secret society. Hence the direction of the Apostle Peter, " Let no man suffer as an evil doer," was not so superfluous as it seems to us. The Christian Church had grown out of the Jewish, and it often displayed that tumultuous spirit which, according to Tacitus, led to the banishment of the Jews from Rome. There was always a danger of a spiritual principle degenerating into a carnal commandment. This was the very first corruption of Christianity, when the Church, instead of an embodiment of the kingdom, became a society having its own organisation—not a means to an end, but an end in itself. As soon as this corruption began, the Church had descended from its true ideal; it was no longer the visible symbol of an invisible principle. It had ceased to be the body of Christ, the fulness of Him that filleth all in all, and it had become instead a religious society, having in it, it is true, the ark of salvation for a decaying world; but it was no longer that which the German school of Roman Catholic mystics have feigned it to be—the continued incarnation of Christ upon earth, the embodiment in a human society of that Divine life whose fulness fills all in all.

We have only to glance at the meaning of the earliest name for the Church in order to see what it was intended to become. The Church, ἐκκλησία, was an assembly—a jury, as we should say—of citizens, called out for a particular purpose, and set apart from their fellow-citizens only for a definite term. True, there were tumultuous assemblies at times (Acts xix. 32), called by this name; but the intentional use of this term, as applied to a mere mob, is explained by the words of the town clerk, in verse 39: "It shall be inquired into (ἐν τῇ ἐννόμῳ εκκλησίᾳ), by a lawful *ecclesia*." As we should say in modern phrase, a commission of inquiry was to be instituted, a jury of citizens empannelled, and by their verdict the whole matter set right. An *ecclesia*, then, meant, not a permanent assembly, but a special commission to try and decide a special case. The use of the word, by the LXX., as equivalent to קָהָל, confirms this. This word, which we rightly render congregation, is the literal transcript of *ecclesia*. Both retain the same root idea of calling, קהל καλειν. The crier called out certain citizens to meet on a special commission. As long as they were set apart for these special duties they were exempted from every other. But the service was an occasional one, and, so far from implying separation from the general mass of the citizens, implied the very reverse. The congregations of Israel were, in the same manner, only committees, as we should say, of the House, who were to report to the House their proceedings. Sometimes, as in our Parliamentary practice, the whole House was in committee, and then, by a kind of fiction, it reported to itself its own proceedings. It is instructive to trace in this way the true idea of the Church, since otherwise we shall not be able to see the contrast between what the Church was intended to be, and what it afterwards became. Church history, as distinct from the world's history, is probably one of those "after-thoughts of theology" which have done so much mischief in setting men's minds on a wrong track in their search after truth. The primitive *ecclesia* was only a congregation, called at first out of the Israel after the flesh and then out of the Gentiles; but in both cases, whether of the circumcision or uncircumcision, the *ecclesia* was only a temporary arrangement or provision to meet a particular need. Our Lord's phrases have been distorted, and a non-natural meaning given to them, not merely by Roman Catholic divines, but by those also who should know better. His promise to Peter of the keys referred only to "the kingdom of heaven"—*i.e.*, to those spiritual truths of His Messiahship and mission. In connection with this kingdom there was to be an *ecclesia* for all time, which was to embody that truth and proclaim it; and this assembly was to be as imperishable as the principle which it affirmed. As a matter of fact, this has been so. Wherever the kingdom of heaven has been preached, and the keys have been used to unlock human hearts and to open doors barred by prejudice, there an assembly has not been wanting to carry on this work. Thus, the *ecclesia* is the subordinate, not the leading, thought in the Lord's argument. But it is an old failing of human nature to lose sight of what is essential in an argument, and seize on the accidental and secondary part of a truth. The keys have been made the symbol of authority, not of use—as if a key were designed for any other purpose but one. The key is not a symbol of kingly power, like a globe and sceptre; it is the symbol of the chamberlain's office. We find it applied by Isaiah to Shebna, the scribe. The kingdom of heaven, and the mode of opening it by the Gospel key of persuasion and preaching—this is the essential part of the Lord's promise to Peter. The accidental and secondary thought is, that an *ecclesia* should be built upon this truth, and that this *ecclesia* should have this one element of permanence in a world of change, that the gates of the grave should never open to receive it. The "society" of the kingdom was to be as perpetual as the kingdom itself; but its perpetuity is to be sought, not in any single type, but in the fact that, as one type died and disappeared, another was to take its place.

Thus, if we understand the *ecclesia* and its relation to the kingdom, all becomes clear which was before confused. We see, on the one hand, the relation of the Church to the kingdom is that of form to essence, or of a type to its idea. We see, on the other hand, that the relation of the Church to the world is one, not of separation, but of contact and of commixture. Augustine, more than any other divine, is responsible for drawing the contrast so sharply, and in such an external way, between the Church and the world. In this he carried out, only too faithfully, the hard and harsh contrasts of Tertullian on the same subject. The whole of the North African school—Cyprian, Tertullian, Augustine—are responsible for this externalising of the Church. It is the root error of all the Augustinian school, of the sacerdotal party in one extreme, of the Puritans in the other. The Alexandrian school did not fall into this error. They, on the contrary, laid stress on the opposite truth, that God was in the world as the *Logos* or Light of man before He became incarnate, as the true Light which lighteth every man that cometh into the world. They saw and seized the true idea of the philosophy of history. They did not set up a harsh external contrast, like that of Augustine, between two cities, the city of God and the city of the devil—a conception which, however assimilated since and absorbed in our traditional theology, is still, as to its origin, half Manichæan. This is Bossuet's philosophy of history, with his two distinct sections of sacred and profane history, to be read in parallel columns. But the Alexandrian school saw farther than this. They saw the education of the human race under tutors and governors, some Jewish, some Gentile, but all leading up to the fulness of times. Thus Clement of Alexandria taught that Plato was Moses Atticising, and that the Preparation of the Gospel was to be seen in Greek culture as well as in Jewish ritual.

All this bears on the question of the *Ecclesia*. It was

intended to be a little society in the world, and acting on it as leaven or salt does. It was to be incorporated, it is true, as a distinct society, but only in the same way, and to the same extent, as physicians, or painters, or musicians are into colleges' of medicine, or art, or music—for convenience' sake. But a college of surgeons exercising judicial functions, and claiming certain governmental rights, would be an "*imperium in imperio,*" which no well-governed State could tolerate. All weak governments tend to this internal decay by conniving at the *imperium in imperio* principle. It is the weak point in feudalism. We see how it brought the Merovingian dynasty to ruin in France, and it was this which the strongest of our Plantagenet kings stood out against with the true instinct of self-preservation. In the East it has brought Japan to the brink of ruin, and the first sign of the revival of the German Empire is that it applies its blood-and-iron policy to put down this Ultramontane attempt to assert that the Church is more than a *collegium,* and is an actual *imperium.* The assertion of Pope Gregory is the key to all Ultramontane pretensions: *Quod solus possit Papa uti imperialibus insigniis.* We have here, in the boldest form, the claim of supremacy put forth, and wherever this is asserted or implied, there the conflict between Church and State is inevitable. The remedy for this is not merely to assert the supremacy of the State *over* the Church, as the Reformation did; we must go further, and cut down ecclesiasticism to the roots by asserting that the Church is no *imperium* at all, but simply a *collegium*—a tolerated or chartered society, if you will, but still a society embodied for one definite purpose only, as a temperance society is to promote temperance, or an art society is to promote the interests of art.

The members of this society form an *ecclesia* called out, for the time being, from the mass of the citizens, but in no other way distinguished from them, much less separated from them. It is instructive to remark that as long as the Greek and Hebrew idea of the *ecclesia* as a mere club or congregation continued, no collision was possible between the Church and the Empire. On the contrary, as is well known, the Empire protected the infant Church from the persecution of its early enemy, the Jewish Church. In the language of the Apocalypse, the earth helped the woman. But as soon as Latin Christianity arose, and governmental ideas entered the Church in consequence of the Roman type of mind inclining to organisation and hierarchy, then, and not before, we hear of the Church becoming a mark of suspicion and dislike.

The early churches planted by the apostles were little commonwealths of believers organised on a republican type. The *ecclesia* was a club which met weekly to promote the spiritual concerns of its members. In many respects, the Jewish synagogue was the type according to which the early churches even among the Gentiles were organised. The bishop or presbyter —for the two terms denote the one, the rank or age the other, the office of the pastor—corresponded to the ruler of the synagogue. There were elders as well as deacons, to keep order and receive and distribute the alms. But the central principle of the service was didactic, not sacrificial. No part of the ritual suggested, in any way, the thought of the temple services. Altars there were none, priesthood was unknown; and phrases such as those which meet us in the fourth century, rhetorically used, it is true, and not dogmatical and precise, as to the dreadful sacrifice, and the sacred mysteries, and so forth, would have sounded strange in the ears of a Christian of the first century. The synagogue, in fact, and the *ecclesia*, were in early times convertible terms. In one memorable passage in the LXX. version (Prov. v. 14) the two words ἐκκλησία and συναγωγή, destined to have such divergent histories, to be representatives of such contrasted systems, appear in close juxtaposition. In the Jewish branch of the Christian Church συναγωγή was probably long used, as we find from James ii. 2, as the usual name for the place of meeting for believers. We have no reason to suppose that with the same word applied to the building the practices and ritual were not identical, or nearly so, allowing for the differences between those who believed that Jesus of Nazareth was the Messiah, and those who did not. The name synagogue, and with it the ideas which it connoted of doctrinal as opposed to sacrificial and symbolical teaching, passed over from the Jewish to the Gentile Church. We find the term applied to Christian meetings by Ignatius. Even in Clement of Alexandria the two words appear united, as they had done in the LXX., ἐπὶ τὴν συναγωγὴν ἐκκλησίας (*Strom.* vi. p. 633). Afterwards, when the chasm between Judaism and Christianity became wider, Christian writers began to contrast the meaning of the two words as if they had originally diverged from the very first, and endeavoured to show how the *ecclesia* excelled the synagogue. (See

Augustine's, Enar. in Ps. lxxx., and Trench's Synonyms of New Test. s. 1.) But this only proves that, by the middle of the fourth century, one form of Judaism had been replaced by another, and that the didactic element of the synagogue service had been supplanted by the sacrificial and priestly ideas of the temple service. So long as the temple was standing, and real animal sacrifices were offered on the brazen altar, the thought of an order of sacrificing priests would have struck the early Church as an irreverent parody of an old and worn-out ritual. The writer of the Epistle to the Hebrews remarks that this ritual of bloody sacrifices was decaying and waxing old, and ready to pass away. It was obsolete; the life and meaning had gone out of it even before the destruction of Jerusalem had formally put an end to it. "We have an altar," he adds—referring to Calvary, where Christ was crucified outside the camp—"of which they have no right to eat who serve the tabernacle." Selecting the annual sin-offering, not the daily burnt-offering, as the truest type of the sacrifice of Christ once and for ever, he goes on to show that as the sin-offering was burned outside the camp with every mark of abhorrence, so Christ, the despised and rejected of men, suffered without the gate, and he urges his half-hearted brethren to follow him outside the camp of Judaism. He calls on them to dissent from the unspiritual ceremonies of their old cult, and to remember that their only altar of sacrifice was that cross on which their Master was hung up in mockery and derision by the world. This altar of Calvary was the place where His followers could offer the only sacrifice of praise and thanksgiving which is acceptable to God, by becoming, like Him, crucified to the world and its affections and lusts. This is the only intelligible meaning of that much-disputed passage, and it is decisive, if we had no other proof of the ideas of the early Church, as to the absence of priest, of liturgy, or of ritual from the reasonable service of the first generation of believers.

As time went on, however, and as the Jewish temple and its animal sacrifices became a thing of the past, Paganism itself began to feel the same vitalising breath of truth which made animal sacrifices impossible any longer in Israel, since Christ had come, and by His death exhausted their meaning. It was only as late as the Theodosian code that sacrifices were formally abolished, but long before then they had fallen into disuse. Two centuries previous to the external triumph of Christianity, its internal spirit had triumphed. But the consequence was, that as the sacrificial ideas had died out of Judaism first, and afterwards even of Paganism, so they stole in, as it were, by a back door into the Christian Church. Priest and sacrifice suggest inseparable ideas—they stand or fall together. It is absurd to argue as if the sacrificial idea in the Christian Eucharist had brought in after it the priestly theory, or the converse. The truth is, that the two rise and fall together. The priest and the altar are inseparable as the soldier and his sword; the one without the other is utterly powerless. The writer of the Epistle to the Hebrews evidently argued in this way, and having demolished the pretensions of the Aaronic priesthood to be unchangeable in the first part of the epistle, he disposes of the claims of the ritual itself in the second part.

With such a document before them, and with the traditions of the synagogue service as contrasted with the temple, it was not easy for the early Church to go wrong. Indeed, it was not for nearly four centuries that the leaven of Judaising priestcraft began to work. The errors of the first three centuries are on speculative more than on ceremonial religion. Whatever the failings of the Alexandrian schools may have been in the direction of gnosis, it was not an enslavement to the senses, that unmanly, irrational sensualism which is one of the weak attempts of our age to bank out the encroaching tide of rationalism. The ideas of the early Church were moulded in an entirely different school from that of religious symbolism. The Jewish synagogue was only the Greek school of philosophy transformed and elevated. It was more Greek than Oriental in its root idea, which was instruction in righteousness by reading and exposition of the law and the prophets. Naturally, therefore, when the synagogue became a Christian Church, it reverted back at once to its elementary form. The school of one Tyrannus, in which Paul taught at Ephesus, could easily become a place of prayer and assembly for early believers. It needed no furniture or appliances to adapt it to the purposes of the new worship. One simple ceremony, the weekly breaking of bread by believers round a table, was all that marked Christianity as a new religion in the external sense of the word. But this weekly breaking of bread on the Lord's-day was not a strange and unfamiliar ceremony to the Gentile convert, if he happened to be one of Greek origin and familiar with Republican ideas of social life. There was the συσσιτία, or public meal, to which each member brought his contribution of food in a *sportula* or basket. This was one of the ties which helped to bind political life together in Greece. What more natural, therefore, than that it should be taken up into the new religious life of converts to Christianity? There was no solution of continuity thus between the secular and the spiritual. It was only the common meal taken up into a higher region, and given a sacramental or spiritual significance which had its meaning in Christ, the bread of life, the true and only food of the Divine in man. This was the primitive idea of the Communion, which was only obscured in later times when the priestly and sacrificial idea came in from Judaism to blur the simple conception of feeding on Christ, which the early Christians wished to set forth by this ceremony of breaking of bread.

To draw, then, these remarks to a conclusion, the earliest type of the Christian Church was that of the synagogue. Passing over into Greece, Christianity easily accommodated itself there to the Republican type of life. The simple worship and the common meal, the principle of local self-government, and the election of their own church officers by the whole congregation—these popular principles prevailed universally for a century or two, and only gave way at last to the Roman idea of an *imperium* in Church as well as in State. Long before Constantine had begun the subjection of the spiritual to the temporal, the way for that subjection had been prepared by setting up a hierarchy. If the Papacy was "the ghost of the Roman Empire sitting crowned upon its grave," as Hobbes described it, the

Episcopal ideas of Cyprian were anticipations of imperialism, as the Papacy was its afterthought. Byzantinism, or the entire subjection of the spiritual to the secular, would have been impossible if the worldly spirit of domination had not first invaded the Church. By lording it over God's heritage, bishops prepared the way for their own subjection to Cæsar. Thus it is that Cæsarism and Clericalism are inextricably mixed up together. By a fatal necessity, or rather, we should say, by a Providential arrangement, which calls out one form of corruption to check another, State interference in religion and a selfish grasping at power on the part of the ministers of religion go together. The remedy against the one is a reform of the other. To disestablish a Church which is hierarchically organised and endowed without at the same time disendowing it, would be to do a wrong to the lay members. It would be to take away the restraining power of the State, and leave the laity, as in Belgium, and to some extent in Italy, at the mercy of a sacerdotal caste. No State should expose any of its subjects to such a trial as this. Mr. Gladstone has justly remarked, in a recent article on "Italy and her Church," that the Italian Government made a serious mistake in surrendering the *Exequatur* and the *Placet*, and that in abandoning these rights the State committed a breach of trust as well as an act of folly. He illustrates this distinction by reference to the Irish Church Act. Before disestablishment the Irish bishops were appointed by the Crown, and when this right was surrendered, Parliament took care that the laity previously represented by the Crown should continue to be represented by a lay element in the Synod of the disestablished Church. In Italy, on the other hand, the patronage of the Crown has been handed over to the ecclesiastical authorities, without any reservation whatever on behalf of the people for whom the Crown held this patronage on trust. Cavour's maxim, therefore, of a free Church in a free State, has resulted in an *imperium in imperio*, which is always contrary to true policy. If Italy has not been torn in two owing to the machinations of the Ultramontane party acting without check or sense of responsibility on the parochial clergy, it has not been for want of will to work mischief on their part, or from the wisdom of politicians in warding off the consequences of their own mistake, but solely owing to that wonderful good fortune of Italy by which the very stars in their courses seem to have fought on her side. She has been shielded from the consequences of her own impolicy by her alliance with Germany, and by the inability of the Ultramontane party to strike her down by the aid of France. But it is none the less certain that it was a mistake to leave clericalism to work without the check of Cæsarism. If the restraining hand of the State were taken off, then the clerical power should have been reduced still further by disendowing the clergy and calling in the action of the laity. To some extent this is the case. The patronage of many parishes rests with the people; but this is far less the case than in Switzerland, and even in Germany, and to this extent the Church of Rome is more powerful than ever in Italy.

These considerations show us that the separation of Church and State is not to be effected without some regard to the order in which that connection grew up, or to the corruptions of the Church which almost necessitated this alliance. We shall return to this subject in a subsequent chapter. It is enough here to remark that the history of the Church is the best comment on its present condition. It could never have fallen into its present condition of bondage if it had kept itself pure from the taint of sacerdotalism and the organisation which this implies. But as soon as a professional priesthood arose, and this class began to grasp at exclusive power in the Church, it entered on a region in which it had to deal with the State first as an enemy, then as a rival, and, lastly, as an ally and partner in the spoil. In the long list of the captives found in the mystic Babylon at her overthrow, there is the "souls of men." We may take this, without any stretch of fancy, to refer to that slavery, political and religious, which a corrupt Church and a corrupt Empire together helped to rivet, and which has come down to us through the Middle Ages as a dark legacy from the evil times of the old Roman world.

CHAPTER II.

THE MYTH-MAKING AGE OF CHURCH HISTORY.

MYTH and legend have been distinguished in this way —that myth is an idea realised, while a legend is a fact idealised. The one enters the region of fiction at the point where the other leaves it. Where the one begins the other ends. Around a kernel of truth in both cases, a pulpy mass of fiction grows by accretion, the only difference being, that the truth in the one case is lodged in a fact, in the other in an idea. The true fact as a legend is projected into the world of idea; the true idea as a myth is projected into the world of fact. It is needless here to adduce instances of both; all we would remark is, that the legend-making and mythical spirit, as they are both departures from truth, invariably go together. Fabulous versions of fact, and fabulous distortions of ideas, are inseparable. Without some mythical spirit, or the idea of truth gone astray, legends would never grow up; so, on the other hand, without some love of legendary exaggeration of fact, myths, or the floating mist of ideas, would never condense in showers of sentiment.

In the case of the growth of sacerdotal pretensions, we see the action of both myth and legend. Mere legends by themselves would not have produced these corruptions, since facts, however exaggerated, are still facts. The legend of the thundering legion, or of the martyrs who spoke after their tongues were cut out, are only exaggerations, or mere misinterpretations of fact, the mischief of which is comparatively small. There is a foundation of fact for the legend; and when we get at the original tale in its true dimensions, we not only understand it better, but also can allow for the mistake of those well-meaning persons who think to heighten our wonder by piling on additions to the facts of the case. But the action of a myth or a distorted idea is more subtle and far more dangerous than that of a legend or exaggerated fact. A mythical idea works like a poison in the body which it enters. It insinuates itself through and through; it corrupts and depraves the inner sense of truth; and then at last it breaks out in those lying wonders which we know ecclesiastical miracles to be. Without myths there could be no legends; without lying ideas there would be no lying facts. Critics of ecclesiastical miracles begin at the wrong end, in dealing out judgment without mercy on monkish miracles, often repeated in a childish good faith, while they spare the mythical spirit which created the church system, at the base of which these legends sprang up, as mushrooms around a decaying oak.

Let us deal, then, with these two evils in the right order. Let us begin by laying the axe at the root of the tree of sacerdotalism. Half reformers of the Anglican persuasion would cut away some of the monstrosities of modern Romanism, and relegate the ecclesiastical miracles quietly to the dim twilight of the pre-scientific age when they arose. But this is not enough. Church principles are themselves at fault. A distorted and unapostolic myth of the Church as an external organised corporation, having a hierarchical succession of orders from the apostles' days, lies at the root of all legends of monkish miracles. Ecclesiastical miracles stand or fall, as those of the New Testament itself do, with our ideas of the authority of those who wrought them. The credibility of any miracle as a bare fact is not enough; it must be taken, as all candid apologists admit, with the institution of which it is a part. In this sense miracles are rational or not, if consistent with the principle of the institution which vouches for them. Miracles of mercy are rational, for instance, in the case of Christ; but a miracle of pure evil, a mere wonder, would be a case of Satan casting out Satan. This is the true rationale of miracles. If Christ is a myth, then His miracles are legends; and so the school of unbelief in Germany, which began with treating the miracles as legends, went on quite consistently to regard the life of the Christ Himself as a myth.

We must deal in the same way with ecclesiastical miracles. Either ecclesiastical ideas are true, and then ecclesiastical miracles are also credible; or, on the other hand, the ecclesiastical idea is itself a myth, and then these miracles grew out of it in the way that legends grew up in classical Rome. In Livy's pictured page we see exactly how the process went on with pagan Rome, and in Church history how it repeated itself in Christian Rome. The myth, or after-thought of Roman greatness, suggested the necessity for these portents and prodigies, which thicken the farther back we go in the annals of Rome. Childish as these legends mostly are, they would never have been heard of unless the success of Rome as the one conquering city had excited a craving for annals corresponding to the illustrious deeds of Rome in her after-history. The same case as this is of every-day occurrence among ourselves. A man springs from obscurity and achieves fame, and the Heralds' College is ready to find a coat of arms and biographers to invent a pedigree for him. Nothing makes success of this kind like success, and the history of Rome, pagan and Christian, is alike a comment on this sarcasm. The legends of Livy and the annals of Baronius are parallel histories. In both cases the myth of Roman greatness itself, the after-thought of history, suggested the legends of early and later times.

Let us deal with the myth first. The idea of Roman supremacy and of a centralised system of Church government grew up early; we cannot say how soon. The generation after the apostles knew nothing of it, for we have fortunately one genuine document—a letter of the Church of Rome to the Church of Corinth, which goes by the name of the Epistle of Clement. The remarkable fact is, that the name of Clement, its reputed author, never once appears in the letter from beginning to end, although later authorities, Clement of Alexandria, Origen, and Eusebius, all ascribe it unhesitatingly to Clement of Rome. Now here we trace the myth to its very *nidus*. A congregation of believers "sojourning in Rome," address their fellow-believers in Corinth on a matter of order on which they are appealed to. The same contentious and carnal mind which the Apostle Paul rebuked in the Corinthians is still at work there. But how is it met and dealt with? Not by authority. The apostle claimed authority, and threatened to come to them "with a rod"; and in one place commanded them by his spirit, as if he were present among them, to cut off the incestuous person.* Does Clement, the so-called successor of the apostles, claim any of the apostles' authority? His name does not appear on the letter. From aught we should know from internal evidence, he may have had nothing to say to the letter at all. At the same time, we have no reason to reject the external testimony which ascribes it to him. On the contrary, we hold it as a decisive, because undesigned, testimony as to the mythical growth of the whole episcopal theory which culminates in the Papacy. The after-thought of such men as Origen and Eusebius, judging the first century by the third and fourth, was very naturally this: that a letter from Rome could only come under the *bulla* or seal of its bishop. True, the bull is wanting, but then it must be put to it, so the myth thus grew that a letter from the Church of Rome could only be considered as an epistle from Clement, the reputed Bishop of Rome. Under modern criticism the myth disappears, and melts into thin air; but early ages were not critical, and so one myth brought in another, until the whole sky was darkened with the mists of Church authority, and it fell, at last, in the thick rain of the superstition of the Middle Ages.

One myth, as we have seen, led to another. The

---

* Vide Hilgenfeld's " Novum Testamentum extra Canonem receptum." Prolegomena to St. Clement, p. xxii.

myth of bishops (now elevated above presbyters as a distinct order) ruling over churches suggested that other myth that the greater churches, the patriarchal churches of Rome, Alexandria, Antioch, and Ephesus, were all, like that of Jerusalem, planted by apostles. The greater the Church, the greater the necessity for tracing its rise up to some apostolic founder. Rome, the greatest of all, must have two apostles for its founders; it must rear its head above other churches, and "*securus judicat orbem*," on the foundations of both Peter and Paul, the apostles of the circumcision and of the uncircumcision. What if the evidence that Peter ever visited Rome at all was hazy in the extreme, and at best more than doubtful? No matter; the mythical spirit comes in to eke out the legendary love of exaggeration. "*Possunt quia posse videntur*" is the explanation of cases like these. They are probable, because possible, and possible, because highly convenient for those whose pretensions to supremacy they are thus brought in to prop up. This underpinning of old ecclesiastical buildings was known to the Church school of divines long before it was attempted by Church architects. The latter are only copyists of the former. So deftly have they done their work, that it has taken centuries of criticism to take down the substructure of myth and fable on which the Papal supremacy rests. Even before the Reformation, Laurentius Valla saw that the Donation of Constantine was a fiction, and that the Decretals, as they were called, of the early Popes were forgeries. The temporal power rested on the one, the spiritual on the other; and yet, though the Donation of Constantine has long since been treated as a clumsy forgery, the claim to temporal power has only been renounced when wrenched from the hands of those who claimed it. In the same way the spiritual supremacy, resting on certain Decretals forged by the monk Isidore, of Sevile, has passed out of count on both sides; and the chronicle which contains these Decretals is a literary rarity. Still, the pretensions which they support have not been abandoned. When the foundations are taken away, the building still keeps up. The ignorant credulity of one class, and the interested assumptions of another, are enough, between them, to keep up an ecclesiastical edifice a long time after its foundations have been undermined.

It is necessary to understand this myth-making temper, or else we shall fail to understand the Middle Ages. It accounts for the steady growth of Church principles during the eighteen centuries from the apostles' days to our own. As soon as the primitive idea of the Church as a voluntary society was lost, or replaced, as it tacitly was,—no one can tell how, why, or when,—by the governmental, all flowed from this by a necessary law of development. The Church, which was meant to grow by one law, viz., that of assimilation, soon began to grow by another, viz., that of accretion. The transformation began in very early times—too far back for criticism to trace. All that we can say is, that in Clement's time it had not begun, and that by Cyprian's time it was in full force. It was a case like that of petrefaction, in which a log of wood placed under a dripping well is changed particle by particle. The stalactites thus assume the grain and fibre of the wood, so that it is not for some time suspected that timber has been changed into stone. This is the only account we can give of the contrast between the New Testament idea of the Church and that which meets us in divines of the Anglican and Roman school of theology. Between these latter, the difference is one not so much of principle as of detail. Both hold to the external and governmental idea of the Church, and whether the process is to stop at the supremacy of bishops or of metropolitans, of patriarchs or of popes, is a matter of detail on which none but trained theologians care to dispute. It may be that the Anglican has the better of the controversy in overthrowing the supremacy of the Pope. But the Papal party, in return, can make short work of the fiction of patriarchal supremacy or episcopal autonomy. The truth is, that as the Church grew she organised herself for the better, as they say—for the worse, as we contend. The result of this organisation was, that the Church became a corporation, and as such a centre of power, with which the State could treat on more or less equal terms. Hence all theories of the alliance of Church and State rest on this assumption, that the Church is an organised society; and without organisation, or that reduced to a minimum, the alliance theory is out of the question. We thus come back to the point from which we set out, that Cæsarism and clericalism are inseparable, and are both permitted of God, the one to check and restrain the other. To argue the question of Establishments and State Churches on the narrow ground either that we find them in the Old Testament, or do not find them in the New, is to betray a shallow view of the problems of life, of which each person is called to give some practical solution. The roots of the controversy lie deep down in the spiritual experience of each individual Christian. Those who have not broken the shell of their Judaism, which is applicable to nominal Protestants as to others, can know of no other protection for their spiritual life than an external organised society. This once conceded, the rest follows with inexorable logic. Given the Church as an organised corporation, having a succession of office-bearers from the apostles, and holding property in trust for ecclesiastical uses, it is only a question of time when a Constantine shall knock at the door of that Church and ask admission at first as a proselyte, then as its patron and *summus episcopus*. We have no right to object to the Establishment principle as begun by Constantine, unless we go on to see that the Clericalism of Cyprian necessitated the Cæsarism of Constantine. We cannot stop short in our objections to State Churches at any one stage of the declension of the Church, and say, "Here the apostacy began;" "Here the Church and the world became united and mingled their waters, which up to this time had flowed in separate channels." All reformation to be final must be thorough. If we are to speak of a Church of the future at all, it must be one in which we go back, not to the so-called primitive times of the fourth, or even of the second century, but we must go up at once to the fountain head, and model our churches after societies as simple as that which met in the upper room of Jerusalem, or the house of Crispus and Gaius at Corinth. How it will fare with Anglicanism, or Presbyterianism, or even some types of organised Independency, it is impossible to say. It is, probably, this fear of an unorganised Christianity, a mere "century of sects," as men said in Milton's days, which attracts so many to the opposite or governmental principle, the only legitimate outcome of which is a spiritual despotism like that of Rome. Our protests against sacerdotalism are unmeaning unless they mount up to the origin of all sacerdotalism. As soon as the principle is conceded that church officers of any kind may have dominion over our faith, there is no point at which we may pause in the fatal descent. Historically, as we have seen, prelacy soon developed into the patriarchate, and that into the Papacy, and it is vain to say, as the Anglicans do, that we may take our stand at the transition point where the first stage passed into the second, or the second into the third. All is orderly and continuous, and the assumption of Papal supremacy is quite as legitimate as that of the patriarchal, and the patriarchal as that of episcopal prelacy. *Obsta principiis* is the only safe motto in cases of this kind. It is the first step which commits us to the second, and the second to the third.

The defenders of prelacy have put forward this apology for it, that it was the front which an organised Church body presented to the Gnostic and other heresies of the second and third century which saved the Church. But for the unity of action, as they tell us, of a synodically governed Church, Christianity would have perished under its own dissensions. We are not insensible to the force of this argument. If there had been no internal necessity for it growing out of the corruptions of the times, we do not suppose that any body of Christians would have ever consented to submit to a centralised authority. The genius of Christianity is so clearly Republican, that it must have been under the pressure of some overwhelming sense of danger that the Church ever submitted to a spiritual despotism. But this argument either proves nothing, or it proves too much. It is only an apology for episcopacy, and tells us nothing more than this, that in the moral government of the world one evil is raised up to counteract another. In this sense it proves too little, or it proves too much, for it implies that such was the anarchy of the primitive Church, that nothing but spiritual despotism could be devised to counteract it. It is an apology for episcopacy like that of French Imperialists for the revival of the Empire. So great was the dread of Socialism, that society called out for a Saviour, and what it sought for, it found in the sham Cæsar of the Tuileries. The truth is, in both cases, that men made an excuse of their selfish fears. Cæsarism, whether in Church or State, was a short cut out of difficulties which they had not the manliness to fight with the fair weapons of controversy and argument. Necessity is the tyrant's plea, and authority is the coward's plea; but, like all acts of cowardice, it recoils on those who are guilty of it. As a result of this submission to spiritual despotism, they obtained a momentary lull from controversy, but at what a price. Differences composed in this way by conciliar authority were not set at rest, but only put off to a more convenient season. Each dispute composed in this way only broke out afresh. We see it in the history of the Arian, Eutychian, and Nestorian controversies. From the fourth to the seventh centuries the Eastern Church was distracted with controversies as to the person of Christ, and as soon as the Church had pulled up one bundle of tares, another had sprung up to choke the wheat. The misfortune, too, was that in rooting up the tares they plucked up the wheat also. The condition of Eastern Christianity at last became so corrupt and powerless, that it had lost all internal energy. The canker of Byzantine Cæsarism had eaten into its very vitals. The Church became the tool of the State in carrying out its despotic restraint of all liberty of thought and action, and when the time had arrived, both perished together, not long after the rise of the Saracen power.

The state of things was only a degree better in the West. Here, at least, the Frankish Empire was raised up to put some slight restraint on sacerdotalism, and to allow some little liberty of independence of thought. The Byzantine Cæsarism which first patronised the Church, and then extinguished it and crushed its individuality, was checked by this providential circumstance, that the Popes, in order to protect themselves against the incursions, first of the Byzantine Cæsar and afterwards of the Lombards, appealed for help to the Franks. That help was willingly given, and the Pope, in gratitude, crowned Charlemagne, on Christmas Day, 800, as Cæsar Augustus and Imperator of the West. On this day, on which, as historians have remarked, ancient history ended and modern begins, a rivalry was set up between Pope and Emperor; and it is to this rivalry of their successors, which neither Charlemagne nor Leo III. could foresee, that Western Europe owes her liberties. Any advantage which the West has over the East arises from the happy circumstance that Cæsarism and Clericalism were not centralised, as at Constantinople. In Byzantine Christianity the Patriarch became the tool of the Cæsar, and so both perished together. In the West, on the other hand, Pope and Kaiser struggled together for supremacy during long centuries, and it was out of this struggle that our liberties, civil and religious, have grown. Sometimes, as in the case of Frederick II., resistance to Papal supremacy took the extreme form of a rejection of the religion whose chief ministers set themselves above the civil power; but Frederick was an exceptional character. He was a Voltairean king, of the type of Frederick of Prussia, five centuries before his time. But, in the majority of cases, the dispute was carried on within closed lists. Pope and Emperor tilted against each other on this single question of the supremacy. In fact, the contention turned, as we see in Dante's treatise, "*De Monarchiâ*," as to which of the two lights, the Pope or the Emperor, was the greater; which was to rule the day and which the night. Dante discusses the question in the spirit of the scholastic philosophy, and chops a good deal of strange logic in support of his proposition that Rome is the legitimate mistress of the world, and the Emperor—not the Pope—the legitimate lord of Rome. Assuming that the world is a Monarchy, and ought to be subject to one master, he disposes of the claim of the Pope to be that master: "God's vicar or minister, by whom I mean the successor of Peter, is, in truth, the keeper of the keys of the celestial realm." He sets forth and assigns to each of these two powers their place. Man being dual, he is subject to two orders, temporal and spiritual, the Empire and the Papacy; he is fitted for two forms of beatitude—earthly and heavenly—to which the cardinal and theological virtues severally lead him. God alone is above the two chief rulers of mankind. Pope and Emperor alike take their authority from Him, nor is either subject to the other. Their spheres are essentially different. In like manner the sun and moon rule the sky, and are distinct. The only question, then, that arose was this, Which of the two was the greater light? The sentence of Innocent IV. is well known— that as the moon receives her light from the more brilliant star, so kings reign by the chief of the Church, who comes from God. Dante, as a Ghibelline, decides otherwise. Rome, he says, should have two suns to point out the two ways to God and the world.

> " Duo soli aver che l'una, e l'altra strada,
> Facean vedere, e del mondo e di Dio."—*Purg.* xvi. 106.

He compares the Pope to the camel which is unclean, because "while it can ruminate it does not divide the hoof;" whereas in the case of the Pope, "the sword is joined to the crozier, and ill beseemeth it that by main force one with the other go."* In the anarchy of the Middle Ages Dante saw no safety for society but in a return to the centralised monarchy of the early Roman Empire. His theory was the old *urbis et orbis*, modified by Christianity. He would set up a system of checks by which the civil and the spiritual—both claiming a certain supremacy, and both deriving their authority from God—should make a united Christendom

* For fuller illustration of Dante's views on Church and State, see the "Introduction to the Study of Dante," by John Addington Symonds.

out of the distracted mass of petty princes and imperial free cities, which waged continual war on each other.

Whether Dante's ideal of a centralised Monarchy for Europe, in which Pope and Emperor held alternate and divided sway, was only a dream or not, it is at least a fact that neither Pope nor Emperor succeeded in wresting the supremacy from each other. Under Gregory IX. and Frederick II. the conflict came to a head, and both combatants left off as they began, broken and exhausted, but unable to crush the other. Meanwhile, it was out of these disputes that the liberties of modern Europe arose. Nothing is so sophistical as the attempt of modern Ultramontanes to show that the Popes were often the champions of popular liberties. It happened so; but this arose from the necessities of the case. In King John's case the legate and archbishop side with the people, and wring from the King the Great Charter which he signed at Runnymede; but at the Constitutions of Clarendon the struggle is against clerical assumptions, and then the Crown and people combine against the clergy, as in the former case clergy and people combine against the Crown. The real danger to liberty has been when a Byzantine union of civil and ecclesiastical power has occurred, as was more or less the case in almost every country after the Reformation, and down to the time of the French Revolution. It may be said that popular liberty had never fallen so low as in France under the centralised despotism of Louis XIV., when Church and State were one machine, moved at the will of one man. In this respect the rise of modern Ultramontanism is by no means an unmixed evil. It is a question whether the so-called Gallican liberties were not more inimical to real liberty than the wildest assertion of Papal supremacy as made by the Jesuits. On the other hand, as is well known, the Jesuits actually favoured liberty as a check and set-off to the absolutism of kings. Thus it is that, as during the Middle Ages the contentions of Popes and Emperors in some sense neutralised each other and favoured the growth of popular liberty, so under the centralised bureaucratic systems of modern Europe the resistance of Ultramontanism is a useful check. Neither priests nor kings can be regarded as safe guardians of the liberties of the people; but when they fall out, as they often do, it happens, as in the proverb—that honest men come by their own. Cæsarism and Clericalism are, and always must be, the foes of liberty. Cæsarism is the negation of civil, as Clericalism of religious, liberty. They are often allied, and their alliance, as was seen in the case of Alva and the Jesuits in the Netherlands, is the deathblow to all liberty. Happily, however, their interests sometimes clash, and then we see the unnatural result of the Jesuits extolling regicide, and actually applauding democracy; on the other hand, we have anointed kings, like Frederick of Prussia and Joseph of Austria, turned Voltaireans, and striking at the principle of authority in religion without considering that they are actually undermining thereby their own power. In the moral government of the world it thus comes about that one evil is permitted, or even raised up, to check another. Priestcraft and kingcraft combined form the most intolerable form of misgovernment under which mankind can groan. Such was Byzantinism as it existed for centuries in the Lower Empire, and such was the system which Laud, Strafford, and Charles attempted to set up in this country. Happily for England, they signally failed, and all three conspirators paid the forfeit with their lives. It succeeded, unhappily for her, only too well in France, and the penalty she paid for submitting to the Oriental despotism of Louis XIV. was a century of degradation, followed by the upheaval of the Revolution, from the effects of which she is still suffering. The lessons of history, then, are so plain that he who runs may read. Christ came to give deliverance to the captive; but when His Church becomes a spiritual despotism, she naturally allied herself with the powers of this world. By a kind of fellow-feeling, she assimilated her system to that of the Imperial power. She courts its alliance, and lends and gives support to its system of authority, and to the general repression of free inquiry in all matters, temporal and religious. By this degrading alliance she has signed her own death-warrant. She would perish in her own corruption but for reforms from within, which ultimately take the shape of revolts from the principle of authority altogether, and the assertion of the counter-principle of the supremacy of conscience, and the duty of men to prove all things and to hold fast that which is good. This is the stage in our religious progress which we have reached at present. The Reformation, which does not go on to assert the ultimate principle of Protestantism, is doomed beforehand to defeat. It may exist on sufferance as modern Anglicanism; but it is pressed in on both sides by two opposite principles—

that of authority or of private judgment, to one of which it must ultimately surrender at discretion. It may boast for a time that it has struck out the golden mean between too great stiffness in refusing and too great facility in yielding. But this golden mean turns out, on examination, to be only a leaden mediocrity, as Archbishop Parker describes it in one of his Zurich letters to Bullinger. There is no satisfactory Reformation which does not bring us back to the ultimate principle on which Christianity rests. If it is a spiritual religion appealing to the enlightened conscience, and resting for its evidence on the personal experience of those who have tasted that the Lord is gracious, then we do not see how we can get beyond the sect principle in religion. Christ's people are as strangers and pilgrims; they hold the truth in a mystery; the world, as it knew not their Master, so it will not know them. They are, and must continue, a sect everywhere spoken against. If, on the other hand, their religion is one of dogma and definition, to be taught by an order of trained clerics, then at once the door is open for the principle of authority, and, where authority enters in, it is impossible to draw the line and say it must stop here or there. A dogmatic theology involves, from the nature of the case, a hierarchy to define and sustain it; and this leads us on to the subjection of that hierarchy to some power greater than itself, and whose springs of action the world understands. The supremacy of the civil power is one of the first necessities of modern civilisation; hence, to escape from the civil supremacy, a Church must go back behind the Middle Ages, when the Papacy first advanced its pretensions; behind even those primitive times of the fourth century, when Church and State were co-ordinate powers. We must get up to the age when the Church met in the upper room, and when Paul preached in his own hired house, no man forbidding him.

Thus, the only road to a reformation in church matters lies in a return to primitive simplicity. We have to pierce through the cloudy myth and legend out of which so-called church principles arose. It is the method of authority in matters of religion—in other words, the dogmatic principle—which brings in its train, by an inexorable necessity, both endowment and establishment; the endowment of Clericalism and the establishment of Cæsarism. There is only one remedy against these evils, which is a return to Republican simplicity. Hence it is that they are only half consistent who ask for the separation of Church and State, and would leave the Church under the rule of an autocratic and dogmatic hierarchy. Synods, and the representation of the laity, may be some sort of safeguard, as in Ireland; but the true safeguard is the Congregational principle—that each body of believers holds, direct from Christ, the head of the Church, not mediately from some synod or central conference. We shall see in the next chapter that all attempts to break out from these Caudine Forks of Cæsarism and Clericalism have failed. The Church has been destined to march underneath them, in order to teach her the original mistake which she made, and to point out to her that she yielded exactly where her Divine Master stood firm. She accepted endowment— in other words, she yielded to the first temptation of commanding these stones to become bread; she accepted establishment, in bowing down to the ruler of this world in return for temporal power; and, lastly, she committed the crowning act of impiety in the Papacy, casting herself from the pinnacle of the temple, as it were, and claiming special protection from the angels so as not to dash her foot against a stone.

CHAPTER III.

THE THREE TEMPTATIONS OF THE CHURCH.

THE three temptations of Christ at the opening of His ministry—the lust of the flesh, the lust of the eye, and the pride of life—seem to suggest the three stages through which the Church has declined from the standard of primitive purity. She has been tempted in the same way as her Divine Master was—through appetite, through ambition, and through spiritual pride and presumption. Alas! unlike Him, she has yielded to these three forms of temptation. Where He stood, there she has fallen, and in each case her yielding to one form of temptation has only laid her open and exposed to a fresh assault of Satan. Not to press the comparison too far, we may describe the stages of her decline and fall as follows:—The first corruption of Christianity was the lust of the flesh. Led into the wilderness of persecution, she was there an hungered of the good things of this world. The lesson which she was placed there to learn was that of entire dependence on God—that man does not live by bread alone, but by every word that proceedeth out of the mouth of God doth man live. Dependence was the law of her being; but, instead of that, she lusted after endowments and emoluments, and what she longed for she was given, even as the Israelites were given meat for their lust in the wilderness. An organised hierarchy and a settled provision for their maintenance, other than the freewill offerings which came in day by day—this was the first temptation which assailed the Church. It was when she yielded to this that Christ's religion developed externally into a cult, and internally into a dogma, requiring in both cases a trained professional class to perform its ceremonials, and to unfold and maintain its dogmas. Having yielded to this form of temptation, organisation having prepared the way for endowments, and made them in a sense necessary, the Church was prepared to listen to a second suggestion of the tempter. Taken up into an exceeding high mountain, she was shown the kingdoms of this world and their glory. The cross in the air, it is said, converted Constantine, and the politic Cæsar made a convenient profession of the new religion, the symbol of which he set up as his *labarum*, or standard. But Constantine would never have discerned this sign in the skies, unless he had first perceived that there was something in the Christianity of his day which he could mould to his purpose and shape to his will as a political instrument. The kingdoms of this world were offered to the Church, as they were to her Divine Master; but, unlike Him, she had neither the faith to wait on the Divine will nor the spiritual discernment to see that these gifts of worldly grandeur were only Dead Sea fruits, which would turn to ashes on her lips. Having thus made her first descent from primitive purity, she had now to undergo a second transformation. From a spiritual commonwealth as a kingdom of priests, she had descended to adopt the Judaical idea of a sacrificing and sacerdotal caste, separate from the laity; and now this caste is ready to be taken over and salaried by the State. They are to become Cæsar's servants, and do his bidding. Cæsarism, or the second stage of the apostacy, would have been impossible unless she had first yielded to clericalism. As it was, the development, or downward descent, as we hold it to be, was inevitable. Launched on a career of worldly aggrandisement, she passed on by slow but certain stages of growth to the last form of the apostacy, which we may compare to the pinnacle of the temple. This was reached when hierarchy, culminating into Byzantine State Churchmanship, at last put forth the monstrous pretension of a universal bishop, *urbis et orbis*. It is significant that when John, the Bishop of "New Rome" in A.D. 589, had assumed, in a public document, the title of "Universal Bishop," it was Gregory the Great, the then Bishop of Old Rome, who withstood him to the face, because he was to be blamed, in the same bold way that one apostle withstood another when guilty of an inconsistency. Writing on this subject to the Emperor, Gregory adds: "I confidently affirm that whosoever calls himself, or desires to be called, Universal Priest, is in his pride going before Antichrist, because through pride he prefers himself to the rest." To his brother patriarchs of Antioch and Alexandria he wrote: "This name 'Universal' was offered during the Holy Synod of Chalcedon to the Pontiff of the Apostolic See, a post which, by God's Providence, I fill. But no one of my predecessors consented to use so profane a term, because, plainly, if a single patriarch is called 'Universal,' the name of patriarch is taken from the rest; wherefore let your Holiness, in your letters, never call any one 'Universal,' lest in offering undue honour to another, you should deprive yourself of that which is your due." To John, the Patriarch of Constantinople, who had assumed this title, he wrote that "the sole Head of the Universal Church is Christ," and asks him what account he will have to render to God at the last day, if he thus tries to subject to himself as Universal Bishop the members of Christ, all of whom are equal. It was not long before the successors of this Gregory assumed those very marks of the Antichrist which a Bishop of Rome had denounced as the signs of His coming. Pride, the sin through which the angels fell, was, according to Gregory, the mark of the apostacy. And yet this Bishop of Old Rome, who could see the mote in his episcopal brother's eye, could not discern the beam in his own eye. As early as 606 he had assumed that title himself, and from this date, according to many interpreters of prophecy, began the 1260 years of the wilderness state of the Church. It is unnecessary to state here whether we agree or not with this year-day theory of prophecy, and this marking of distinct dates in the roll of prophecy as it unfolds itself. It is enough here to remark that as pride and presumption was the third and last temptation which Christ resisted, so it was the third and last form of the Church's apostacy. The singular thing is, that those who can see the nature of the apostacy as it culminates in the Papacy, claiming, as Hildebrand and his successors have done, a universal bishopric and supremacy in Church and State, do not see that this is only the outgrowth of a previous stage of corruption. What is new Pope but old Patriarch writ large? The Anglo-Catholic as well as the orthodox Greek Church agree in inveighing against the last stage of the development. But they have no right to complain unless they carry their protest one stage further back, and renounce the hierarchical spirit altogether. Thus the three stages of decline are those, when, from taking the stones of endowments and dignities for bread, the Church began to crave for the kingdoms of this world by an alliance with the State, and ended at last in confounding Church and State alike in that "masterpiece of Satan," the one universal monarchy of the Mediæval Papacy. This is the pinnacle of the temple of pride, the certain mark of the predicted apostacy; but the apostle reminds us that the principle was already at work in his day, and actually calls attention to that withholding or hindering power which kept back for a time the full manifestation of the mystery of iniquity. For the first three centuries Cæsarism and Clericalism were opposed; this was the letting power of the Roman Empire allowed by Providence. But as the Empire began to decline, it laid hold of Clericalism to prop itself by, and the alliance of the two was Byzantine Christianity, when the Church was favoured and patronised by the State. The last stage of all "this strange eventful history" was reached when the Empire or civil power, having altogether fallen to pieces in the West, there was room for the manifestation of the mystery of iniquity—a Church, that is, which had completely transformed herself into a worldly power, while she laid claim to be a spiritual one; a Church which, in the apt language of the Apocalypse, had horns like a lamb, and yet spake like a dragon. Popery has been called Satan's masterpiece; if so, it is because it is such a perfect counterfeit of a holy and pure original. It is a masterpiece of a kind with that of the forger and utterer of base coin. In dealing with it, it is impossible to say whose image and superscription it has, Cæsar's or God's. It is neither wholly secular nor wholly spiritual: if it were either one or the other, we should know how to deal with it. Hierarchical pride, for instance, is a corruption of a spiritual truth, and Erastianism is an outbreak of the merely secular spirit in religious affairs. We can deal with these. But the Roman or Ultramontane spirit, properly so-called, differs from both—or, rather, is a combination of both, as Corinthian brass is of various metals melted up together. There is no greater proof of the strong delusion than the fact that an amalgam results utterly unlike any other. But the strangest part of this progressive development of error is that ecclesiastics, as Gregory of Rome in the case of John of Constantinople, can see the error in others, not in themselves. Prelates object to patriarchs, patriarchs to popes. Each strikes at the evil one stage lower down in the scale of development than that which they have descended to. The half-reformed Anglican often leaves nothing to be desired in his zeal against Popery, except the charity and intelligence to see that the beam is in his own eye.

To deal even-handed justice all round, we are compelled to carry the question of State Churches a stage farther back than is generally done. To strike at the principle of an Establishment or State-endowed Church, while we leave untouched the underlying evil of the hierarchy, is to do as with Nebuchadnezzar's tree in the vision—it is to cut down the trunk, while the roots are left in the ground to be nourished with the dews of heaven, only to grow again as the opportunity comes round. There is a certain solidarity in evil as in good, a fatal consistency with which one development of the apostasy involves another in its train. It is not a bald truism to say that no lie is of the truth. On the contrary, it suggests the solemn warning that every lie has its antecedent and its consequent. It springs from a previous apostasy: it results in some still deeper form of corruption. We cannot draw the line, as the dogmatic Anglican or the Lutheran would do, at any one century in Church history, and say that up to this stage the Church was pure and primitive, and that after this we may trace the workings of the apostasy. The apostle, in his letter to the Thessalonians, distinctly teaches the contrary, and points out that there was the germ of this principle already working in the Church, there was *the* apostasy, the well-known and well-defined departure from the truth (the article here is emphatic), which was like the leaven of the Scribes and Pharisees, of which the Lord had already warned His disciples. We are at a loss to identify this in any other way than as the sacerdotal or hierarchical spirit which began, even in the apostles' days, to lord it over God's heritage, which elevated Church "offices," introduced at first simply for convenience of administration, into "orders," having an indelible character attached to them like the Levitical priesthood. The Church, from a mere assembly of believers, an *ecclesia*, or body called out from the rest of mankind, and separated in that way for certain functions to be discharged for the good of others, grew into an organised body, having a life of its own. The more the Church and the world were contrasted in one sense, the more the dominant military spirit which then held the world together passed into the Church. Perhaps on account of its having to do battle with Cæsarism, the Church braced itself up to the conflict by adapting to itself the spirit of military organisation ; Loyola, we know, in passing over from one form of knight-errantry to another, transferred to his new cult and order the military rules and iron discipline which made the Spanish infantry the admiration of Europe in the sixteenth century. These Spanish priests, as the Jesuits were known in Germany and elsewhere, were only Spanish soldiers who exchanged one cloak for another. It was much the same with the early Church. It is true that there was a primitive age, the age of martyrs, emphatically so-called before martyrdom became the new road to saintship, and before hero-worship had infected the Church with a dangerous form of self-righteousness. It could be said of the first martyrs that they overcame by the blood of the Lamb, and they loved not their lives unto the death. But this age was soon succeeded by the apologetic, and that by the dogmatic or creed-making age. Then it was that the evil which was only a germ before burst out into full luxuriance. With the age of Cyprian the monarchical theory of the Episcopal office began to display itself. After a brief struggle, Episcopacy trampled down Presbyterianism, as Presbyterianism a generation before had got the better of Independency.

But the law is inexorable that "they who slay by the sword shall be slain with the sword, they who lead into captivity shall be led into captivity." The Anglican divine points with undisguised satisfaction to the triumph of Cyprian over the Novatian schism, as it was called. Cyprian, the bishop of Carthage, not only got the better of Novatus, the presbyter, in argument, but also deposed him in virtue of his superior Episcopal authority. But the Anglican forgets that it was this Episcopal monarchy which paved the way for patriarchal, and, finally, for papal, absolutism. There is no drawing the line, as Dr. Pusey attempts to do, at some arbitrary point in the fourth century, when prelatical Episcopacy had not yet developed into the papal system. The stages of descent from Republican simplicity are clearly marked out. There was first the Independent form, when each church was a little society or club, having no fixed government at all, but only certain bye-laws or rules, agreed on by all members, as in any other Greek Club or Hetairia. Then followed the Presbyterian type, when the Churches began to confederate under their Presbyter, or Episcopos —for the two terms were then interchangeable, the former referring to person, the latter to the office; the one derived from the Jewish synagogue, and the other from Greek life. It is at this Presbyterian stage that Clement's Epistle to the Corinthians was written. These Corinthians, with the democratic, insubordinate spirit common to the Greek character, and which the apostle himself had noticed only to reprehend, had deposed from the bishopric some worthy presbyters, who had been appointed by them, or afterwards by other men of good repute, with the consent of the whole Church—"men who have blamelessly ministered to the flock of Christ with humility, quietness, and without illiberality, and who, for a long time, have obtained a good report." "These," he adds, "we think, have been unjustly deposed from the ministry. For it will be no small sin in us if we depose from their bishoprics those who blamelessly and piously make the offerings. Happy are the presbyters who finished their course before, and died in mature age, after they had borne fruit, for they do not fear lest any one should remove them from the place appointed for them. For we see that we have removed some men of honest conversation from the ministry which has been blamelessly and honourably performed by them."*

Three things are apparent from this short extract, which contains, we may remark, the pith of this much-disputed epistle of Clement. (1) That the constitution of the early Church was popular, not hierarchical; (2) That there were no "orders," but only "offices," in the Church; and (3) that among these offices the Presbyter and Episcopos are interchangeable terms, implying that in Clement's time there was a Presbyterian parity, not Episcopal primacy. It was only a short step from Independency to Presbyterianism; but in passing from the Greek or Republican, to the Roman or Monarchical type of the Church, the struggle lasted nearly a century. From Cyprian of Carthage to Cyril of Alexandria we may extend the period during which, with more or less bitterness, the strife had gone on. In Jerome's time it was so completely settled in

* Clement, Ep. i. ch. 44.

favour of Episcopacy, that Jerome the Presbyter can only utter a lament of dissatisfaction at the loss of Presbyterian parity as a thing of the past. But the victorious party had to learn that the development of the hierarchical principle was not to stop with the triumph of Episcopacy over Presbyterianism. Episcopal monarchy was, in its turn, to submit to Byzantinism, or the supremacy of the State over the Church; and when that passed away with the decline of the Roman Empire, there grew out of it the last form of the Apostacy—the papal absolutism, which is the last and worst development of the hierarchical principle. It is a remarkable illustration of the apostle's reference to the withholding power of Cæsarism that exactly as the power of the Roman Cæsar declined, so the Roman patriarch began to assume his insignia and titles. Like young Harry V. taking up the crown when his father was asleep, so the Church of the West acted towards the later Byzantine Empire. The declining power of the Greek Empire tried for some centuries to resist the usurpation of temporal power by the Bishop of Rome. It was all in vain. One by one the Imperial titles and dignities passed over from secular into spiritual hands. The Pope assumed the title of *Pontifex Maximus*, and the Pontiff at last became the civil as well as ecclesiastical lord of Rome, with a diadem to his mitre. To this there was added a double diadem, and at last the triple crown was assumed by Boniface in token that the mystery of iniquity—the full alliance, or rather fusion, of Cæsarism and Clericalism—was complete. The apostacy, which was but a germ in the apostles' day, was now finished, when it sat in the temple of God, and declared itself to be God.

Thus the transformation of Christianity from a spiritual power acting by simple attraction on the hearts of men, into an external power acting coercively by laws and penalties, constitutions and rescripts, was not a sudden process. It was a slow and silent deterioration, begun by the introduction of a leaven or hidden principle foreign to the body itself. The two parables of the mustard-seed and the leaven here occur as throwing light on each other. As far as the first parable is concerned, all is simple and self-evident. Christianity grows as a tree from its seed, outwards from within; from the germ to the sprout, from the sprout to the shrub, and, lastly, from the shrub to the tree, we can mark the several stages, and trace its orderly growth. But with the leaven it is different. Its action is also that of a kind of growth outwards from within; but it is not by simple assimilation of foreign elements to itself, taking up inorganic matter and making it part of itself, which is the mystery of life. Making that live which of itself cannot live—this is growth. In the case of the leaven, it is not the assimilation of one body to the laws of another, but the change is reciprocal. The leaven corrupts, and is corrupted; it destroys the Church, and is, in its turn, destroyed by it. It is a case not of growth, but of fusion. Fermentation is a kind of marriage of two bodies foreign to each other, and the product is a third thing—a progeny partaking of the nature of both parents, but, strictly speaking, different from either. It is this latter simile which expresses the change which took place when Christianity and the Roman Empire came together. Rhetorical writers have described this conflict and the triumph of Christianity over Paganism. L. De Broglie writes* :—"Founded on the same day as the Christian Church, and thereby associated, though with a very different title, in the promotion of the same work, the Imperial monarchy of Rome was not called to the same destiny. Their point of departure alone was common to the two. While, despite the severest trials, the Church took root, grew, and expanded over the whole earth, the Roman monarchy, in the full brilliance of its prosperity, at first became enfeebled, was then rent piecemeal by discord, and was finally dissolved. The progress of the one and the decline of the other were in almost exact correspondence."

This is a true account of the matter, if we regard the single parable of the mustard-seed. Christianity grew and overcame Paganism, and cast it out from its place of power and throve in its stead, assimilating to itself all that was great and noble and good in Paganism. But besides this account of the matter, which goes little further than its external growth, there is the fusion, or rather confusion worse confounded, of Christianity as a dogmatic monarchical system, with the dogmas and hierarchies, Jewish and Gentile, which preceded it. In this case we take up the parable of the leaven. One school of interpreters understand the leaven to be unmixed good; the opposite regard it as unmixed evil. Both miss the mark; it is mixed good and evil; it is the production of a new and third thing out of the commixture of Christianity and heathenism.

* "L'Eglise et l'Empire Romain, au IV. Siècle," ch. 1.

Christianity was the leaven which leavened the whole lump of heathenism; but the converse is equally true—heathenism, in its turn, leavened the whole lump of Christianity. One class of writers have attended to one class of phenomena, and another to the opposite. The consequence is, that to the one the history of Christianity has been little else than that of growth and advance, in spite of some adverse events, as Mosheim calls them, in his pragmatical style. To the other class, it has been one continued corruption and apostacy from the very beginning. The one is right in considering that Christianity has leavened the world with truth, but wrong in overlooking the fact that the world has, in its turn, leavened the Church as much. But the other school of thought is also right in saying that the history of Christianity is little else than one long apostacy from its true ideal; they are only wrong in the uncharitable inference that the Church has consequently altogether failed of its mission, and that, were it not for an elect remnant—the hidden people of God, scattered everywhere—judgment would have long since fallen on the world and consumed these sinners together.

The true view we take to be this: that its assimilation of the world to itself, by growth, as the grain of mustard-seed, and also its internal assimilation to the world, as the leaven and the lump are when mixed—that both these processes have gone on together. Both are part of God's purposes. Christianity has failed of its true ideal as the kingdom of God among men; but, nevertheless, the Church, with all its faults, as a corporate body has done much, and has much yet to do. Its failure has arisen from its yielding to the three forms of temptation we have glanced at—bread, power, and the pinnacle of the temple: endowment, establishment, and, as the climax of the two former, spiritual pride.* The Church of Constantine's time had committed the first of these three sins. The Church of the Byzantine age, as the creature of the civil power and the instrument of the Cæsars' despotism, had yielded to the second of these forms of temptation. It was reserved for the Papacy to reach the pinnacle of the temple, and to commit the last sin of spiritual pride and presumption, in which a Bishop of Rome arrogates to himself the twofold office of arch-priest and king, and claims the two swords of temporal and spiritual dominion. It is this impiety which marks the last stage of the apostacy, but there is no one point in the fatal descent where we can say, Here the evil began, and here the Church introduced an element entirely foreign to her primitive constitution. The truth is, the leaven of the Scribes and Pharisees was in her from the very beginning. The one temptation led on to the other. Having reached the stage of a tolerated religion, she longed to become a corporation, and to hold property in trust, nominally for the benefit of others; to redeem captives, emancipate slaves, relieve prisoners, and other such works of mercy. This position of recognition she attained to under Constantine. The stages by which the Church passed from a persecuted and private sect to

* Readers of Swift's "Tale of a Tub" remember the three grand ladies which Peter, John, and Martin fall in love with—the Duchess d'Argent, Madame de Grands Titres, and the Countess d'Orgueil. This is a humorous way of describing the three forms of temptation to which the Church has yielded herself—the lust of the flesh, the lust of the eye, and the pride of life.

the dignity of a dominant and intolerant State religion, were these three. It was tolerated as a private sect by the edict of Gallienus; and this toleration was so evidently the result of terror, that a change in the Emperor's temper or circumstances would inevitably have restored the old persecution. But by the Edict of Milan, under Constantine, a few years later, the new religion was placed on a position of equality with the old religion of the State, but not substituted for it, according to a very common impression. Christians and all others were to be permitted in all liberty to follow the religion they preferred. It appertained to the tranquillity of the times that all should adopt the religion they liked best; *in colendo quod quisque deligeret liberam haberet facultatem.* It is true that special favour was shown to the Christians. But this had reference to past persecution and injustice; their confiscated property was to be restored or made good by the Imperial treasury. If the actual holders desired indemnity, they were to apply to the prefect of their province, and their case would graciously be taken into consideration. Christian places of worship were to be rebuilt, and all appertaining to them guaranteed for the future against spoliation. But though this was a decided advance on the bare toleration of Gallienus, it was many stages short of what Christianity was destined to become as the dominant State religion. The stages by which this advance was made are many. No less than eighty "Imperial Constitutions" mark the seven years, 315—321, which followed the final overthrow of Licinius; and, doubtless, the majority of these were tinctured with the new ideas. Constantine, we may say, elevated Christianity to an equality with the old religion. Gratian and Theodosius established its supremacy, and destroyed the possibility of all rivalry for the future on the part of Paganism, which they degraded and oppressed. Honorius withdrew even the small eleemosynary support which these emperors had conceded to the professors of the old faith, and punished with heavy penalties any officials who neglected to carry out his edicts against them. Then came the sack of Rome under Alaric, which finally swept away the temples and other monuments of the old religion which had not been converted to the uses of the new; and when the deluge of invasion had passed away, a new world had emerged from the ruins of the old. Rome as a city was now Christian in a sense it had never been before.

A century elapsed from 312 to 410, from Constantine's victory at the Milvian Bridge to Alaric's sack of Rome, when the only spot in the city which the barbarian respected was the shrine of the apostles Peter and Paul —this century marks the transition from a persecuted to a dominant sect. We have seen that the first stage was the toleration, and the second the endowment and recognition, of the Christian Church. The third stage is its complete establishment as the *religio civilis* of the Cæsars and the Empire. This stage has been aptly described by Dr. Döllinger and others as Byzantinism, or that of the Establishment of the Church culminating in its complete subjection to the State. In the case of a Church monarchically constituted, it was only too ready to bow the neck and wear its golden fetters. The governing power of the civil society found itself brought into the closest relations with the governing power of the religious society, as questions arose which required their common action. The bishops thus, of necessity, became a kind of Privy Council to the Emperor. The troubles in the African Church, and the prominent part taken by the Emperors in the suppression of the Donatist schism, drew the bonds of the connection still closer, and definitively committed the State to a line of policy determined by the circumstances of the Church. The great Arian schism and the Council of Nice, occurring as they did only a few years after Constantine's politic conversion, riveted the yoke of Cæsarism still more firmly round the neck of the Church. All that was wanted was to adapt its organisation to the civil divisions of the Empire; and that, with a hierarchy ready to hand, was easily effected. The existing civil divisions of the Empire were adapted by the Church. The bishops were given "dioceses," so named from the civil divisions of the Empire, and the clergy were "parochialised" in the same way. The seven "dioceses" of the old Empire not only gave their name to the new ecclesiastical divisions, but the limits of both exactly corresponded. The seven dioceses included some hundred and eighteen provinces, and these were made similarly available. Each province, of course, contained several cities of importance, with the lands attached to them. These lands were called παροικίαι, or parishes, a term properly applicable to those who dwelt in proximity to each other. The Church system accepted the arrangement, and has perpetuated the use of the term. The English parishioner little dreams that in the use of this familiar word he is recalling the territorial arrangements of that great Empire which once ruled the world.

Yet so it is, and the same associations are connected with all the great officers of the Church. To the parochial cities are attached bishops; to the provinces, metropolitans; to the dioceses, patriarchs. The patronage of the Church, which before had rested on the clergy and people—"*cum clero et populo*"—was now transferred to the Emperor as the only representative of the people under a despotic system like that of the Empire.* These rights were at first only asserted, not exercised, and even in the case of the great patriarchal sees of Constantinople, Antioch, Alexandria, and Rome, they were claimed as splendid prizes with which the civil ruler was enabled to stimulate the affection or reward the fidelity of his followers.

This change of attitude on the part of the Church towards the Empire was such, that there was no halting midway in the position of a tolerated and protected sect. It must be admitted, in justice to the Church of that day, that there was no middle course between persecution and patronage. It is an old remark that in Rome there was but one step from the Capitol to the Tarpeian. Under an intolerant despotism like that of the Cæsars, Christianity must either retire into the catacombs, or come forth as the ally of the State and wear the Imperial purple. Byzantinism, as it is called, or the subjection of the Church to the State, is its inevitable condition under a centralised despotism. Such was the jealousy of the Emperors, that they could brook no rival near their throne, they could not tolerate even the old

---

* We are indebted for these details to an interesting work of Mr. Sheppard's on "The Fall of Rome and the Rise of New Nationalities." The reader will find full particulars in Bingham and Wittich.

collegia, or independent guilds, which had come down from the ancient times of the Commonwealth. When the day came, therefore, that the persecution of the Church ceased, she had to consent to wear the Imperial purple as the very condition of her existence. But even her best friends are not blind to the fact that this new position of patronage brought with it very serious drawbacks. Thus M. Capefigue, himself a decided Ultramontane, has to admit this. He remarks:—" There are in the history of all parties two periods, two situations, entirely distinct—that of opposition, and that of accession to authority; and of the two, the latter trial is frequently the more severe. It frequently happens that a party whose capacity for attack and destruction is admirable, hesitates, trembles, and is lost when called to the direction of affairs. In this respect, Christianity itself seemed better suited for patience, suffering, and martyrdom, than for the duties of government." "This change in the seat of Empire," he continues, "forms a revolution of immense importance in the history of Christianity. It would have taken a long time at Rome for a man to purify himself from Paganism and assume the *rôle* of the neophyte. At Constantinople, a city entirely new, not a trace of Paganism remained. It was no longer the martyrs' tomb which served to sustain the sacred mysteries, but vast altars of porphyry or marble. Gold glittered everywhere, and Constantine took as his model the Biblical splendour of Solomon. The bishops, priests, and deacons, were no longer dressed in the simple garment of linen or coarse stuff, which belonged to the epoch of persecution and martyrdom; they were clothed as the magistrates of Greece, or the satraps of

Syria or Persia. The bishop bore on his head the mitre adorned with precious stones; in his hand he grasped the pastoral staff in the form of a sceptre; his finger was ornamented by an amethyst of large size. The dalmatic and chasuble were of silk. The priests and deacons adopted splendid ornaments, rich girdles, robes, and tunics. To the change, then, in the seat of Empire may be ascribed the origin of ecclesiastical luxury and Catholic magnificence. The idea of the power of God revealed itself with such grandeur, that it was natural to crave after its manifestation by the pageantries of worship; the splendour of the altar is another homage to the Lord."*

Nor was it only in externals that the result of this "alliance" was seen. The price which the Church had to pay for all this magnificence was in the decline of her spiritual independence and the loss of internal self-government. Gibbon has asserted, and Hallam has accepted the statement, that there were no fewer than eighteen thousand posts in the Church which were filled by popular election; but virtually the Emperor appointed the patriarch, the patriarch the metropolitan, the metropolitan the bishop, and the bishop the subordinate clergy. And further still, what the Emperor did at the seat of government, the Imperial prefect imitated on a smaller scale in his province; so that, upon the whole, it cannot be denied that, practically speaking, ecclesiastical appointments were from very early times under political influence. Already, thus early, the question of investiture, the fruitful source of strife during the Middle Ages, had begun to appear. The right was

* Quoted from Sheppard's "Fall of Rome," &c., p. 661.

claimed by the Emperors of placing the consecrated "pallium" on the persons of the bishops at the time of their election—a significant action involving the claim of temporal jurisdiction over themselves and their dioceses.

We have said enough to show that by the middle of the fourth century the Church had fully entered on that stage of her downward career which may be described as the apostacy. Clericalism and Cæsarism, the subjection of the laity to the priesthood, and of the priesthood to the civil power, had become fixed forms in the Church. The connection between these two forms of corruption is such, that the one inevitably brings the other with it in its train. It is wisely ordered that it should be so. Clericalism, as we see it full-blown in the form of modern Ultramontanism, is such an intolerable slavery, that the nations subjected to it appeal unto Cæsar; they "fly from petty tyrants to the throne." Dr. Döllinger, in his earlier writings, before his present breach with the Roman Curia, makes much of the evils of what he calls the Cæsaro-Papacy, or the Erastian type of subjection of the Church to the civil power, common to all Protestant countries where there is an Established Church at all. But he forgets that Erastianism, though an evil in itself, is a remedy against a greater evil—that of ecclesiasticism. A Cæsar-Pope is a step of emancipation from a Pope-Cæsar. The Act of Supremacy made a Henry VIII. head of the Church; but this need not shock those who had seen an Alexander or a Leo head of the Church. Of the two, it was an infinitely less evil. It was the first step out of bondage, and it teaches us this, that the complete emancipation of the Church from State control and patronage can only be attained when the Church returns to her primitive simplicity, and by renouncing ecclesiasticism renounces also those assumptions of spiritual authority which necessitate the assertion of the Erastian principle.

Our survey of the course of early Church history brings us back to the point from which we set out. The decline of the Church is marked by her yielding to the three forms of temptation which her Divine Head resisted and overcame. When she is again led of the Spirit into the wilderness of poverty, and submits to what worldly Churchmen are pleased to call "spoliation," then she will be like that Church of the Apocalypse against whom the dragon in vain lets loose a flood of waters. Then the earth will help the woman; then she will see her triumph in the man-child caught up to the throne of God; and then, in the fulness of time, God will avenge His own elect, overturn the power of Satan, and bring in the true kingdom of God among men.

CHAPTER IV.

CLERICALISM LEADS TO CÆSARISM.

In all inquiries such as this, of the relation of the Church to the State, there is a previous question which underlies the controversy, and determines our attitude to it: What is our idea of the Church? Is it or is it not an external society or corporation, with an organisation of its own, called a hierarchy or priesthood, and transmitting certain supernatural powers by something like succession from the apostles?

If the Church is a corporate body of this kind, then it is clear that it must hold some relation to the supreme corporate body, the State; and the more intimate that relation is, the better it will be for both parties. No State can tolerate an *imperium in imperio;* and the evil of the Papacy is precisely this, that it is a State within the State—a society owning a foreign allegiance, a corporation holding property, and otherwise organising itself, with little or no reference to the civil power.

If, on the other hand, we have reason to think that it was not Christ's intention to found a corporation of this kind; if He came preaching, not a new theocracy to replace the old Jewish, but only to set up the principles of the kingdom of heaven in the hearts of men—then the question is greatly simplified. When we say that we are Christians, what do we mean, and what is our relation as Christians to the civil power? A hierarchical system must assert itself in some way or other, and strike out some form of alliance or concordat with the State. Not so with a purely spiritual system, like the kingdom of God. That does not depend on organisation at all. Its bye-laws are the fewest and simplest. Its civil status is merely that of a club or guild for purposes of mutual edification. It has no centralised authority. If it holds property, it is only under trust deeds, which may be revised at any time by the Court of Chancery. An institution of this kind is no menace to the State, and as it barely exists in the eye of the law, it may be tolerated, and even indirectly encouraged, as a means for the moral education of the people, by the State with perfect safety.*

It will be found that all controversies on the relation of Church and State hinge on the question, What is our idea of the Church? To ascertain this at the outset is to clear the ground of much useless controversy with those with whom we never can agree, since the principles from which we set out so widely differ. Those who hold that the Christian Church is only another name for the kingdom of God, have no difficulty on the

* The anonymous epistle to Diognetus, one of the few undoubted remains of early antiquity, points out how Christians are in the world but not of it, and that the relations of Christianity to the world is that of the soul to the body invisible, but the source of its life and motion. This conception would have been foreign to later times, when the Church began to embody itself, and in this sense, as an external corporation, to set up as a rival of the State.—See Chapter VI. of the "Epistle to Diognetus"—"What the soul in the body is, that Christians are in the world."

subject of Establishments, the only tie which holds its members being a voluntary one. Independency of the State is, therefore, the natural outcome and development of a spiritual society of this kind. Whether, then, the Church is a spiritual society, held together by no other tie than allegiance to its unseen Lord, whose life flows from the Head to the members; or whether it is an organised hierarchy, holding a deposit of doctrine and ritual, known as " the faith "—in either case, we may apply to it the remark of an eminent historian, quoted by Neander (K. G. VI. p. 2), respecting the kingdoms of this world, that they are best preserved by the same means by which they were first founded: "*Imperium facile his artibus retinetur quibus initio partum est.*"

As all organisms have their own law of growth, Christianity will develop according to one of two fixed types: it is either a voluntary society with no higher organisation than the congregational, ending, at most, in a federation of Churches, each independent of the other, and all alike subject to the civil power in every matter which does not touch their allegiance to Christ; or it is a centralised hierarchy, holding a distinct corporate life of its own, which at one time asserts its independence of the State, or even its superiority to it, as the Roman hierarchy did, and at another time claims special recognition and exceptional privileges in return for its subjection to the powers that be, as the Greek and Anglican Churches do.

Disestablishment, then, is not a simple question which can be discussed upon its abstract merits, independent of the nature of the Churches themselves, as some politicians think. It is like begging the question to speak of liberating religion from State patronage and control; for if we understand religion to mean Christianity regarded in its single aspect as the kingdom of God, it never took a shape which the State could patronise; its purest form was in those little religious republics which were founded in the cities of Greece and Asia Minor. Such a religion cannot be liberated from State control and patronage, for it has never enjoyed it.

His kingdom is not of this world, it never has been, and, more than that, it never can be. It must first suffer a silent transformation, such as Christianity underwent between the second and fourth centuries as it passed from the Greek to the Roman type of organisation, before it becomes an institution which the civil power can embrace, assimilate to itself, and use for purposes of police. That transformation, as we know, actually occurred. But the change necessitated a new relation to the State.

As a hierarchical Church it is, and must ever continue, of the nature of an Establishment. A connection of some kind it must keep up with the State, and that connection will vary with time and circumstances. It may be a mere concordat, as between two independent and sovereign powers, the Church and the State, or a union as close as that which ties the Greek or the Anglican communion to the supremacy of the civil power; but a connection of some kind there must be. According as Christianity in its constitution is congregational and popular, or hierarchical and centralised, will it naturally ally itself with the State or not. It is evident, from the nature of the case, that a loosely-organised popular Church never can become an engine of State, much less can it set up an *imperium in imperio;* but, on the other hand, an organised hierarchy always must stand in the relation to the State of an equal, either as its rival or its ally.

Behind the Establishment question, therefore, and antecedent to it in time, as well as prior to it in real importance, lies the pretended power of the keys. The Reformation has only half done its work by depriving Rome of its pretended jurisdiction and claim to supremacy. If National Churches are set up, as was the case in Germany and England, hierarchically constituted with a sacerdotal order, and claiming a pretended succession from the apostles, the vital element of error is still in the system. It may lie dormant for a generation or two, as we see in the case of Laud, before it sprouts out again into a new form of spiritual despotism; but the elements of mischief are all there, and those only are to blame who set up a prelacy, and then complain that it is constantly degenerating into something like the Papacy.

So constant is this relation between clerical organisation and its tendency to develop into State-Churchism, that we may classify the Churches of Christendom either in the order of their hierarchical development or of their dependence on the principle of Establishment. The most hierarchical Church is that of Rome: this Church not only feels some attraction towards dominion, but is actually a *condominium* with the State. In its most arrogant form as Ultramontanism, it sets itself, in fact, above the State, and claims the obedience of the Sovereign as the Viceroy of Him who is King of kings and

Lord of lords. These pretensions are a little antiquated now, and never would have been ventured on, even in the Middle Ages, but for the break-up of the Roman Empire, and the attempt of the German people to set up that ghost of a dead past—the Holy Roman Empire of the German people. This, in its turn, encouraged the Popes to meet one false pretension with another; but whatever excuse they had from the example of fictions invented by the civil power, this does not diminish the guilt of those who first degraded the Church into a hierarchy spiritual in name, but secular in spirit. The Cæsaro-Papacy was thus fiction piled on fiction, and lie added to lie. First the chair of Peter was set up, and the pretended power of the keys asserted; then the forged Decretals and the false Donation of Constantine were added: the whole resulting in one of the most amazing fabrications of political arrogance devised to hold the world in awe by the pretension to spiritual power.

The Oriental and Orthodox Church comes next after the Roman as a hierarchically-governed Church making pretensions to the power of the keys. As it is second only to Rome as a sacerdotal system, so its pretensions to wield political power and to share the two swords with the State are second to those of Rome. As a spiritual despotism, it is an admirable contrivance in the hands of a despot like the Russian Czar. He has moulded it accordingly to his purposes. He has set up a Synod instead of the old Patriarchate, and his *aide-de-camp* presides in that Synod as the Emperor's mouthpiece. The connection of Church and State in Russia is that known by Church historians as Byzantinism— a despotic State directing a despotic Church, and converting a contrivance for repressing the spiritual liberties of mankind into an instrument for still further repressing their political.

When we turn to the Anglican, we find a Church only a degree less sacerdotal than the Russian, as that, in its turn, is less so than the Papal. In this case, too, its political *status* exactly corresponds to its place in the scale of hierarchically-governed Churches. It is a mere accident and no breach of the law we are pointing out, that modern Anglicanism sometimes uses the language of Free Churchmanship, and sometimes even threatens what it will do when disestablished and disendowed. But this is mere bravado—the threats of partisans who would shrink from being taken at their word, and who know well, or ought to know from the case of the Non-jurors, how soon a sect withers away whose roots are not deep down in some eternal principle of God or of human nature. Anglicanism is, and must continue to be, a politico-ecclesiastical system. It is vain to pretend that it could live on as a Free Church and under a purely voluntary system. Voluntaryism presupposes a popular government: a hierarchy would abdicate its functions if it descended to cater for popular support. Hence it is that, if Anglicanism were formally disestablished to-morrow by Act of Parliament, it would re-establish itself informally the day after; and this is the real *crux* of the question, as all who can reason on the subject now see. This is the argument, which is the only one that has the smallest weight for maintaining the present arrangement popularly known as the union of Church and State. When two ride together, it is said one must sit behind the other; and at present the Church sits on the pillion behind, and must take what course her lord and master, the State, assigns to her. But if she were free, she would take her own course, and a very mischievous one that would be according to those who are shrewd observers of the reactionary tendency of Churchmen.

Now, we do not dispute this statement, nor do we question the fact that a Church like the Anglican will develop two tendencies—the one in the direction of sacerdotalism, the other in that of a love of political ascendancy. The two tendencies are inseparable, and spring from the same root, which is the carnal mind— the mind of the disciples before the ascension of Christ, not of the apostles after that event; of Peter and John as natural men, not of the same Peter and John as spiritual.

But what we wish to point out is that, if we are consistent, we shall lay the axe at the root of the tree, and not merely lop off the one branch of Establishment while we leave the roots of sacerdotalism in the ground to spring up in a Disestablished Church. True that our political action cannot go farther than this. When the State has repealed the two Acts of Supremacy and Uniformity—the two pillars, as we may describe them, on which the house of the Establishment rests— the State Church will then come down with its own weight. But the sacerdotal element latent in Anglicanism will not be much affected; on the contrary, it is likely to flourish with all the more vigour from the withdrawal of the restraining force of the Erastian or mere State-Church party—just as the Pharisees would have flourished all the more if their rivals, the Herodians, had been cut off in some way by the downfall of Herod's power. We have, then, to see that our convictions are thorough-going, and that our views of spiritual Christianity are so clear as to enable us to dispense, not merely with the political support of the State, but also with those props to faith which a hierarchy and its dogmatic system are supposed to lend. This is the weak point of the Disestablishment party, and it is well that they should know the weak as well as the strong points of their cause. As long as the majority of professing Christians are carnal, they will say, "I am of Paul" and "I of Apollos;" and where this spirit exists, there is the hierarchy in its germ. Nothing, then, but a purely spiritual conception of the Church, such as the kingdom of God reigning in the hearts of men, will ever counteract these ideas of a hierarchy of which Establishmentalism is only the last word. Anglicanism, then, as we judge it, is the third in the scale of hierarchical Churches; and, next to the Greek and the Roman, it is most dependent on political support for its existence. We do not say that it is absolutely impossible that it should become a people's Church, for institutions will sometimes live on, and even seem to gather strength, under conditions the very opposite to those which are natural to them. Witness a peasant priesthood in Ireland, with a hierarchy ranging from a cardinal to a curate or hedge schoolmaster, all drafted from the same class in life as that to which they minister. But the exceptions in such cases as these can be accounted for, and, if so, they prove the rule. Our statement is that a hierarchical Church is one that must incline to an Establishment: hence, to create a Free

Church in the full sense of the word, we must do more than merely lop off her political privileges. To suppose that the prelatical spirit will end with the expulsion of bishops from the House of Lords, is to take a very simple view of human nature. The roots lie down deeper than our Tudor or Stuart legislation; the *origines prelaticæ* date farther back than the Plantagenets or the Conquest. We may trace them up to the day when the Bishop of Rome, as *pater patrum*, became the *Papa* of the West. The germ of it is in Cyprian and the third century. Probably, if we had all the records of the early fathers, we should say it was earlier still.

It may seem invidious to seek in even lower strata of Church organisation than Anglicanism for illustrations of the law that the hierarchical spirit is the real root of that love of religious ascendancy of which Established and National Churches are everywhere the expression. But, not to touch on the Continental Churches, we see in Presbyterianism another illustration of the intolerant spirit which grows out of a hierarchical type of Church government when in alliance with the State. In Holland, the Calvinists were intolerant, because they enjoyed political ascendancy; and the Arminians, perhaps for no better reason than that they were the weaker party, and had to go to the wall, began to preach toleration and the rights of conscience. It may be said of Churches, as of poets, that they are cradled in wrong, and what they learn in suffering that they tell in song. The Arminians, or Remonstrants of Holland, set up, as Laurent points out, the doctrine of the supremacy of the State, and the right of all private persons to redress from the Civil Courts, as a remedy against the tyranny of opinion in Church Courts. They denied, *in toto*, the power of the keys, claimed as much by the Reformed Church of Holland as by the unreformed Church of Rome. They went as far as to deny the Church any regulative powers whatever; and in their apology for the Remonstrance, they state the reason to be that otherwise there would be two co-ordinate powers in the State, which is contrary to the essence of sovereignty, and opposed to reason. A man might as well have two heads.*

Under the name of liberty of the Church, these Dutch Calvinists claimed a right *circa sacra*, which did not end with sacred things strictly so-called. This new theocracy, for it amounted to that, was as harsh and inquisitorial as that of Rome, without its excuse. A magistrate of Middleburg, who was expelled by the clerical party, took his revenge on them in a satire, which had an immense sale at the time, and was even translated into English, with a eulogistic preface by Selden—in itself no mean proof that the evils of Clericalism were as keenly felt in England as in Holland.

What is called Erastianism is only the same protest against sacerdotalism in another quarter. Erastus was physician to the Elector Palatine, and smarted under the intolerance of the Calvinistic party, then dominant at Heidelberg. His advice to the Elector was to allow no *imperium in imperio*, such as Presbyterianism had set up; and the Erastian party are logically right. The instant that a Church ceases to be a purely voluntary and spiritual society, it must set up something like a

---

* Duas enim summas potestates in uno populo dari, ipsius summitatis naturæ repugnat.—"Apologia pro Confessione Remonstrantium," ch. xxv. p. 277.

condominium, and the question is, How far can the State tolerate this? If the State is itself popular, and not bureaucratic, the conflict may be adjourned; and there need be no collision between two sovereignties, since both Church and State alike are held under the people as supreme. This is why in the Swiss Republics a Presbyterian form of Church government, though Established and State-paid, has not been a menace to liberty. But in centralised and bureaucratic States a collision inevitably occurs between the Church Courts and the Civil, and one of the two must give way. The law of self-preservation being the first in politics as in life, statesmen are not to blame for asserting an extreme Erastianism in face of clerical pretensions. If all parties were wise, the Church would cease to be a theocracy, and then Erastianism would disappear with the cause which produced it. But how can we complain of the seventeenth century for not seeing a truth which the nineteenth century is only groping after? An Established Presbyterian Church seems to invite the growth of Erastianism as its natural and necessary antidote; and whenever the two are opposed, it is needless to add that the weaker has to submit. If this were all, the hardship would not be so great. Of two evils we should choose the least, and Erastianism is undoubtedly a less evil than Clericalism. But we must not blind ourselves, on the other hand, to the evils of Erastianism. The *jus circa sacra* is too great a trust to put into the hands of any absolute and often irresponsible prince. What mischief it has wrought in Germany is almost incredible till we have studied the question thoroughly, and ascertained the true causes of the rise of Rationalism. The Professorate in the Universities, the training, in other words, of the religious teachers of the age, is one of those *sacra;* is it to be wondered at, therefore, that secular powers should administer their patronage for secular ends? Water, we know, cannot be forced in our houses above the height from which it is turned on in the reservoir. The Church of Christ has brought in all this flood of Rationalism on herself by allying herself with the world-power for dogmatic and controversial purposes. She has forgotten the golden rule, that none but spiritual persons can do spiritual work. A Presbyterian National Church is more even to blame on this account than an Episcopal, for presumably she had more light, and at least held a purer theory of the relation of the Church to the world. She never committed the same act of spiritual adultery, as we may describe it, of accepting an Act like the Act of Supremacy. Indeed, she always protested against it, and asserted the headship of Christ in deed as well as in word. But the *ignis fatuus* of Nationalism blinded her, as it has other Churches as well, and for it she sacrificed many precious grains of truth. She denounced the sectaries, and emphatically rejected the new and damnable doctrine of toleration and the rights of conscience, which Baptists and Independents proclaimed, as if they were pestilent heresies. The Presbyterians, indeed, were so enamoured with the Old Testament theory of National Churches, that they landed themselves in worse inconsistencies even than the Anglicans. The latter, at least, were consistent in preaching up passive obedience and a theory of the Divine right of kings, which would have been extravagant at the Court of Louis XIV., and was simply contemptible at that of Charles II. Anglicanism had taken the State to itself as its master, and though its master was one who dawdled away its time between Hobbism and Popery, this, at least, was not so foreign to the genius of a system, which is itself a curious compound of the two. But what had Presbyterians to say in the camp of the royal martyr? Milton, in his Defence of the English People, uttered a warning voice, but in vain. "Woe be to you, Presbyterians, especially if ever any of Charles' race recovers the sceptre! Believe me, ye shall pay all the reckoning."

History, then, is full of illustrations of the evil of Clericalism in alliance with the State. It is only half the remedy to free the Church, as it is called, in the phrase of the age, from State patronage and control. The Church, or rather the people of the Church, must also free themselves from Clericalism, or that power of the keys which is dear to the professional theologian. Only half the battle is won by Disestablishment. The more dangerous part of the fight remains in guarding against the re-establishment, in some informal way, of a so-called Free Church, full of the hierarchical spirit, full of tradition and dogma, and only yielding itself apparently to popular movements, in order to check and defeat them, like Charles II. signing the Convention of Breda with the intention of breaking it at the first opportunity.

The conclusion we have reached at this stage of our inquiry is this—that Disestablishment is only part of a larger question, and that to carry it by a mere *coup de l'Eglise* in Parliament would be a barren gain to the cause of the Free Churches. A hierarchical Church is, ought to be, a State-governed Church. To liberate it is, as it were, to let loose on society a class of sacerdotalists, who might become the same danger to the State that the clerical party are in Belgium or in Italy. Cavour's maxim of a free Church in a free State is a mischievous sophism or a great truth, according as it is carried out in a thorough-going spirit or not. If it means that there are to be two dominions side by side, two co-ordinate authorities, one of them a so-called spiritual, but thoroughly secular power, to enforce its laws in its own way, then we should say that Bismarck's way of dealing with the Church is preferable to Cavour's. A free Church implies a spiritual Church, or at least a society whose bye-laws are only those of an ordinary club, and which, therefore, cannot in any case come in collision with the laws of the land. But if marriage is to be regarded as a sacrament, and orders as indelible, and vows as irrevocable ; and if the rule of *non possumus* is to be acted on, that the Church may acquire property, but never give it up—then to treat such a Church as free is to give up State sovereignty. Italy, on account of her own weakness, and the malicious jealousy of France, hounded on as she is by the clerical party, has had to make this compromise, and give currency to a phrase whose hollowness no one knew better than its astute author. Germany being strong and united, and mistress of herself, used no such misleading phrases. Her statesmen are Erastians, as some would call them, of the extremest type ; but it is an Erastianism not only excusable, but absolutely justifiable, under the circumstances. The Romish hierarchy is both endowed and established in Germany. If they wish for more liberty, they must take it on the only terms which a strong State could consent to. It is only in Turkey and Egypt that there are capitulations exempting Franks from being arraigned before the Turkish tribunals; but even there those capitulations are found intolerable, and are at last surrendered. It is not in this way that the question of Disestablishment is to be carried out, and Nonconformists who now call for it would be the last to agree to it, if it were to be granted on these terms. If we are thankful for anything, it is for the lessons of even-handed justice which the three centuries before and since the Reformation have taught Europe. We should divide the six centuries since Hildebrand into two equal portions, and say that during the first three the Church has tyrannised over the State, during the last three the State has tyrannised over the Church. There has been injustice on both sides. The Erastian idea has arisen to chastise the Church for yielding to the Hildebrandine. At last, let us hope that the one wrong will be purged by suffering the other, and a really free Church will emerge in Europe side by side with a really free State. Both sides will have to give up much, and the bureaucracy or political hierarchy will have to abate its pretensions as well as the spiritual. We are at present still in the midst of the fight, and the party cries which we hear of Disestablishment on the one hand, and of the duty of maintaining a national profession of religion on the other, are rather misleading than otherwise. The knot lies at the point where the kingdom of heaven touches earth. As soon as the Divine idea becomes incorporated in any one society, much more in one that claims to be the Church Catholic and Apostolic, it is at once an institution of time, to be dealt with and regulated as any other by law and precedent. It is an eminent jurist who has seen more clearly, perhaps, than any divine, the only conditions under which the Church can liberate herself, and get out of the meshes of statute law. Puffendorf, in his treatise, "*De habitu religionis Christianæ ad vitam civilem,*" has seen to the bottom of a question which may be said to have been the conflict of ages. He sets out with asserting that the Church never can be a State within the State, but simply an association submitted, as such, to the control and inspection of the civil power. "The capital question," he adds, "is to ascertain whether Jesus Christ ever meant to establish some spiritual power to which His followers were to submit themselves. If we admit that such a power exists, then there is nothing for us Protestants to do but to recant, and to make our submission again to the Pope. But we have only to read the Scriptures with an unprejudiced mind to see that the Founder of Christianity never meant to invest His apostles with any such power. He was a master who taught His disciples. He came with a revelation of the Word of Life to those who had ears to hear it. He came to teach poverty of spirit, and meekness of heart. His commission to His apostles was to preach the glad tidings, not to set up a new government in the world. And in what does this good news consist? That the kingdom of heaven is opened, that the end of all things is at hand, and that it is the duty of all to repent. Again, what is the meaning of the remission of sins? Did the apostles exercise any special power or jurisdiction in their remission? On the contrary, it is by faith that we obtain that remission, and the kingdom of heaven is opened to all them that believe. This is the teaching of Christ and His apostles. There is in it not a shadow of claim to anything like power. As for the Church, it is only the company of the faithful; but does this association confer on it any new rights, or give it any coercive authority or empire? Its mission remains the same, which is to teach and to preach the remission of sins. When it acts, it acts as all free societies do, by way of common consent, not by way of authority or command. This Church cannot pretend to be a State within the State, for if it were a power, then one of two things must occur: either there would be two sovereign powers, and then anarchy and dissolution of the social tie; or the State would be subordinated to the Church, in which case it would cease to be the State. Is it, think you, to set up anarchy, or to organise a theocracy, that Jesus Christ has come into the world?"

The knot is here cut, and nothing more need be added to this conclusion. The question of Establishment is, as we have seen, a question of what we mean by Church and State. As all are agreed as to the meaning of the latter term, and no one disputes its claim to supremacy, the key of the controversy lies in the equivocal term Church. The word is everything or nothing, according to our views of spiritual truth. The High Churchman is commonly said to be one who lays great stress on the corporate idea of the Church, and the Low Churchman the one who takes the opposite view of the matter. But suppose we go one stage lower than the ordinary Low Churchman, we reach the point where Churchmanship, as we may call it, evaporates altogether, and nothing remains but a sublimated faith or a Divine Person, allegiance to whom is the only tie of spiritual fellowship. This is the true starting-point of our inquiry —the place where we can see room for a free Church in a free State. As soon as Christians are ripe for this— and some classes are ripe for it by their not being ashamed to own that they belong to a sect and discard altogether the phrase of the Catholic Church—then we have reached the stage of religious voluntaryism in which the Disestablishment question becomes easy and self-evident. To educate Christians for this is the task of the Free Churches; to prepare Churchmen for it the duty of those who have parted with all hierarchical ideas. Organised Christianity and Establishments are on the same plane of thought, and, therefore, with thorough consistency, those who have moved off from the one are prepared to recede from the other.

CHAPTER V.

TENDENCY OF ALL ORGANISED CHURCHES TO GRAVITATE TOWARDS ESTABLISHMENT.

IF we look at the question in the light of pure reason, we must admit that a legal Establishment of one form of religion in preference to every other is a two-fold wrong—a wrong to the religion so preferred, and also a wrong to those which are passed by. It is a wrong equally on the assumption that one form of organised Christianity is more of God than any other, and on the opposite assumption that all are alike developments on man's part, as well as accommodations on God's part, to the varying growths of society. Lastly, it is a wrong whether we hold that the free play of conscience requires that no temporal inducements should be held out to men to embrace one form of religious truth in preference to every other, or whether we say, with "jesting Pilate," What is truth? and therefore regard all State profession of religion as an organised hypocrisy. Earnest men, then, of all schools alike, whether sceptics or religionists, may look on a State Establishment as a mischievous contrivance for smothering convictions and impressing on dead creeds the air and appearance of living beliefs.

Thus, if we follow the logical order, we should condemn all Establishments in the abstract, and then combine to put an end to that particular form of Establishment which prevails in this country. Still, the majority of men do not follow the logical order—or rather, we should say that the question does not present itself to them for settlement in that order. To them the concrete presents itself before the abstract, the particular before the general. It is only when the shoe pinches, as we should say, that they begin to see how barbarous and ignorant our method has been to fit the foot to the shoe, and not the shoe to the foot—in other words, to provide a religion for the people, and then to expect religious convictions to shape themselves according to the pattern of uniformity set up by the State. The mistakes of over-government in trade, and other directions, were pointed out by Adam Smith and his school in the last century, and have been slowly remedied during this century. But we still go on perpetuating this mistake in religion, partly because men of the world are too indifferent to the rights of conscience to see that it is a wrong to repress its free play, but principally because even those who see the abstract reason for Disestablishment do not see the practical necessity for dealing with our existing State Church.

It is not our intention, then, to add another to the many excellent treatises on the abstract question of Establishments in general. No words of ours could add to the weight of the testimony of such a thinker as Vinet. It is both more modest and true to fact to say that all that we have ever learned of the supremacy of conscience and of the duty of preserving a sacred recess, into which truth only can enter as light enters a room when the windows are unbarred, has been learned at the feet of Vinet. Milton would have taught this truth in his day, but the seventeenth century was not able to bear it. We make a great mistake if we fail to see that the century after the Reformation was a dogmatic stage of the human mind; men had only broken off one yoke of authority to impose on themselves another. It is difficult to say whether the Synod of Dort or the Council of Trent was the most intolerable form of dogmatism; the only result of the Reformation for the first century and a-half seemed to be that, whereas the spirit of inquiry had to reckon with only one infallible Church it had now to reckon with four; there were the Tridentine, the Anglican, the Lutheran, and the Calvinist Churches—all equally intolerant, and equally persuaded that with them alone lay the one deposit of Divine and infallible truth. The persecution of opinion as such was held to be a duty both of Church and State; and toleration itself, as we gather from Sir William Browne's essay on the subject, was only tolerated as the excuse of indolent minds who had no genius for disputes on religion. Toleration, in fact, was a cry of distress put up when the oppression of some dominant Church could be borne no longer. Hence it was that toleration was held more or less by the sects which were persecuted, and rejected by them as often as the wheel of fortune brought them to the summit and their adversaries under their feet. The Arminian Baptists, it is true, came very near the admission of this truth; and the Cambridge Platonists, though more a sect of philosophers than of religionists, exalted it almost into a dogma of belief. It is to the honour of the Society of Friends that they have never wavered on this subject. Their testimony has been uniform, because of all the sects they are the only one which rested it on a religious and not merely on an ethical principle. In the doctrine of the inner light of conscience they may be said to have found the key to the connection between natural and revealed religion, which was almost lost to the Church during the reign of dogmatic systems resting on the principle of authority.

Others have clearly pointed out the evils of State Churches; but no one has ever gone to the roots of the question so thoroughly as Vinet. He has elevated individualism into a principle. He is a believer in the reality of the fall, and the consequent contrast between the actual and the ideal of humanity, as deep as either Augustine or Pascal; but he has not fallen into their mistake, and set up a rival society, called the external historical Church, as the antidote and corrective to the evils of that other external society known as the State. This was only to set up one Establishment to check another, which has ended, as we might expect, either in their coalition, which is the most monstrous form of tyranny, or their open collision, which is a state of anarchy scarcely less deplorable. All this Vinet has seen and described with a penetration and point which leave nothing to be desired. On this subject we are content to sit at his feet and confess ourselves to be his disciple. He has seen, more than any other writer whom we can refer to, that "the fiction of a State Church is, of all things, the best adapted to put consciences to sleep, and that the more this institution puts on sonorous titles and pompous insignia, the more fast and profound will the sleep of those consciences be."

"Nothing," he adds, in another paragraph, "intimidates or perverts the religious sentiment so much as contact with the civil power. Religion in the hands of the last inevitably becomes a species of police. Conscience, hurt and alarmed, retires within itself, creates within itself in secret a religion which is exclusively its own, leaving to shallow souls the religion of form or the forms of religion. But when, on the contrary, it is free from all impure contact, the religious sentiment spreads itself abundantly throughout life and society, penetrates the masses, filters through to the seat of power, forms without contract or convention a Christian nation, a Christian Government. Authority then takes its tone from public conviction, and is thus the most precious of all expressions of society; its morality is Christian, its policy is Christian, because morals have inscribed this necessity on its mandates."

On this subject we have nothing to add. We can only say of those who do not see the force of these arguments that they are defective in spiritual insight. They neither understand the fall which is the cause of man's present duality, nor the plan of redemption which is the means of his ultimate restoration to unity with himself. For the present there must be two distinct spheres of action—the secular and the spiritual, the State and the Church. Pelagians and Pantheists quite consistently deny the fall, and, consequently, this dualism, out of which the contrast of Church and State arises. Hence it is, as Vinet remarks, that "Spinoza, as well as Hume and Hobbes, gives up religion to the civil Government. Thinkers of the Materialist or Fatalist school are firm upholders of a State religion." The advocate for State Churches does not even know, or at least forgets, the lessons of history, which invariably teach that religion recovers new life in proportion as it withdraws out of the State's sphere of attraction, and the State withers and paralyses whatever it touches in the spiritual domain. When Bonaparte restored altars he did not restore religion; she was recovering without him: he stifled her in the purple, and under his icy hand the sacred oil, which had begun to flow in the fire of trial, was soon seen to congeal again. Advocates of Establishments have, indeed, so little to say on the abstract ground that they now prudently keep off from it. They have changed their note, and as the system of State Churches can no longer be defended on the dogmatic grounds formerly taken up, they generally content themselves with the argument of an indolent and half cynical Conservatism—that it is one thing to establish a new Church, another thing to disestablish an old. It is an argument founded on the philosophy of indifference, and is well summed up in the old saw, *fieri non debet factum valet.* In general, as Vinet observes, the system of State Churches defends itself chiefly by attacking others. It contents itself for the most part with contesting the worth and, above all, the possibility of the opposite systems proposed, and trying, by way of exclusion, to establish the right that is denied to it. How true this is we may judge from the case of all the three essays to which the Peek prizes in support of State Churches were recently awarded. All three essays, and the first, in order of merit, the most distinctly of the three, renounce and even repudiate, with something like contempt, the old-fashioned syllogism of our boyhood—

> "The State is bound to maintain the truth;
> The Church, as by law established, is that truth;
> Therefore the duty of the State," &c., &c.

The fallacy lying in the undistributed middle term truth is now so apparent, that we need not waste argument on persons so prejudiced as to cling to it in spite of its obviously equivocal use. No intelligent mind, able to write for or adjudicate on such essays as the three to which the Peek prizes were awarded, would repeat arguments like these, which have only to be thrown into the form of a syllogism to show their fallacy. The ground is now, as Vinet remarks, one of an attack on Voluntaryism rather than of defence of Establishmentalism in itself. According to the first of the three writers, all tolerated—*i.e.*, law-protected—Churches are of the nature of Establishments. No society that touches earth at all, as it must do, if it have any property even in a building in which to meet, or any bye-laws to regulate the relation of its members to each other, can withdraw itself from the cognizance of the laws of the land. But, as in many cases of sophistical reasoning, we have here a sounding truism covering a mischievous paradox. The supremacy of the law is what every one admits; yet it is equally a maxim of law that every man's house is his castle. The wind of heaven may enter it, but no one may pass the threshold without a warrant to show that the law has been broken by the owner. This maxim—if it, too, is not a mere sounding truism—implies, that the law may protect institutions without being called on to go a step farther and patronise them, much less accord to them exclusive privileges and advantages. That every corporation, ecclesiastical as well as civil, is amenable to the law, is only to affirm the Act of Supremacy, which, if it had stopped short at that negative point, would have never met with a dissentient voice in England outside the Ultramontane party. But it is like asking an inch and taking an ell to go on from that to the statement that, since all Churches have a temporal side on which they are amenable to the courts of law, the Executive should therefore take them in hand and convert them into departments of State, or, worse still, establish one sect to the exclusion of the rest. In reply to the charge that the Establishment is a State-made and a State-paid Church, Anglicans are in the habit now of replying that it is neither the one nor the other. They say that the National Church is simply the old historical Church of Augustine's planting, which fell in the eleventh century under the centralising tyranny of the Bishop of Rome, and from which the Tudor kings delivered her, not without much robbery and spoliation on their part. They compelled her to pay the price of redemption from Rome by subjecting her to another yoke—viz., that of Parliament and the civil power, which was only a little less galling than that of Rome from which she was delivered. This Anglican theory, which we do not intend here to discuss, is like many other theories of history—difficult either to establish or to refute. It has some facts in its favour, many others against it; at all events, it is only a theory—a subjective way, that is, of marshalling facts whose truth depends on the point of view through which we look at them.

Our intention is not to refute this new theory of an Establishment, but only to remark that it is new. It is an instance of the way in which the old dogmatic argument of the theocracy has given way under its defenders. State Churchmen have nothing to say for a State Church *per se*, but only for the particular arrangement which still has the force of law in this country. So selfish and sectarian in this sense has Anglicanism grown, that its advocates had scarcely a word to say for the Irish Establishment, which they let go by default. If the principle of Establishments were not worm-eaten by scepticism on all sides—the deepest sceptics being its loudest advocates, the political Conservatives—we should have heard something of the principle when it was challenged in Ireland. Men who have a conviction do not desert it when it does not work true in details; but, retaining the principle, try it again and again until a machinery is found adapted to the motive power within. In the case of Anglicanism, it is changing front every day, and it is impossible to say how much it holds of the Establishment principle at present beyond sticking close to the endowments, which it claims by a sort of Divine right as given to God in times of superstition, and inalienable now, because there is a Divine law that endowments may increase, but never may decrease.

The modern argument for Establishments, then, merely amounts to this: that, since all Establishments imply endowments, conversely all endowments imply Establishments; which is about as logical as to say that, since all black sheep are ruminants, all ruminants are black sheep. Vinet has exposed the fallacy in the aphorism on the difference between civil and religious marriage: "Every citizen is not a believer, but every believer is a citizen. Religious laws can only bind those who believe in them; but civil laws bind every man who lives among men." It is thus an argument against endowments, and one in favour of Voluntaryism, pure and simple, that all endowments and trust-deeds entangle those who hold them with the affairs of this life contrary to the word of the apostle. Like a wise teacher, he does not condemn those things *in toto*, but he points out to us what they lead to. An endowment is, we admit, a *quasi*-Establishment; it is a step in the direction of a State Church. We admit this; but, if warned by history of the fatal descent from holding property under the State to becoming its servant, may we not choose the nobler alternative of refusing altogether to tie up the grace of God in a trust-deed, like the sword of the giant wrapped in an ephod, and becoming rusty because unused? The experience of the Free Churches as to endowments does not encourage them to repeat the attempts of their fathers of last century. If wise men, they let them go by default, and cast themselves on the people, as the mendicant orders did in their early and better days. To do so is to cast away the only apology for Establishments which the modern intellect can offer. The argument of these advocates of State Churches only amounts to a kind of *tu quoque* against the Dissenters, which confirms Vinet's remark, that modern Establishmentarians attack others rather than defend themselves. If Establishmentalism covers all tolerated Churches, then the National Church, as she is called by way of emphasis, is only one of many cults all claiming equal rights to be regarded as national. If this means anything, it means concurrent endowment with concurrent Establishment; and how would its advocates like to work out their own principle? The first result would be the repeal of the Act of Uniformity, and the throwing open of cathedral and other pulpits to Churchmen and Dissenters alike. The State is not going to enforce the limitations of a sacerdotal sect on the one hand, and allow it, on the other hand, to claim all the privileges of the National Church. This is that way of playing fast and loose with the subject which prevails in clerical circles. The Church is broad and national on the one hand, narrow and denominational on the other. Talk of its endowments and its right to them, and then it is to be treated as a National Church; talk of the rights of others to go shares in these good things of this life, and then it is narrow and exclusive, resting on the figment of apostolical succession.

We conclude, then, this chapter, as we set out, with the remark, that it is not enough to show that the old arguments for State Churches from the duty of the State and from Old Testament example are all obsolete. No one admits this more readily than the modern advocate for Establishments. Not one of the three writers of the Peek prize essays condescends to notice the old apologies for Establishments, which did good service in the old days of dogmatic theology and the right Divine of kings. The modern argument for a constitution like ours in Church and State is, that it exists and has its roots in the past. No one, it is said, would dream of setting up such an institution as the English Establishment; but, finding it in existence, we should be rash indeed to think of pulling it down. What these reasons are for keeping up what it would be absurd to call into existence, we forbear to inquire; but the reason avowed by men like Sir John Lubbock is, that to clear it away would do more harm than good. "It is one thing," said Sir J. Lubbock in an election speech at Maidstone, "to disestablish a weak Church; quite another thing to abandon all control over a remarkably strong one. The result of the separation would be," he went on to say, "not merely to disestablish and disendow the Church of England, but also to create and establish a gigantic, powerful, and wealthy ecclesiastical corporation independent of State control. Thus," he added, "the true effect would be, not to disestablish the Church, but to disestablish the State." This is the old argument paraded so often in Germany, that the only remedy against Ultramontanism is Erastianism. We do not see the absolute necessity of being driven to an alternative between two forms of evil; we are not reduced to the hopeless condition of the chickens, who were consulted whether they would be roast or boiled, and who were so illogical as to answer, "Neither." Those who argue in this way are scarcely sincere in saying that they fear the outbreak of an Anglican spiritual despotism worse than that of Rome. What they really mean, if they said out their innermost thoughts, is, that they dislike all strong assertion of individual conviction on religious subjects which the sect principle implies. State religions, as Vinet observes, have no more zealous champions than the adversaries of all positive religion. Spinoza, as well as Hobbes and Hume, gives up religion to "the civil Government. Thinkers of the materialist or fatalist school are firm upholders of a State religion." On this account it is that the real foe which the Liberation Society has to fight is not the old-fashioned dogmatist, whether Evangelical or Anglican. They are stiff for existing endowments and but little else; and, if the endowments were left to be disposed of as they pleased, would only be too thankful to be relieved of the control of the State. But the real champions of Establishment, pure and simple, are the Erastian or Broad Church party—the Herodians of modern religion, who hate spiritual religion as much as the Pharisees do, but who are too wise to let their hatred appear. It is all hidden under a mask of comprehensive charity. What they desire, however, that they dare not avow. The system of State Churches can only be advantageously defended from the point of view of Pantheism. This is one of Vinet's penetrating remarks, in which he shows how much farther he sees into the question than writers who have only a slender acquaintance with recent German thought and its tendencies. To understand, for instance, Rothe's State Churchmanship, we must know his Pantheistic leanings; and the school of English Broad Churchmen are much nearer to Rothe's position than, perhaps, they are themselves aware of. In Arnold and Stanley's case, the old Hooker argument for the civil supremacy over the ecclesiastical has been worked up to mean something which the judicious Hooker little thought of, and which, if he were consulted about, he would distinctly deny that it is fairly filiated on him.

But, be that as it may, these are only instances of

what occurs every day. Men take their side, and then find reasons for doing so, and invent high-flying theories which are said to cover their case, but only do so in the very limited sense that a kite in the air covers the boy who is flying it from a string. We have seen too many such theories rise, dance in the light, and then, like bubbles, burst from their own emptiness, to care to argue down theories which are only invented for argument's sake. With regard to these theories set up to prove Establishments, we may leave them to die out like the older Ptolomean astronomy, which it took a century from Kepler to Newton to dispose of. In this respect, theories die hard. It was so with the Newtonian philosophy: the elder Bernouilli died a Cartesian, the younger grew up a Newtonian. It was not because the father was a less eminent mathematician than the son, or less capable of comprehending the *Principia*, that the task of abandoning the old philosophy was too much for him. It required a generation to bridge over the abyss between the vortices of the one philosophy and the attraction principle of the other. So it will be with this question of Disestablishment. When the time for the change has come, the great mass of mankind will pass over from one abstract principle to another under the driving impulse of an imperious necessity, and will scarcely feel the wrench it has been, so lightly do theories sit on the consciousness of most men. The *quomodo* and the *quando* will teach them the *quia*. There are only two points which we have any need to enforce in this stage of the argument:—1. The necessity for disestablishing a Church which is already denationalising itself and becoming every day more of a sacerdotal sect; and 2. The duty of securing revenues for national purposes which, if left much longer under present trusts, will soon lose their national character and be regarded as private trusts.

If we can establish these two principles, we shall prove all that we have attempted to do, and to that task we now address ourselves in order.

CHAPTER VI.

THE "FREE CHURCH IN A FREE STATE" THEORY CRITICISED.

THE aspirations and tendencies both of statesmen and Churchmen are alike in one direction. Under a vague sense that there is no union but by subjection either of Church to State or the converse, both sides repeat, with more or less sincerity, the celebrated formula of the Italian statesman—A Free Church in a Free State: *Libera Chiesa in Libero Stato.* But, before those aspirations can become realities and those tendencies shape themselves in facts, a revolution must occur in men's ideas as to what the Church is. Her liberation from subjection to the State can only be effected on one condition, viz., that the Church shall renounce her hierarchical character, and abjure that usurpation of the rights of the entire community as kings and priests unto God. In God's moral government of the world, we often see one form of oppression or repression of Divine truth called in to check and neutralise another. Church history for fifteen centuries may be summed up as the struggle of Cæsarism against Clericalism. The liberties of the people have been held in pledge between these contending powers. At one time the Church was the champion of popular liberties, and at another the State.

The cause of truth has stood aloof from both; but at one time it has been forced to appeal to Cæsar against the hierarchy, and at another to the hierarchy against Cæsar. Even in the lifetime of the Apostles, the germ of this long struggle of centuries is seen when the Apostle Paul was challenged by the Roman governor Felix whether he would go to Jerusalem, and there be judged of those things which were laid against him: he refused, and appealed unto Cæsar. The reason of that appeal was, that the Apostle correctly judged that he would be more likely to receive fair play from a civil than from a clerical tribunal. In the language of the Apocalypse, the earth has thus helped the woman, and swallowed up the flood of waters which the dragon has let out of its mouth. The waters are the symbol of a wild and raging world-power, such as the Jews again and again stirred up against the Christians. The dry land, on the other hand, is the symbol of fixed government based on laws and resting on disciplined military strength. We see, then, the sense in which Paul appealed unto Cæsar, and the history of spiritual Christianity for eighteen centuries is little else than a repetition of this incident under varying circumstances. It has been the conflict of Cæsarism against Clericalism, of Erastianism against Ecclesiasticism, of the Byzantine type of Imperial ascendancy against the Roman type of Papal or Clerical. In the one case, it has been the State-Church; in the other, the Church-State. The Imperator of New Rome has claimed to be Pontifex Maximus; while the Pontifex Maximus of Old Rome has retaliated by laying claim to the purple, and, on the credit of forged documents—such as the Donation of Constantine and the

Decretals of Isidore—has laid the foundations of a kingdom which is little else than a parody of the old Imperial rule on a shrunken scale of grandeur.

It needs but little spiritual discernment to see that the true bride of Christ—the spiritual society which He has left on earth as a witness to her unseen and ascended Lord and Master—has as little to say to the State-Church on the one hand, as to the Church-State on the other. The Byzantine and the Roman type of theocracy are alike alien to her; between Erastianism and Ecclesiasticism she stands, as Paul on Mars' Hill between the Stoics and Epicureans, having as little in common with the self-sufficiency of the one as with the self-pleasing and expediency of the other. All that can be said in excuse for the two systems is, that the one has been raised up to check and neutralise the other; and the error of true Christians has been that, in flying from the one, they should have thrown themselves into the embrace of the other. To use the lively language of the prophet, it has been "as if a man did flee from a lion and a bear met him." The true Church, like the young David, has been delivered alike from the paw of the bear and of the lion. Nothing more distinctly shows how incomplete the Reformation was than this. It was nothing more than a single stage in advance—not a complete recovery of primitive purity. The Reformers, with scarcely an exception (Hooper in England, Zwingli in Switzerland, and, to some extent, Knox in Scotland, are the only exceptions we can name), set up one form of theocracy to encounter and put down the other. Erastianism, or the supremacy of the civil over the spiritual, is said to be of the genius of Protestantism, and this verdict is true, if we look to the results of the Reformation. The Reformers were in such haste to rear the walls of their spiritual Zion, that they forgot the wise precaution of Nehemiah and Ezra. They made league with one class of enemies of spiritual truth to counteract the other. This was Luther's grand mistake in Germany. Finding that some of the petty princes befriended him—partly from respect for his convictions, but principally from dislike of the Kaiser, who was a foreigner—he put himself and his cause too much under their protection. He was thus led into many inconsistencies, such as his approving of the double marriage of the Elector of Hesse, and taking the part which he did against the peasants in their rising against their feudal oppressors. This determined the whole course and after-development, not of German Protestantism only, but of the political history of Germany. The supremacy of the Prince in religious affairs, or what has been called Byzantinism, was thus riveted like a yoke round the necks of the German people. The Erastian maxim, *Cujus regio, ejus religio*, became the law in Germany, and absolutism in its worst and most degraded form, the type of Byzantine Cæsarism, has reigned almost without a check down to this day.

It would lead us too far afield to follow the results of this degraded type of State-Churchism in Germany. But it is not going too far to say that, but for this corrupt type of theocracy, in which the king was also high priest, the exact reverse of the Roman theocracy in which the high priest is a prince, we should not have seen that plague of Rationalism which has nearly killed out vital Christianity in Germany. The rise and spread of Rationalism are co-extensive with the erection of Universities planted by the State, and of theological faculties supplied by professors exclusively appointed by the civil power. There is nothing in the German intellect more Rationalistic than in the Scotch or English; but Germany wanted those safeguards, which, to some extent, existed in England, and still more so in Scotland. The Church exercised some control over the Universities with us; but in Germany it had next to none—or, rather, to speak more correctly, Church and Universities were alike under the bureaucracy, and treated alike as branches of the civil service. With us there was a certain Protectorate allowed to the State over religious affairs; but in Germany the Protectorate was merged in a complete and centralised system of police supervision. Professors and pastors were alike regarded as public officials—appointed, paid, and dismissed at the will of a Minister of Public Worship, who was responsible, not to public opinion, but to an absolute Prince, who lived in a little Versailles, and who mimicked the state and pretensions of the King whose maxim was—*L'Etàt c'est moi.*

In this sense, there is great truth in the remark of Vinet: "The Church-State, properly so-called, is an invention of the Reformation, when, afraid of its own principles, it denied it in action after having proclaimed it in words. The Reformation, in separating itself from the Roman Church, which was neither the multitude nor the civil power, was constrained, in order to find a head, to address itself either to the people or the civil power. Its principle would have led it to choose the people, but in general it had not courage for this; and, in order to possess a present and visible authority, it addressed itself to the civil power, of which it made a bishop. Such is the character of State Churches. This may be briefly designated as the Episcopate of the civil Government. Thus, then, the real State Churches are not so old: they only date from the sixteenth century, and may, without doing them injustice, be called abortions of Protestantism. For Protestantism, in consecrating the principle of individuality, pledged itself to a republic, bound itself to liberty; whereas we see that it weakened and infringed its principle at the very moment of proclaiming it."

The Reformation in England took the same channel as in Germany, and, under Elizabeth and James, rapidly sank into a kind of modern Byzantinism, in which the Prince was Patriarch or Bishop of Bishops. James I. shrewdly discerned that Presbyterianism was religious Republicanism, and he hated it accordingly, as much for its political as its religious tendencies. Anglicanism, or a kind of acephalous hierarchy—the arrested development of the hierarchical movement in the fourth century before episcopal monarchy had developed into the imperialism of the Papacy—was just the instrument which he desired. He found it ready to hand. To make himself a Protestant Pope was an ambition dear to the heart of a Royal pedant, who was nothing if not a theologian. The grotesque part of the affair is, that, having purged himself of one-half of Calvinism, and that its nobler element, he could not shake himself loose from the other element—its narrow predestinarianism; and so he presents the incongruous spectacle in history—ludicrous, if not contemptible—of a prince putting down Scotch Calvinism with one hand, and building it up with the other; sending his envoys to Dort to spin metaphysical cobwebs with which to catch Remonstrants in Holland, while he was openly persecuting those Independents in England whose theology was entirely in harmony with that of the State Church of Holland. His successor, Charles I., was both more logical and trenchant—so trenchant, indeed, that he brought himself and his two chief advisers in Church and State, Strafford and Laud, to the block. His ideas of Protestant Popery were decisive. A list of the Bishops, drawn up for his use by Laud, with the letters O and P—Orthodox and Puritan—pointed to the only end of such a conflict. Orthodoxy meant a kind of reproduction of the orthodox Church of the East, with a Cæsar for its chief priest, and subjection to this Cæsar the one rule of the realm in Church and State. The rebellion was so clearly on his side, that it is a disgrace to history that the phrase should have been used in the other sense, and the question prejudged in this way. For this the State Church is more responsible even than the servility and prejudice of historians like Clarendon and Hume. The State Church of Charles II.'s day, when it took in hand a revision of the Liturgy, introduced into its Service-book a form of prayer to commemorate the Anglican martyr, which is one of the strangest compounds of prejudice and passion on record. It set apart a day, in its ecclesiastical calendar, to commemorate the Royal Martyr, and, strange to say, this unauthorised canonisation of Charles came down unchallenged almost to our day. At last it has been removed, with the other two State services, from the Prayer-Book. But the Church which read history in this way must expect to be judged for its conduct. It cannot quietly discard these services out of its public offices, and escape in this way from the consequences of its own partisanship. The Church of Rome is, in this respect, to be admired, if not imitated. She, at least, has the courage of her convictions, and does not in one age repudiate her own solemn deliverances in another. But the Church of England, which is better or worse than that of Rome in this respect, is plastic as was the Byzantine Church, of which it is a debased copy. The chief mark of constancy in the State Church of this realm is, that it has faithfully reflected the theological tone and temper of the powers that be with the colour and complexion of the times. We may speak of its Tudor period, of its Stuart and of its Brunswick varieties; and, on closer inspection, we may see that it has varied exactly as the Sovereign. The Church of Charles I. was not that of Charles II. As the first Charles was a better man and a worse king than his son, there was the same contrast between the Churches of the two periods. Laud was a better man than Sheldon, but a worse Church ruler. If William III. had lived long enough, he might have weeded out from the Bench the sacerdotal and non-juror element altogether which came in with the days of Tory reaction under Anne, only to be extinguished by Hoadleyanism and indifferentism under George I. To criticise such a Church or write its history is only to write the history of the reigns under which such-and-such Archbishops received their mitres, and were sworn in as members of the Privy Council. Consecration, in fact, during the Hanoverian period, was looked upon as little else than the ceremony by which ecclesiastical judges were sworn into office. The Bench of Bishops and of Judges were the prizeholders of their respective professions, and the only difference between the two was decidedly in favour of the legal. The bar was an open career; and Court favour, though it went for much, did not reign supreme in the legal as in the clerical profession. Happily there is in our day a better public opinion at work everywhere, and our Bishops, as a rule, are generally selected for their merits, though there is still room for family influence and Court connection to assert itself.

Thus the Church of England has been all through its history a faithful reflex of the age itself. We sometimes hear the phrase, "an old-fashioned Church-of-England man," as if there were some *prisca fides*, some deposit of tradition in the Church of this realm, as there is in the Greek and Roman Churches. As for the sentiment, facts are against it. The non-jurors thought themselves true Church-of-England men, but their school of thought died out in a little schism or sect. Their legitimate successors are the school of the Tracts for the Times, and where that is leading to scarcely admits of a doubt. Its first tendency is towards Disestablishment, and its end must be absorption in that great maelstrom of priestcraft, whose centre is in Rome. The Church of England, then, only exists, as its Erastian supporter, Dean Stanley, shows, in the Privy Council. Paraphrasing the question, "What is the German Fatherland?" he shows it is not in the bishops, or in Convocation, or even in Pan-Anglican Councils, that the vital element of the English Church lies. Its pineal gland, if we may borrow a metaphor from the body, is in that meeting point of head and body, the neck of the institution, where a ganglionic knot of ecclesiastical lawyers interpret those Articles which divines, under Royal authority, drew up three centuries ago.

If this is not modern Byzantinism, then we fail to understand the meaning of words. It is Clericalism controlled by Cæsarism, and, as we might expect, the most ardent clericals chafe under the control, and long to break loose. Such, however, is the dislike of Clericalism by our age that it actually favours Cæsarism, since it is supposed to keep the former in check. Hence, as the ichneumon was worshipped in Egypt on account of its destroying the eggs of the crocodile, so Cæsarism, which, by itself, is as irrational as the Egyptian worship of the cat, is justified in this country on the ground that it restrains Clericalism. But this is short-sighted, as we believe. Left to itself, Clericalism would not really make much way in this country; it would decline into a sect, and die at last from want of vitality in the robust air of our popular Protestantism. Thus Cæsarism and Clericalism at present go hand in hand in the Church of England. Our only hope is, that the evil may produce its own remedy. Tired and worn out by the intolerant pretensions of a sacerdotal sect, the people of England may rise and assert themselves, and sweep away Erastians and Ecclesiastics together. We are out of patience with the way in which Clericals and Cæsarists throw the blame on each other. It reminds us of the Jewish fable of the blind man and the lame man, who together robbed an orchard, the lame man plucking the fruit and the blind man lending him a back by which to reach the bough. They were both to be beaten with rods, and, to make the punishment more impressive, it was in the same way that the crime was committed that the retribution came. So it is with the Pharisees of the Church, who throw the blame on State control, and the Herodians, who retaliate that but for sacerdotalism, the nation would long since have passed an Act of Comprehension as a sequel to the Act of Toleration. Both are right and both are wrong— right in what they assert of their rivals, wrong in what they say in their own excuse.

The inference is, that the only remedy is in a complete destruction of this Cæsaro-Clerisy. The only way to destroy it is, as in chemistry, to set up a new affinity— to draw off the Erastian party in one direction, and the Ecclesiastical in another. If we completely secularise the one and leave the other a sacerdotal sect, we shall put an end to this dangerous compound—the State Church—which is an explosive element in modern society. There will be a struggle, and it will cost much effort to do this. The roots of the system are deep down in the soil. The very corruptions of the Church are among its strong points. Its law of lay patronage, and the way in which the purchase system, intolerable now in the army, is tolerated still in the Church, enlists a host of supporters for such an institution among the upper and privileged classes. The question of Disestablishment is fast becoming one of the lower and middle stratum of society against the upper. In favour of the State Church there is the entire weight of the Court, the peerage, the landed proprietary, and the plutocracy, with a few insignificant exceptions. It is not probable that with our existing House of Commons this will be effected; but it will fare differently when the working-man's candidate and the agricultural labourer's representative sit side by side on back benches in the House of Commons, and begin to watch and control the votes of the governing classes.

Then the Cæsaro-Clerical Church of England will go to pieces, and we shall see Cavour's sentiment modified into a federation of Free Churches in a Free State. One Free Church might be a menace to liberty; not so with a federation of churches loosely cohering together, and acting on each other in a spirit of healthy rivalry. American voluntaryism has its own faults, but they are those of human nature, and if it is not the Millennium we could wish for, it is a decided advance to the stage of perfect liberty of thought and opinion, essential to the life of a spiritual religion.

CHAPTER VII.

THE THREE EVILS OF THE ENGLISH ESTABLISHMENT.

PASSING on from the general course of Church history, let us glance at the special features of the English Church Establishment. No other National Church in Europe presents us in the same way with the two tendencies of authority and of private judgment—the Catholic and the Protestant, as we commonly call them—so intimately linked together, and acting and reacting on each other. Here, if anywhere, Church principles may be studied, and the efforts of State Churchism, for better and worse, seen to the greatest advantage.

It has been said by modern apologists for the Establishment that it is an unfounded assertion that the State at some time agreed to set up and establish one particular Church; that, setting out from the abstract principle that it is the duty of the State to maintain a religion, it went on to pronounce which form of religion it should be; and that finally, out of a number of contending sects, it came to a kind of judgment of Paris, assigning the golden apple of supremacy to the Episcopal Church. We admit that if the opponents of Establishments were to argue in this unhistorical way, it would be easy for professors of history to point out their mistakes. But this is the common case of a caricature. A writer is represented as saying something supremely ridiculous, and then he is refuted out of premises which have been laid down for him by another. Instead of unfair arguments of this kind, let us meet these professors of history on their own ground, and point out the gradual stages in which a State Establishment of religion grew up in this country as in the rest of Europe. By limiting our point of view to our own country, we shall better understand the course of events elsewhere.

So far from saying that the State entered into an alliance with the Church at any particular point in the history of either, it would be more correct to say that all modern civilisation is Christian. The result is, that the State grew up under the shadow of the Church, not the Church under the shadow of the State. The course of history is traced, not by the approach and ultimate alliance of two independent bodies, but conversely in the gradual assertion by the State—first, of its own sovereignty, and then of its supremacy over the Church, and, lastly, in our day, of its entire neutrality and indifference to it. Thus the three stages of English history are marked by a Pope's Church claiming a certain supremacy over the State; a King's Church, in which the tables are turned, and the supremacy is that of the State over the Church; and, lastly, a People's Church, in which the supremacy lies with the people at large, and is localised in each congregation, not centralised, as at present, in the Crown and Parliament.

This is the true course of development. It falls in with, and corresponds to, Herbert Spencer's law of evolution, in which societies, like organisms, are simple at first, and become complicated as civilisation advances. In the earliest state of society, the legislative and the executive are one; the King and his Council advise, and then put their own decisions into execution. It is for rulers to command, and for people the simple duty is to obey. Then, as civilisation advances, the ruling power separates out into three distinct branches—the executive, the legislative, and the judicial. On the complete independence of these three elements of the sovereignty, the stability of a country depends. We may measure the growth of civilisation by the recognition of this principle of the interdependence, as well as strict subordination, of these branches of the constitutional tree. Civilisation is the evolution of structural variety out of simplicity. A rude and primitive society is like a twig —one single shoot out of the ground. But an advanced and civilised society is like a tree, where from one root there are many branches, and these boughs so widespreading that they may be broken off without endangering the life of the tree. Thus, in the civilisation of a tribal state of society like that of the Saxons in Britain twelve centuries ago, it is absurd to speak of the alliance of Church and State. The question even of the supremacy, or which is king in Britain—the Pope or the Basileus or Bretwalda—had not yet arisen. Both claims slept in the bosom of a yet ungrown society, as the peculiarities and distinctions of sex sleep in the new-born infant, or the music of the moon in the plain brown egg of the nightingale.

A French writer has described the growth of modern society as born *sur les genoux de l'église*. So far from the State having been the nursing father of the Church, the very reverse is the case. All our modern institutions have grown up under the shadow of the Church. It would be ungrateful not to admit this. But while we owe a debt of acknowledgment for what the Church did in the past, we have a duty to discharge for the present and with a view to the future. Progress is marked by the law of evolution. The State grows into an institution, having laws of its own. Take the judicial, for instance. During the Saxon period, the Court of the Hundred holds ecclesiastical as well as civil pleas. The Bishop sits as assessor with the Eaorlderman or Sheriff in the Court of the County. During the Norman period, the law authorities, civil and ecclesiastical, separate, and each takes its own course. They enter into a struggle with each other, which is not finally settled until the Reformation, when the supremacy of the Crown is asserted once and for ever, and the Canon or Pope's law has to become the Crown law. The same course of emancipation of the State from the Church is to be traced in the progress of education. The Universities were nothing but Church schools, and when we inquire how it came about that the Colleges at last overshadowed the University, the explanation is, that the Colleges represented the regular clergy, which, in the thirteenth century, completely eclipsed the secular. The Colleges bore the same relation to the Universities as the monastic system in general to the diocesan and episcopal form of Church government. It is true that when the Papacy could not control the two orders of mendicant and preaching friars which overran Europe in the thirteenth century, it wisely resolved to utilise their zeal to reduce to obedience those other children of the Church more unruly than they were. In this it acted on the same astute policy as Henry VII., who sent over as his deputy to Ireland Silken Thomas, the Lord Kildare, saying, "Since all Ireland cannot control him, he shall control all Ireland." In the same way, the Papacy converted the Orders into a body of Janissaries by which it hoped to regain the spiritual allegiance of Europe, which it had nearly lost under its schisms and the rivalries of disputed elections to the Papacy. It was in this way that, as the Orders springing up out of finally succeeded in mastering the Church, so the Colleges outgrew the Universities, and almost asserted their independence of them. These monastic institutions, which grew up *in gremio Universitatis*, were as undutiful as modern society itself, which has been nursed *sur les genoux de l'église*, only to rebel against its mother. In any case, the course of modern progress has been the same, whether in the Courts of Law, at the Universities, and throughout society. It has been the liberation, not so much of the Church from State control and patronage, as of the State from Church control and patronage. The history of the relations of Church and State has thus been not unlike the rivalry between Jacob and Esau. The younger brother, the supplanter, obtains both birthright and blessing, and the elder serves the younger. So in the same way, Hellenism, or secular society, is made to serve under Hebraism, or ecclesiastical, all through the Middle Ages. But at the *Renaissance* and the Reformation the tables were turned. Hellenism, like Esau, has the dominion, and breaks the yoke from off its neck. The State was subject to the Church during the Middle Ages;

the Church has been subject to the State for the three centuries since the Reformation. Perhaps in both cases we should not be ignorant concerning this mystery; that, as Jew and Gentile, according to the apostle, have alternately ruled and served, so Hebraism and Hellenism, or Church and State, culture and Christianity, the spiritual and the secular, have alternately played the part of tyrant and slave. It is intended that by-and-by they may see that their true relation is one not of competition for the mastery, but of kindly co-operation. They are not to be organised into one compacted system, but to interact on each other as light, heat, and electricity do in nature.

It would clear up much confusion of thought on the subject of the alliance of Church and State if we would bear in mind that as institutions grow, so our ideas of them are insensibly modified. We forget that we cannot look back at the England of the ninth century, and see it with the same eyes as the men of that age did. We insensibly assume that their point of view was ours, and that if Church and State were united then, it was because statesmen and Churchmen both wished to unite them; whereas the real state of the case is that their union arose from the simple and homogeneous state of society. Religion, morality, and law, as Professor Stubbs observes, seem to be regarded throughout the period as much the same thing.* The principle stated by Tacitus, that among the ancient Germans good morals were of more avail than good laws are elsewhere, "*plus ibi boni mores valent quam alibi bonæ leges.*" The relation of the Church to the State was

* Vide Stubbs' Constitutional History, Vol. I., p. 234.

thus close, although there was not the least confusion as to the organisation of the functions, or uncertainty as to the limits of the power of each. It was a state of things which could only exist in a race that was entirely homogeneous, and becoming conscious of political unity.

The law of development is, in fact, the key to this question of Church and State in England as elsewhere. As society grew and became more complicated, Church and State assumed each its own jurisdiction. They were at first one, as children laid in the same cradle and growing up in the same nursery. Next they were united as man and woman are when fully grown and prepared for entering into that partnership for life which we call marriage. The third state of their evolution is when this union or alliance is found to lead to contentions as to the supremacy, and when, to use Cecil's illustration to Elizabeth, two cannot ride on horseback without one sitting behind. This is the stage in which we are at present. The State is in the saddle, the Church on the pillion behind. But there remains a fourth and the final stage, when Church and State shall alike feel that they have outgrown the nursery and the partnership stage of alliance, and when each must take its own course separate from the other. To this all things point at present.

If we were to mark out the epochs of English history corresponding to these several stages, we should say that England was in the first stage down to the time of the Norman Conquest. Hooker's theory of the identity of Church and State is an utter anachronism now, and it was partially so in Hooker's day; but it expressed as fairly as any theory can the facts of the case in the Anglo-Saxon period of English history. Bishop and Earl then sat in the same County Court. There was scarcely any distinction between civil and religious offences—all crimes were alike against God, the King, and the Church But with the Norman Conquest an important change is apparent. The most important measure of the reign of the Conqueror, as Mr. Stubbs has remarked, was the separation of the Church jurisdiction from the secular business of the Courts of Law, and is, unfortunately, like all other charters of the time, undated.* Its contents, however, show the influence of the ideas which, under the genius of Hildebrand, were forming the character of the Continental Churches. From henceforth the Bishops and Archdeacons were no longer to hold ecclesiastical pleas in the Hundred Court, but to have Courts of their own to try causes by canonical, not by customary, law; and allow no spiritual questions to come before laymen as judges. In case of contumacy, the offender may be excommunicated, and the King or Sheriff will enforce the punishment. In the same way, laymen are forbidden to interfere in spiritual causes. The reform is one which might very naturally recommend itself to a man like Lanfranc. The system which it superseded was full of anomalies and disadvantages both to justice and religion. But the change involved far more than appeared at first. The growth of the Canon law in the succeeding century—from a quantity of detached local or occasional rules to a great body of universal authoritative jurisprudence, arranged and digested by scholars who were beginning to reap the

* Vide Stubbs' Constitutional History, Vol. I., p. 283.

advantages of a revived study of the Roman civil law—gave to the clergy generally a far more distinctive and definite civil status than they had ever possessed before, and drew into Church Courts a mass of business with which the Church previously had only an indirect connection. The question of investitures, the marriage of the clergy, and the crying prevalence of simony within a very few years of the Conqueror's death, forced on the minds of statesmen everywhere the necessity of some uniform system of law. The need of a system of law once felt, the recognition of the supremacy of the Papal Court as a tribunal of appeal followed of course, and with it the great extension of the Legatine administration. The clergy thus found themselves in a position external, if they chose to regard it so, to the common law of the land—able to claim exemption from the temporal tribunals, and by appeals to Rome to paralyse the regular jurisdiction of the diocesans. Disorder followed on disorder, and the anarchy of Stephen's reign, in which every secular abuse was paralleled or reflected in an ecclesiastical one, prepared the way for the constitutions of Clarendon, and the struggle that followed, with all its results, down to the Reformation itself. The same facility of employing the newly-developed jurisprudence of the canonists drew into the Ecclesiastical Courts the matrimonial and testamentary jurisdiction, and that most mischievous, because most abused, system of enforcing moral discipline by spiritual penalties at the instance of men whose first object was the accumulation of money.

The able writer from whom we have quoted the above has observed with great truth that the history of institutions cannot be mastered, can scarcely be approached, without an effort. True as this is of civil, it is especially true of ecclesiastical institutions, whose origin is partly secular, partly spiritual. The Church enters into conflict with the State like those heroes of Homer who are demigods—the child of a mortal and an immortal. Achilles, when wronged by Agamemnon, does not redress his wrongs or revenge them as one man with another. He complains to his mother, Thetis, and thus brings the gods down into the conflict. In the same way, the Church of the Middle Ages fought for a carnal prize—the dominion of men's conscience—with spiritual weapons, the fear of the unseen world and its powers; and the result was that in many cases, though not in all, she prevailed as Achilles did over Agamemnon. But the result was a revolt, not merely against Rome, but against the intolerable tyranny of the subjection of the laity to the clergy. It was the clerical courts, more even than the Papacy itself, which brought on the Reformation in England. The first act, then, of the Reformation, and the keystone of the whole, was the Act of Supremacy and the enforced submission of the clergy to the civil power. Convocation silenced or reduced to a mere assembly for voting supplies, and the Bishops' Ecclesiastical Courts reduced from courts of record to the mere registry of wills and marriages, the subjection of the Church to the State was nearly complete; and what Henry began Elizabeth carried still farther. She claimed, and all but exercised, the right of deposing as well as of making bishops. Consecration was a mere ceremony carried out under a Royal order, equivalent to a patent. In every act and relation of life, the clergy were made to feel that the Church was the second, not the first. The iron entered into their soul, and the little finger of the Royal supremacy which was near was thicker than the loins of the Papal supremacy which was far off.

It was in this way and by these means that our much-lauded National Church arose. It was national, it is true, in the sense that its tyrant was a Tudor, not a Farnese or a Medici; but as for liberty, either of self-government or growth from within, there was none. The rule *cujus regio, ejus religio*, which we think so degrading in Germany, and which only grew up there into a maxim of State after the Peace of Westphalia in 1648, was acted on in the most unblushing manner in this country a century before. Under Henry VIII., the Church was tossed violently, like a ball, between Lutheran and Catholic formulas, according as the King's mind wavered. When he reformed, it reformed; as he relapsed, it relapsed; and sturdy old Latimer seems to have been almost the only prelate who dared even to comment on this "mingle-mangle or hotch-potch," as he called it, of old and new doctrine. It is not surprising if there were many vicars of Bray. The Bishops were, in too many cases, mere trimmers, and Cranmer the most disgraceful of all, whose death scarcely redeems a career of pliable courtiership, in which he seems to be only a debased Wolsey, a Ximenes without his greatness. This taint of Erastianism which came in with the Reformation has never been purged out of the English Church. It is, in fact, the most Erastian Church in Christendom, not excepting even those of Germany, where Erastianism arose, and where it was hurled as a term of reproach by Calvinists against Lutherans. The Calvinistic Churches, to their honour be it said, have always resisted this taint of secularism more steadily than the Lutheran; but no Church on the Continent, Lutheran or Calvinist, has ever submitted to the yoke of Royal supremacy so slavishly as the English. It has even gloried in its shame, and all that it means by calling itself national is, that it is anti-Papal. It is not national in any other sense. It has never reflected the religious feeling of the great mass of the people. It has been at one time a Crown Church, and, under the Stuarts, the servile supporter of the Prerogative. Later on, it was the Church of the Peerage and the privileged classes, as Warburton describes it in his day; and latterly it has become the Church of the Plutocracy, and finds its chief supporters among the newly-risen moneyed classes, who use it as the readiest passport into good society. Its very corruptions, of which the purchase system is the most glaring, are, in fact, the secret of its strength among that class. The attempt to remove this scandal of the sale of livings (euphemiously, it is only the advowson or right to appoint which is the matter of sale) has been dealt with very cautiously by the Bishop of Peterborough; but it has failed, as all who know the strength of these vested interests knew it would. In fact, the Church of England is, for better or worse, what the eighth Henry made and left it. It has ceased to be the Pope's Church, but it is not the People's Church. It is still, as it has always been, the Church of the Crown and the upper classes, and, as long as their influence is predominant, it will continue to exist on its present foundations. When, for any reason, the balance of power is transferred from the upper to the lower section of the middle classes, then it will fall from the withdrawal of its natural supports in the privileged classes, and, above all, in the plutocracy.

Applying, then, the law of evolution to the English Church, we cannot admit as Mr. Freeman assumes, that since she was not set up and established at any one point in her history, that for this reason she ought not to be disestablished. Our argument is, that the Church, in the estate of prelacy, grew in this country and extended its powers side by side with those of the Prerogative. During the Saxon period, which was the infancy of our constitution, Church and State grew up side by side. There was no thought of union or even of rivalry. The law of differentiation had not begun to divide and distinguish between the provinces of the secular and the sacred. One law, as in the Mosaic polity and that of Mahomet, covered all cases. The distinction of later times into canon and civil law was unknown. With the Norman Conquest and the rise of the Papacy under Hildebrand, which was coeval with it, the distinction of Church and State begins to emerge. The two are allied, as the two swords given to Peter, as the sun and moon of the political firmament; but there is room for rivalry, and a contention, accordingly, for supremacy begins. On this contention the history of the Middle Ages mainly turns. All the strife about investitures is nothing else than the result of the consciousness that Church and State had entered into partnership and afterwards disputed for the mastery. At the Reformation we reach the third stage of this long process of evolution and differentiation. The State has now grown, and by the law of specialisation has branched out, into a constitution, with an Executive and a Judicature. Slowly the professions—law, physic, and divinity—have broken off from each other, and each has taken its own line of study, and holds property under distinct charters. Then army and navy, in the same way, have become distinct branches of our national defences. Endless are the ramifications and subdivisions to which this specialising tendency has progressed, and is progressing still. We may trace it in the history of our Poor-law. At first it is a benevolence collected by churchwardens and placed in a basin every Sunday on the altar; it is then a rate; and, in the last stage of all, we have guardians, unions, a Poor-law Board, and all traces of its original religious use have disappeared. The same order of emancipation of the State from Church control and patronage is going on everywhere. The monk's hood on the graduate's shoulders, the coif on the serjeant-at-law's wig, alike point to clerical traditions which long clung to our Inns of Court. This tendency to differentiation, which is the law of growth in the physical world, is also the law in the political. It explains what some call an advance and others a decline from primitive ideals, but which all admit is inevitable—the slow and final separation of Church and State. As in physiology organ and function are correlates, and as we rise in the scale so organs increase in complexity and functions differ proportionably, so it is in the body politic. It is not one member, but many; and the more advanced our civilisation, the more entirely the functions of the spiritual break away from those of the secular.

Thus, as the pre-Reformation age marked the subjection of the State to the Church, and the post-Reformation the subjection of the Church to the State, there only remains that we should now fall back on the primary relation of all, which is that of the isolation of Church and State. We must leave the Church to act on the world, not as an organised body in alliance with, and more or less in dependence on, the State, but as a purely spiritual system, acting on society as the leaven *hid* in the three measures of meal. It is by chemical affinity, not by mechanical incorporation, with the State, that Christianity is to act on the age in the future. This is the Reformation of the future; but, to attain this, we must break up the existing Establishment. No mere reform of abuses will suffice when the institution itself is little more than a compromise between Cæsarism and Clericalism. Attack the clerical element, and it takes refuge in its Erastian tendencies as subject to the State. On the other hand, attack its Erastianism, and it defends itself as a great spiritual society resting on the apostolical succession.

Let us notice in order some of these evils.

I. The first of the evils of State connection, though not the greatest, is Prelacy. By this we mean the arrangement which elevates the highest class of Church officers into Peers of Parliament, and by attaching baronies to their sees converts them into great officers of State. Into the constitutional argument for such an arrangement we need not here enter. It is obvious that it grew out of the necessities of the case in early times, and that when a Norman King summoned his great vassals and those who held *in capite* of the King to a Council of State, he should summon Bishops and

Abbots who held lands, the investiture to which was jealously claimed as a Royal Prerogative. In these times not to summon the Bishops and great Abbots would have been to admit that they held these lands otherwise than of the Crown; and knowing that the dispute as to investitures was the key to the controversies between the Crown and the Pope all over Europe, the summoning of Bishops to sit in Parliament as Barons was the reverse of a privilege. It was a dignity they would have been only too happy to dispense with. So difficult is it to throw ourselves back into former times, that we are in danger of regarding the Baronial Bishop of the age of the Edwards as the special mark of the Crown's favour. The very reverse was the case. The jealousy of the Church was extreme on the part of the Crown. Every effort was made to curtail their independence, and one of the means adopted to rivet the yoke of the Royal supremacy round their neck was thus to summon them to Parliament. Those Abbots only escaped whose lands were held by some base tenure. The Bishops and greater Abbots would have readily consented to be exempted from this feudal burden of attending Parliament. The clergy were regarded as a caste by themselves, with their own Convocation, in which they voted the supplies required by the Crown from them as a separate Estate of the Realm. It was not till a century after the Reformation that Convocation consented to surrender its right to a separate taxation of the clergy. Though in a sense, then, the Church of England was constituted in the " Estate of Prelacy" long before the Reformation, Prelacy, in the modern sense of the word, as an exceptional privilege of one order of the clergy, only dates from the power of Parliament to control the Crown. We may fix that date from the meeting of the Long Parliament under Charles I. Hence it is that Milton strikes at Prelacy so fiercely as the blackest feature in the Church of England of that day. In the narrow and intolerant mind of Laud, Prelacy had shaped itself into a new engine of oppression to restrain the rising liberties of the people, and to check the growth of the Constitution. The Prerogative, in spite of all the extravagant assertion of the Stuarts and their Court flatterers, was really weak in England. Without a standing army, and with no fixed revenue and no means of extracting it except by a vote of Parliament, the Stuarts might have clung to the fiction of the Divine right of kings, and the pretension would have been as powerless in Charles' hands as it had been in those of his father. Unfortunately for the King and his cause, he found an ally in Laud willing to do the work of Thorough with all Strafford's daring, but with a subtlety which Strafford never could descend to. Prelacy, in a word, was the engine used by Laud, as a standing army trained in the Irish wars was the instrument on which Strafford relied. Laud's idea of Prelacy was probably that of the great Cardinals Ximenes and Wolsey. He was not a mere statesman in cassock like the French Cardinals Mazarin, Richelieu, and Fleury, who ruled under weak kings like Louis XIII. and Louis XV. His ambition, probably, went further than theirs. He dreamed of turning the tables on the State, and using the Royal supremacy to reverse the subjection of the clergy to the laity, which had been riveted by the Act of Submission of 1532. Much as Laud extolled the Royal Prerogative, he was no mere courtier like Williams and Mainwaring. He had vaster schemes behind, and probably meant to use Charles as a puppet much as Mazarin and Richelieu had done in France, only for different ends. Their minds were essentially political; his was ecclesiastical through and through. Hence it is that Milton and the Puritans came to hate Prelacy with such peculiar intensity. To them it was the representative of a hateful combination of reaction, civil and religious. It concentrated in itself all that was illiberal and anti-popular in Church and State. It is true that this type of Prelacy has never reappeared in the English Church. Laud was the last of the prelates or prince-bishops, in the active and mischievous sense of the word. When the phrase has been applied to a Bishop Barrington of Durham, or a Bishop Sumner of Winchester, it has meant nothing more than that an amiable and courtly divine was the fortunate holder of overgrown revenues in the Church. A nineteenth century prelate is a peer with an establishment on a somewhat reduced scale, who, much against his will, has to put on lawn sleeves when he sits in the House of Lords, and who lives in a second-rate country-house, which, unfortunately for him, is misnamed a palace. To these modest dimensions has Prelacy shrunk in our days. Whether as the spiritualty they are of much use to the order of temporal peers among whom they are supposed to mix, we have never been able to gather from the admissions of peers themselves. As to Burke's rhetorical phrase about religion raising her mitred front in the homes of kings and nobles, facts decidedly bear in the opposite direction. The upper classes, if they want spiritual consolation at all, generally seek it, as all other people do, from some godly minister whom they respect for his own sake, not for any official rank which he happens to hold in the Church. As a matter of fact, men of rank rather dislike a successful Churchman, and his spiritual peerage is no commendation to him in the eyes of the class of hereditary peers. Prelacy, then, is an institution which is dying a lingering death. As it exists in this country, it is little more than a harmless survival of a state of society which has disappeared. It only creates a smile when the Archbishop of Canterbury claims that he holds a kind of midway position in the State as a great statesman as well as a Churchman. Thus it is that the attempt to conserve the old principle of a dominant Church by giving it an air of comprehension which cannot belong to it defeats itself, and we fall back on the position that the only solution of the question is, to throw the region of spiritual beliefs open and unenclosed—a kind of *ager publicus* or folkland, to be enjoyed in common by all, the only interference on the part of the State being to protect the rights of all in its equal enjoyment.

II. Another evil of the English State Church, for which there is no remedy but disestablishment, is the patronage system, with the corresponding abuses of the purchase of livings. Into the history of this question we need not enter. Abuses have generally, if not always, an historical rise in the dim past, and they hide their sources, as great rivers do, in distant and ill-explored mountain regions. The feudal lord who created a benefice by bestowing certain lands and paying tithes of his own and his tenants' produce, at first as a voluntary and afterwards as a compulsory tax, naturally acquired the patronage of the benefice, and so became the *advocatus* of the living, which in course of time became his *advocatio*—hence the word advowson. All this is only what we might expect from the nature of the case, and, being in harmony with the ideas of the age, no special abuse grew out of it at first. But, as time went on, as the feudal system died out, and the modern proprietary system of holding land took its place, manors changed hands, and so manorial rights came into the market. Ecclesiastical patronage being one of these manorial rights, it, too, became a matter of barter and sale. At first these rights were appendant, and such rights were conveyed with the manor as incident thereto by a grant of the manor, only without adding any other words. But where the property of the advowson has been once separated from the property of the manor by legal conveyance, it is then an advowson in gross, and is annexed to the person of the owner, and not to his manor or lands. Many reforms have been suggested for this abuse of patronage, but they all fall short of the true point of efficacy. The only remedy is to lay the axe at the root of the tree of patronage altogether, and restore to the *gemeinde*, or *commune*, or congregation of Christian men, their ancient right to call their own minister. It has been conceded in Scotland by a Conservative Ministry, who have shown the wisdom which consists in locking the stable-door when the steed is stolen. In Scotland, where the abuses of patronage were infinitesimally small, but the resistance to it stern and unyielding—there politicians have conceded the point; whereas in England, where the evils are crying, but the resistance languid on account of those who object having long since seceded—in that case no attempt at reform has been made. We can account for this on the principle that politicians move on the line of least resistance. Where the reform is easy and the demand for it loud, there they yield without much pressure; where, on the other hand, the reform is troublesome and the demand for it not so pronounced, in that case they hold back, and wait for pressure from without before they move at all. In the case of the English Church, it is clear that lay patronage and the purchase of livings having been so long recognised by law, the remedy will not be so simple as in the case of Scotland. There is no solution of the question but one, which is, to invest the parishioners with the freehold of their own church and its ecclesiastical revenues, and to create a corporation aggregate of the parish to succeed to the rights of the corporation sole on the next avoidance of the benefice. In that case the parishioners will have to deal with the patron, and to compensate him for the loss of his rights of presentation. This they could do by a charge on the revenues of the parish. After that lay patrons have been compensated in this way, the surplus might be applied to educational purposes, or some such similar object on which the parish should agree. Into the details of this scheme for extinguishing lay patronage, we do not intend to enter here. They have been clearly and lucidly brought out by Mr. Hopgood in a pamphlet lately reprinted from the *Contemporary Review*.* But

---

* Disestablishment and Disendowment of the English Church. Reprinted from the *Contemporary Review*. With Introductory Remarks by James Hopgood. Williams and Norgate. 1875.

the point we wish to enforce is this, that there can be no reform of Church patronage in this country on any other terms than total disestablishment. It is not to be supposed that patrons are going to surrender their rights to the people, and to step aside even with compensation, in order to see a scheme of endowed Congregationalism take the place of the existing system. The Church will either continue on her present foundations, or move off altogether and become a free and people's Church. But she cannot halt at some half-way house, and carry out her endowments with her into the open air of voluntaryism. Prelacy, patronage, and the purchase system, have grown up together in that exclusive aristocratical state of society in which the Church has lived and moved and had its being ever since the Reformation. They must all stand or fall together. We have seen from an historical survey of the English Church that it always has reflected the state of society of the age in which it either took a fresh shape or made a new point of departure. During the Middle Ages it became a Papal Church, because the Papacy was then the great paramount power in Europe and the visible centre of union in Christendom. At the Reformation it took a fresh point of departure, and, with the supremacy of the Crown over the Pope, the Church became an Erastianised Establishment, which, as Vinet well remarks, was one of the results of the Reformation all over Europe. In our day, the principle of the supremacy of conscience has asserted itself at last, not as a mere barren formula, but as a point of departure for religious organisation. Spiritual truth is at last being left to its own free development, and men are left to aggregate themselves religiously in what confederation they please, uncontrolled by any authority, secular or ecclesiastical. This brings us to the sect principle of religion, which, no doubt, is only a transition to a higher and more universal Church of the future. Still, to attain this, we must be prepared to pay the price, and to accept the break-up of our existing organisations as the only way of reaching it. The English Church is an anachronism as it is; it represents nothing but a survival of obsolete ideas of Churchmen who were also great officers of State, and of public men who in return undertook to regulate the Church. Prelacy, or the intrusion of ecclesiastics into worldly affairs, and patronage, or the assumption of one lay person to appoint a teacher for a whole community—these correlative evils of Clericalism and of Cæsarism arose together, and can be reformed only in one way,—by leaving religion to the free action of the individual conscience, and by reducing to a minimum the corporate idea of Church authority.

CHAPTER VIII.

SCEPTICISM AND SUPERSTITION THE OUT-GROWTH OF STATE-CHURCHISM.

WE have shown that the tendency of State Churches is to develop those two forms of error which we describe as Cæsarism and Clericalism. Endowment and Establishment tend to foster those two tendencies which are known as Erastianism and Ecclesiasticism—the two parties, as we may call them, of the Herodians and the Pharisees. Some Churches lean more in the one direction, others in the other; and the same Church, as we see in the case of the English Church, has inclined at one time in the Erastian direction, and at another towards the Ecclesiastical type. Generally, it will be found that when she was most favoured by the State and lapped in political privileges, she has leaned to a servile type of Erastianism. Then, again, as soon as these privileges have been threatened, and there has been a whisper in the air of religious equality, or, at least, of concurrent endowment, she has recoiled from these hateful concessions in the direction of sacerdotalism. It was the remark of the late Sir Cornewall Lewis, one of the acutest thinkers of his age, that there is danger in a Colonial Government leaning on a single party in the community for support, for the instant that this party which has enjoyed a monopoly of State patronage is threatened, it passes from the extreme of loyalty to disloyalty. The Crown connection party in a colony is often the most difficult to deal with when the Governor attempts in any way to. dispense with it. It is precisely the same with a State Church. The most Erastian Church is ready to become the most Ecclesiastical, and to set up the most extravagant claims of independence from the State, after having leaned on State support and fawned on it for its favours.

These are some of the evils which Cæsarism and Clericalism bring in their train. But this by no means exhausts the list. The Erastian and Ecclesiastical tendencies may be said to be confined, in a great measure, to the clergy. We have also to consider how the system of political Churchmanship works in the case of the laity. As a rule, laymen are indifferent to either theory, as such. They have no great interest in Church theories in themselves, and, excepting the lawyers, whose leanings towards Erastianism are easily accounted for, it cannot be said that the laity, as a rule, have much sympathy with Church questions, as such. With the exception of a few sentimental young men affected by Ritualism, the great mass of the laity, in their recoil from sacerdotal pretensions, fall into a kind of indifferentism which is only one remove from utter scepticism. The fashionable religion of our day is the modern form of Hobbism, which holds that "religion, like pills, is best swallowed whole, not chewed." Men of this class are quite consistent from their point of view, since State control is the best check to that which they dislike—the strong sense of personal religion commended to every man's conscience in the sight of God. It must be admitted that this class of sceptical State Churchmen constitute, after all, an insignificant minority of highly-educated men. Their "sweet reasonableness" of a religion which is only a form of ethical culture never has, and never will, lay hold on the great mass of mankind. To the great majority a religion is worthy of State support, not because it is a reasonable hypothesis with regard to an insoluble mystery, but because it is a true and authentic record of the Divine will. That this should be doubted by many within the pale of the Establishment, and denied by all without it, is fatal to its claim as an Establishment; and no one will question that we have reached this stage at present.

There is nothing so difficult to attack and deal with as this scepticism which conceals itself beneath the folds of an Established Church. No one who observes the currents of thought in modern society can shut his eyes to the fact, that two opposite tendencies are set up and fostered by this dangerous inducement to conformity which a State Church holds out. It fosters superstition in one class and scepticism in another. There are the Hobbists, who say that nothing is so certain as that we cannot assert that the opposite may be true. All religions are only guesses in the dark—approximations to an insoluble problem. Thus they stake their belief in a highly-dogmatic Church, on the quaking foundation of scepticism, as to any certainty in revealed truth. They repeat the cynical sentiment of the philosopher of Malmesbury, that orthodoxy is the religion which the head of the State approves of, and heterodoxy what he disapproves of. It is the mischievous maxim of the

German princes which has done so much to undermine all faith in religion cynically put, *cujus regio ejus religio*. On the other hand, this wave of scepticism from the side of the Hobbists is met by a counter current of superstition and blind reverence for Church authority as such. Priests and philosophers have ever been at work to destroy the simplicity which is in Christ Jesus; but at no time have they obtained such a following as at present among the semi-educated and fashionable classes of modern society. The rise of Ritualism has been coincident with the rapid increase of wealth and luxury among the commercial classes. Concurrent causes have been at work in both cases. Wealth calls for new outlets for indulgence and enjoyment, and art is the first to dip its feet in the golden Pactolus which flows from our mines and manufactories. But worship is akin to art, or has long considered art as her handmaid. It is but a step, then, to call in art to assist in making worship more stimulating to the wealthy classes, who are jaded already with excitement and sated with pleasure. This is the true *rationale* of the rise of Ritualism; it is the expression of a craving for worship released from the dulness and dryness alike of the old Church and Chapel of last century. We are not insensible to the reasons for the reaction, and if it had ended here, few would have had much to complain of in Ritualism. But the roots of sacerdotalism lay in the Anglican Church; they were left there for peace' sake at the time of the Reformation, in the hopes that they would die away in the ground. Unfortunately it has been otherwise. Sacerdotalism and the æsthetic craving for ceremonial in religion have come together and formed an amalgam which, like the Corinthian brass, is found to be the hardest of metals because it is the result of a fusion of several. Thus it is that a sceptical tendency in one class is met by a superstitious in another, and in Oxford perhaps more than anywhere else these two tendencies are focused and come to a head in the rivalries of the schools of the High and Broad Churches. The two parties meet on the common ground of a State Church, and though the difference between the two is this, that while the High Church, like the Ultramontanes, would wish to see the spiritual ruling the secular, and the Broad Church would reverse the relation, they are agreed in desiring to keep up the connection. Neither party is prepared to see the Church reduced to that state of republican simplicity in which, with little organisation and no wealth or influence to attract the worldly, she would be regarded simply with indifference by politicians, and passed by as much as the questions which exercise musicians or mathematicians are by those whose interests turn on the affairs of this world.

It is for this reason that if the Church is to be disestablished it should be done quickly, before this superstition and scepticism have eaten into the vitals of society, as they are threatening to do under a system which favours a hollow conformity. We are too prone sometimes to thank God that English society is not as French; whereas, among the upper classes at least, the resemblance between the two is as fully marked as are the contrasts. In both there is a blind fear and hatred among the upper classes of what is called democracy. The reign of privilege is threatened: feudalism, or the government of a conquering race—the Franks over the

Romanised Celts in France, the Normans over the Anglo-Saxons in this country—is nearly extinct. The reason for it has long since disappeared with the fusion of the two races; but, as we know, institutions cling on to life long after the reason for their existence has passed away. Hence it is that the traditions of feudalism as a governing caste in Church and State are strongest at a time when the institution itself for any practical purpose has disappeared. The stern facts of history die out in a haze of sentiment as the sun sinks to his rest in a blazon of orange and purple and gold. The reaction, as it is called, in France is fiercest at the time when the Revolution has triumphed all along the line. The more the principle of authority is questioned in all matters, religious and secular, the more passionately it asserts itself. All despotisms die hard, a spiritual despotism hardest of all. So heroic are its struggles to assert itself in the teeth of the age that it sometimes awes its conquerors, as the majesty of Imperial Rome awed the barbarians who viewed it, and led to the epithet, the Eternal City. It was given this name by the Saxon pilgrims who saw it in the eighth century at the moment of its utter ruin. In the same way the Church of Rome, that ghost of the Roman Empire sitting crowned on its grave, has struck even Liberals like Macaulay with a sense of its being perpetual—the Tithonus of Churches which never could die. There is nothing more remarkable than this reaction of Clericalism at the time when its death was watched for. The spirit of sacerdotalism has revived as much in England as in France, and, as a rule, the privileged classes have rallied to it in the hope of finding some succour from it for their own declining status. Thus it is that the battles of the past—Saxons against Normans, commons against lords, Protestantism against priestcraft—are being fought over again in our day. The weapons are different, but the combatants are essentially the same classes. It is fought out in the Press and on the platform, not in the council-chamber and on the battle-field ; but it is none the less a war of classes, and though the event in the long run is certain, we are not to blind ourselves to the immediate results of the struggle.

This being so, it is the duty of those who admit that the Church must be disestablished not to temporise or delay. Even in a single generation that Church has changed her front, and is no longer the same Church of the Reformation that it formerly was. This silent revolution dates from the year 1834. The rise of the new theology was received at first with a chorus of condemnation from the whole Bench of Bishops. Episcopal charges rained down censures on the "Tracts for the Times." A whole literature was called out in reply to them. Authorities were ransacked, and files of long-forgotten worthies, the fathers and founders of the Reformation, were called up from the dust of libraries to rebuke the intruders. The Parker Society publications were reprinted in the vain hope that this cloud of testimony from Elizabethan divines would rebuke the audacity of the attempt. Nothing daunted by this appeal to authority, the innovators hurled back rival tomes into the enemy's camp. The Anglo-Catholic Library of reprints of the Caroline school of divines was projected in reply to the Parker series. It was a veritable battle of the books, and though the weight of testimony rested with the divines of the Reformed school, there was no denying that Anglo-Catholic theology had its *locus standi*, at least since Laud's time, in the English Church. A few years later and the controversy took a new turn. A Cornish vicar refused to subscribe to the dogma of baptismal regeneration, in a sacerdotal sense, which was applied to him as a test of orthodoxy by the Bishop of Exeter of that day. The case went from Court to Court, until the Supreme Court of Appeal, guided, it is said, chiefly by Lord Langdale's advice, decided in favour of an open construction of the dogma, leaving the clergy the liberty to hold the baptismal term "regeneration" in a sacerdotal sense or not. This memorable judgment in the case of Gorham against the Bishop of Exeter has given a set to the judgments of the Privy Council on appeal ever since. It has created, in fact, a new theory of subscription, in which any interpretation is allowed which does not openly impugn the Articles, instead of the opposite, which excluded every sense but one. The three parties in the Church have successively been shielded in this way from proscription by their rivals, and it has been the desire of the lawyers to make the Church broad and comprehensive as it was that of the divines to make it narrow and exclusive.

The result of this politic toleration of divergent and sharply-contrasted theologies has not been an unmixed good. It has preserved the Church from disruption, it is true, or from disestablishment which must have ensued from the forcible expulsion of any one of the three parties by a combination of the other two. In this sense it has saved the Church from breaking up into sects, as Free Churches are in danger of doing. But, on the other hand, this "sticking to the ship" theory, as it has been called, has its drawbacks. In the first place, it lays an undue stress on conformity for its own sake. Unless we set truth above unity, above even brotherly concord, we are in danger of throwing away the substance for the shadow, the kernel of religion for the husk of its outward establishment. In the next place, it generates a sceptical and indifferent state of mind with regard to essentials. Once we are launched down the fatal descent of compromise and the subscription of formularies in a non-natural sense, it is impossible to say where we can stop. All dogmas and definitions are only approximations to the solution of an insoluble mystery, and we end at last by thinking, as Mr. Matthew Arnold is fond of repeating, that one approximation is as good as another, and that the only class who are utterly wrong are those stiff and unyielding Dissenters who will not first conform and then subscribe the Articles in some non-natural sense of their own. The result of this tendency is to foster scepticism, and that of the worst kind—that dry rot of the soul which sets in when we are too lazy to take up the flooring of the house we inhabit, and to see for ourselves on what foundations our faith rests. The evil does not end there. When a Church is held together with external clamps of conformity only, and dissent from its doctrines takes the form not of external revolt but of internal dislike to its dogmas, the malady is then driven in. Those peccant humours of the body which, when they break out on the surface in skin disease, pass away, become mortal maladies when they attack the vital parts. The result of thirty years' struggle in the English Church between two schools of theology has been to generate scepticism in one extreme and superstition in the other. No intelligent friend of the Church, and especially no layman, who values it chiefly as an instrument for promoting practical piety, can regard it now with any other than feelings of deep alarm, rising in some cases to positive aversion. The Church is outwardly the same as ever—her formularies are unchanged; but if we look below the surface and judge her by the prevalent tone of her clergy, we should say that she is not the same Church. The proof of this is to be sought in the tone of her organs. Between the organs of the extreme High and Low Church parties there is a division deeper far than between any two bodies of Nonconformists. To bridge over this chasm is impossible. All the warnings of the moderate men on both sides are thrown away. Perish the Church if she ceases to be Protestant, is the watchword of one party. Away with the Establishment if it hinders the spread of the Catholic revival, is the answer back from the organ of the other party. Terms of accommodation are impossible, and as the school of the *Rock* have the dead weight of popular Protestantism on their side, they are the least willing of the two to listen to anything like a compromise. The conviction that if it went by an appeal to the great mass of the laity they would have to leave the Church has driven the Ritualist party even to desire disestablishment as the less evil of the two. They have practically become Liberationists, not from conviction, but out of sheer despair of holding their ground any longer in the Church in the face of the recent judgments under the new Public Worship Act. Thus it is that forces within the Church as well as forces without have risen up to strengthen the hands of those who see no remedy but one for the present confusions.

It is in cases like these that delays are dangerous. The longer the evil day, as they regard it, is staved off, the worse it will be for those who must go out into a Free Church of the future. Had it been disestablished thirty years ago, it might have organised itself, as the Irish Church is now doing, as a distinctively Protestant Church. But the little leaven has now leavened the whole lump. The clergy are familiarised with a new theology; a College has been founded at Oxford, named after, and as a memorial to, one of the representative names of the Tractarian party. Keble College is more than a literary memorial to the author of "The Christian Year": it is a visible symbol of the triumph of the new doctrine of the Corporal Presence. Between the first and the last editions of "The Christian Year," there is a notable change in one line. It is the Homousion and Homoiousion of modern controversy.

> "Oh, come to our Communion Feast!—
> There, present in the heart,
> Not in the hands, th' Eternal Priest
> Will His true Self impart."

So Keble wrote in 1827; but when he revised the last edition a few years before his death, the reading stood thus:

> "Oh, come to our Communion Feast!—
> There, present in the heart,
> As in the hands, th' Eternal Priest
> Will His true Self impart."

The note accompanying explains, but does not justify, the change. It is only too plain a proof of a change of mind on the part of the saintly writer himself, who was carried on by the fatal spirit of logical consistency to hold the doctrine of the Corporal Presence and of Eucharistical Adoration. That this new doctrine has warped the minds of hundreds of the clergy, and made them unsafe stewards of the mysteries of God in a Church calling itself Reformed, is also undeniable. To this we may add the attempts of Dr. Pusey, the late Bishop Forbes, and others, to construct an Eirenikon, or, at least, to force the Prayer-book and Articles into a certain harmony with the Roman doctrine of the Mass. Desperate as these expedients may seem to any unprejudiced layman, the mischief does not end with the authors of these disingenuous attempts to bring the age back under the yoke of sacerdotalism. These assumptions of the power of the clergy to work some change in the elements by virtue of certain words of consecration are half believed in by those who do not themselves go quite so far in the Romeward direction. Parties, it is said, like serpents, are moved by their tails. To use a less offensive metaphor, the clergy are like mobs, pushed on from behind. Bold and unscrupulous men, often writing as anonymous journalists, put out extreme assertions in Church organs. The statement passes unrebuked, the practice gets tacitly sanctioned, and so the mass of High Churchmen are pushed helplessly on into ceremonies and beliefs which, if stated at first in their naked fulness, they would reject with indignation. Eucharistical Adoration, the Real Presence, Confession, Penance, and Purgatory are now taught almost without reserve. Even in things indifferent, a practice is preferred because it is Roman, and, saving for Celibacy and the Infallibility of the Pope, there is nothing to hinder a formal reunion between the Anglo-Catholic and the Roman Catholic schools of theology. The reunion of Christendom, in the narrow sacerdotal sense of the term, is openly called for, and the weakness of those who allowed Convocation to meet as a mere Clerical Parliament has been taken advantage of to set up a theory of the Church which is Ultramontane in all but name.

The sacerdotal party see their advantage, and do not hesitate to push it on in the teeth of the remonstrance of moderate men. As for the Evangelical party, for some reason, they have lost their old nerve and fibre, and cling on helplessly to State connection as if their only protection against the extreme men who would carry all before them lay in the Establishment principle. They seem to feel that, if disestablished, they would be left in a hopeless minority, and so they unwisely cling on to the Royal Supremacy as their only safeguard against the worse evils of sacerdotalism. This is a shortsighted, and, we would even say, a suicidal, policy. They see the dangers of disruption, but they do not see how to pluck the flower of safety out of the nettle of difficulty. They are blind to the fact that the mass of the laity are utterly opposed to these sacerdotal pretensions. The majority of Englishmen do not even understand what Ritualism means, and flock to churches where an advanced ritual is practised, not for the doctrines, but the music there. This inert mass of unthinking and nominal Churchmen, who are reckoned as proselytes of the gate by the teachers of the new school, would soon go over to the other side if the Church were free, and synodical action, in which the balance of power lay with the laity, took the place of that mediæval sham of Convocation. The Evangelical party act like a flock of sheep driven by their fears into piteous appeals to Prime Ministers to come and put down Ritualism for them. If, instead of this, they boldly took the Ritualists at their word, and appealed to the people, they would rise at once to the level of their high argument. They have lost the direction of affairs at present, but they might easily regain it. Abandoning the ground of appeal to the Privy Council, if they threw themselves on the people, they would probably find themselves supported by public opinion. Ecclesiastical lawyers like the town-clerk of Ephesus, and political bishops like Gamaliel, only dim the spiritual vision of men who profess to be ministers of a Gospel which is not of man or by man. It is these miserable temporalities which hinder spiritual men from seeing things in their right light. The Evangelical party, like the Laodicean Church of old, is rich and increased with goods, and it needs eye-salve, in the first place, to see things again in the same light as its fathers saw it.

We do not know a more miserable confession of impotence than the admission that the Low Church party needs the support of the State to keep down Ritualism. The argument is positively suicidal. We should wish to believe, for their own sake, that it is not true; that they are taking counsel of their own fears, and that fear, as the wise man defines it, is a "base betrayal of the succours which reason offereth." If it be true that the cause of Protestantism has no other bulwark than the State against a flood of Ritualistic and Romanising error, then so much the worse for Protestantism. If it has come to this, that it cannot meet Rome on the ground of argument and an appeal to the laity, it has signed its own death-warrant. Sometimes it seems as if men otherwise able and candid will use a weak argument of this kind because it appeals to the base fears of their audience. Thus the Archbishop of Canterbury, speaking some time ago at Maidstone, told the people that they might get rid of him, but there was another Archbishop (referring to Cardinal Manning) whom they could not get rid of in this way, and that they would then have to deal with him single-handed. If this meant anything more than the old "No Popery" spectre, brought out to awe a rustic audience, it meant that the sacerdotalism now latent in the English Church would then break out in its virulent form, and that we should have a home-growth type of Ultramontanism to deal with as troublesome as that which makes Constitutional government so difficult to carry on in Belgium, Italy, Germany, and elsewhere. For our part, we venture to say that we do not believe a word of it. That the sacerdotal spirit lurks in the English Church is undeniable, and we are willing to admit that Cæsarism is the same check to Clericalism now as the Roman power was to the leaven of Judaism, to which the apostle refers as the lawless one (2 Thess. ii.). But if he who letteth will let, may we not believe that in the latter case, as in the former, when the bulwark of political restraint is taken away, a spiritual epiphany of Christ will destroy that lawless one? This "bulwark" theory is too transparent a sham to deceive any who do not wish to be deceived. If a State Church is the bulwark of Protestantism, how is it that the unwearied enemies of Protestantism are those who have stolen out of the citadel of the Establishment and gone over to the enemy's camp? Nor are these open renegades its most dangerous foes. "Save me from my friends," the State Church may say; "I can deal with my foes." It is those who remain behind the bulwark to sap and mine it who are most to be dreaded. All that the Protestant party can do is to countermine and to carry on underground battles, as we may describe them, in Courts of Arches. These ecclesiastical suits, *sub arcubus*, may be honest attempts to meet sap with sap and mine with mine; but we would rather fight in the open, and, if we must die, like Ajax, let us die in the light. No! the truth is that it is the State Church which makes the evil which it afterwards tries to mend. A Free Church must, in the long run, be a small and a weak Church. As such it will not hold out attractions to men who enter the ministry under secondary motives. It offers too small a scope for ecclesiastical ambition. The disputes of a sect are like storms in a pond in comparison to those in the open sea. The tendency of sects is to subdivide, to weaken themselves by continued secessions; and all this, though it may be an evil from a certain point of view, is not the danger from which we have to protect ourselves by State control and patronage.

On the whole, then, we conclude that the only remedy for the present state of confusion is to let the Church alone to disintegrate itself. At present, by keeping the Church under the control of the Legislature, we secure to it a certain external uniformity which is very dear to the upper and governing classes. But we obtain this at the price of its internal life and spiritual usefulness. Admitting, as we do, that Christianity is the salt of the earth, and desiring to see that salt seasoning the mass of secular life, we cannot consent to an arrangement by which the salt loses its savour. The Church is the spiritual counteractive to the State; it supplies those principles which secular life needs. But we do not go on to argue that it is, therefore, the statesman's duty to incorporate the spiritual society with the secular, and construct a State which shall be one and the same society in its secular and spiritual relations. All history is one long protest against this grand mistake of legislators. The result of this union is either an ecclesiastical State like Judaism, or a political Church like the State religions of Greece and Rome. In the former case, the hierarchy rule the State; in the latter, the magistracy control the Church. But, in either case, the true interests of religion are marred and hindered. History, which records these mistakes, does not record a single instance of the true relation, which is that of a benevolent neutrality. This admission seems to tell against our case, for if what has been will be, presumably we may infer that what never has been never can be. But we are not so sure of that. The history of human progress is the gradual elimination of error. The story of human progress, as Beccaria remarks, presents to us the picture of a vast "sea of error, in which only a few tempest-tossed barks at a distance from each other emerge to the surface of truth." This being so in other things, we are encouraged to hope that the errors of Church history will not be repeated for ever. The theory of perfect indifference on the part of the State has only been slowly reached in America, and even there the theory has still some who distrust it. It was not struck out at a heat there; it was no inspiration of the Pilgrim Fathers, nor even a happy thought of the founders of the Republic, who drew up the Declaration of Independence. Slowly and reluctantly the control of religion has been renounced by politicians there, and it is only in the same timid, tentative way that we can expect the like results in the Old World. We must be patient with men's prejudices, as God is, and trust that the mistakes of the past will compel men at last to see that the only help they can render to religion is summed up in the words of Gamaliel, "Refrain from these men, and let them alone;" or in the answer of the merchants to Colbert, "*Laissez nous faire.*"

CHAPTER IX.

GROWTH OF THE IDEA OF RELIGIOUS NEUTRALITY.

"SEEING that the Royal Academy now usurps the place without discharging the functions of a national institution, it becomes important to consider what, if any, are the available means of reform. That the Society should be preserved in its present state, like one of Sir Charles Dilke's unreformed corporations, for the sake of the picturesque beauty of its decay, is a suggestion which would be scarcely found flattering, even in the eyes of the Academicians themselves. Many of these gentlemen, as we have seen, are fully alive to the magnitude of the interests entrusted to their keeping, and are very conscious of the proved incompetence of the body to which they belong. For it is not to be supposed that the failures of the Academy are merely historical, or that its appropriate labours are now complete. Much remains to be done, although the Academy does little, and the artistic requirements of the time are certainly not to be measured by the capabilities or achievements of a society that is pledged to inaction."

The above remarks on the Royal Academy (quoted

from a letter to the *Pall Mall Gazette*, by Mr. J. Comyns Carr),* might be applied *mutato nomine* to an Established Church. Academies for Art and Establishments of religion labour under the same drawback. They alike degenerate under that law of traditionalism which represses all individuality, and which is the inherent vice of all corporate bodies. The law of decay, written on all such institutions, may be summed up in this law of the conservation of form at the expense of life, which is the opposite of the Darwinian law—that the strong displace the weak. In the case of corporate bodies, as of Trade Unions, it is the weak and the imitative who displace the strong and self-reliant. It may protect the weak in the struggle for existence, but it is at the expense of progress. Every great and beneficial principle, whether in art, science, or religion, has had to pass through the cold fit of national neglect, and the hot fit of State support and patronage. It is difficult to say whether the cold or the hot fit is the most injurious to its best interests. Art has had its Academies, science its Colleges of Surgeons and Physicians, its Royal Institutions and Royal Societies, and religion its State Churches. The result is the same in all three cases. Happily for art and science the fatal embrace of the State has not been thrown round them in the same way. They have never wanted royal patrons and ministers, like Mæcenas and Richelieu, to throw around them the false glare of public recognition. But, on the whole, they have been left alone to an extent which it has not been the good fortune of religion to participate in. How little Academies have

* Vide *Pall Mall Gazette*, March 9, 1876.

done for real art, or Royal Societies for true science, let history be witness. Art, which is imitative, and science, which is only the learning what other men have thought, are not strangled by patronage. For this reason there is a use in colleges and endowments for book learning. All that learning asks for is leisure, and endowments provide that for it. But all true art, which is inventive, and the higher science, which implies research, will never get their meed from Royal Academies and Societies. The endowment of research is one of the dreams of our day; but the dream will never be realised, for there is no testing the true scientist. Learning of all kinds may be tested, and so may be safely endowed; but real invention is like poetry, an inspiration which is its own reward. Much more is this the case with regard to religion. Unhappily for the true interests of religion, politicians have been possessed with the thought that, since it is the most important factor of human welfare, it must not be left out of account in the building-up of political societies. The remark is as old as Plutarch, that you may find cities without walls, or monuments, or palaces of any kind; but a city without a temple to the immortal gods is not to be met with. The inference seems obvious, that what is so important to human welfare must come under the special protection of the magistrate. To him, at least, all religions, whether equally true, as the multitude think, or false, as the philosopher holds them to be, are equally useful. When modern apologists for State Churches appeal to antiquity, it is as well to meet them with the frank admission, that if authority is worth anything, it is entirely on their side.

The precedents, such as they are, only establish one order of things. We meet with only one of two types of society, the Asiatic or European—the one, the religio-political, or Church-State ; the other, the politico-religious, or State-Church. In the one, which is hieratic, as in Egypt, Assyria, and among the Jews, the State is a function of the Church; in the other, which is democratic, as in Greece and Rome, the Church is a function of the State. The only difference is, that what is first in the Oriental conception of things is second in the West, and *vice versâ*. But with this difference: they are at one as to their view of religion as an organised institution with a priesthood and ritual, which is to enter into and take part in the political life of the State. But whether a Church-State, as in the East, or a State-Church, as in the West, it comes to nearly the same thing; and the controversies of modern times, whether on politics or religion, all turn on the question, "What think ye of Christ?" Did He come as a religious reformer, to destroy false cults and set up a pure cult in its place? So thought Constantine, so Charlemagne, Alfred, and all politicians and public men, almost without exception to our day, the exceptions being so few and far between that they are of absolutely no account, unless we weigh authorities as well as count them. Churchmen have not been slow in echoing this commonplace of politicians. Not to speak of sycophants, like the Byzantine clergy of the Lower Empire, or the Bancrofts of our Church, to whom James' utterances against the Puritans seemed the language of inspiration, it is a melancholy fact that no sect (if we except, perhaps, the Friends and the Baptists) have escaped this taint of Cæsarism. They have all worshipped the image which Nebuchadnezzar has set up.

It is a remark of M. de Laveleye, in a pamphlet on Protestantism and Catholicism, that "the action of religion is so profound on the minds of men that they are always led to give to the State forms which they have borrowed from that of religion." This is true; but so is the converse. It is equally true that men are led to give to the Church forms borrowed from those of politics. It was so in the second and third centuries. The absolute and autocratic principle had asserted itself in politics, and it passed into religion. Men in their helplessness crouched, from fear of anarchy, beneath the shadow of a *Divus Cæsar*, and the Church, unconsciously at first, but afterwards more openly, copied this bad example. She abandoned the Commonwealth or Republican, and organised herself on a Monarchical type. This explains the rise of diocesan episcopacy. She was taken up into the political system of the empire, and consequently had to accommodate herself to her new position. At first the purple sat uneasily on her, and her monks and hermits of the desert, who were the Dissenters and Nonconformists of that day, raised their protest, such as it was, against the worldliness of prelatical Churches. It was all in vain. The gold and the iron, the brass and the clay, had become mixed, and the result was that long conflict between a *Kirchen-Staat* and a *Staat-Kirche*, the Byzantine and the Roman idea of supremacy. In the West this conflict was aggravated from the fact that Cæsar's throne was vacant, and an unheard-of claim was set up, based on forged Decretals and a lying legacy, that Constantine had abdicated in favour of Pope Sylvester. That standing difficulty of modern States, Ultramontanism, grows out of this state of things. In a recent paper in the *Fortnightly* M. de Laveleye states this with his usual precision and point:—

"The Catholic clergy claim that to the Pope alone belongs the right of deciding, in the last instance, whether a civil law is binding. They could not, therefore, admit that the lay Government should impose conditions on the nomination of priests. That would have been to recognise the supremacy of the State, and they maintain, on the contrary, the principle of the supremacy of the Church. The importance of the dispute is plain. Nothing less than a question of sovereignty is at stake. Who is to be master in Germany, the civil power—the Emperor and the Chambers —or the Pope? It is the old quarrel of investiture, the old struggle between the Papacy and the Empire. The only way of bringing it to an end would be to adopt the American system of complete separation. But the Germans contend, and perhaps not without reason, that such a system is only good for Protestant countries. In a Catholic country they say it conducts directly to the enslavement of the State and the absolute domination of the Pope, as is to be seen in Belgium. The State professes to ignore the Church, and not to concern itself with it. But the Church only admits the system provisionally, and with a view of drawing from it the means of establishing its own power. It claims that the State should be subjected to its laws; it makes itself master of the instruction of the young, on whom it inculcates its own ideas, and it carries these ideas into triumphant practice the day after it has gained the majority in the country. The struggle is thus made inevitable, and the only alternative is to bow beneath the Sovereign Pontiff, who holds in his hands the two swords—the sword of civil and the sword of ecclesiastical authority. What seems to mark that the conflict cannot be avoided is that it has broken out in all the Catholic countries—in France, in Spain, in Belgium, in Italy, in Ireland. On the other side of the seas at this very moment it is pursued with no less violence in Brazil and throughout Catholic America. The battle that is being waged in Prussia is, therefore, a fact that results from the nature of things—a sort of historic necessity for Catholic countries."

Hence it is that this mistake of politicians as to the meaning of Christ's kingdom has been a "funeral dower of present woes and past" to the Church and the world. If they had left the Church to itself, and regarded it as an insignificant sect of Ebionites or Essenes—the Ebionites or poor ones, the Essenes or pure ones, Puritans (for so the two words mean in the Hebrew)—the leaven of Prelacy and the full-blown apostacy of the Papacy might have been kept out of the Church. But it was not to be. Perhaps it was part of God's purposes that the Church of the future was to learn by the mistakes of the past, as the camel finds its track by the whitened bones of the caravans which bleach the desert. The descent of the Church into the mediæval apostacy was long and painful. Long and painful is her track upward to the spiritual highlands of liberty and independence. A dominant Church becomes a persecuting Church. The age of the martyrs is reproduced within herself, and the mystic Babylon is drunk with the blood of dissenters from the dominant creed. This is the nadir of her descent, and as it is the darkest point so it precedes the dawn. Then there arose new sects of Ebionites and Essenes, Christ's poor ones and preachers —the Peter Waldos, Wiclifs, Husses, and Jeromes of Prague. They are persecuted as before, they are counted as sheep to the slaughter; but still they gather followers. These hunted men band together as David and his outlaws in their caves of Adullam, and at last David comes to his throne, the persecution ends, Protestantism is a religion to be treated with, and even Spanish Philip has to put out his fires in the Netherlands. After a brief reaction and an ill-starred effort of Protestantism to repeat the vain attempt to enforce uniformity, men begin to see the mistake. A new idea dawns on their minds. Liberty, if not equality, is the last word of Protestantism in the seventeenth century. The nobler idea of perfect religious equality has not yet broken on the world. Still the gain has been great, and a point has been made good from which the Church and the world will never again recede.

It has been remarked by Professor Masson, in his life of Milton, that the history of the modern idea of toleration could be written completely only after a large amount of special research. Who shall say on the heads of what stray and solitary men scattered throughout Europe in the sixteenth century, *rari nantes in gurgite vasto*, some form of the idea as a purely speculative conception may have been lodged? Hallam finds it in the

"Utopia" of Sir T. More (1480—1535), and in the discourses of the Chancellor l'Hôpital of France (1505—. 1573), and there have been others. But the history of the idea as a practical and political notion lies within a more precise range. Out of what conflicts and controversies carried on in Europe during the sixteenth and seventeenth centuries was the practical form of the idea bred? Out of pain, out of suffering, out of persecution —not pain inflicted constantly on one and the same set of men, or on any two opposed sections alternately; but pain revolving, pain circulated, pain distributed till the whole round of the compass of sects had felt it in turn, and the only principle of its prevention gradually dawned on the common consciousness.

Thus it is that persecution and toleration are correlated—or rather, to speak more accurately, toleration is a kind of after-thought upon persecution. It is with toleration as with free trade; in both cases the generalisation was only reached after a long induction of instances, and after the opposite theory had been tried under every case and had signally failed. The simplest hypothesis is not the first, on the contrary, it is the last, to be resorted to in any scientific inquiry. It is the same with moral questions. Men tried an enforced uniformity in worship, clung to it long, in spite of the cruelties it inflicted on others, and only renounced it at last when it could no longer be concealed that the evils of State compulsion in religious matters outweighed the advantages.

But toleration is, after all, only a step, though an important one, in the stage to the entire separation of Church and State. It was the Dutch sect of Baptists who seem to have been the first to reach this stage. In a Confession, or Declaration of Faith, put forth in 1611 by the English Baptists in Amsterdam, this article occurs: "The magistrate is not to meddle with religion or matters of conscience, nor compel men in this or that form of religion, because Christ is the King and Lawgiver of the Church and of conscience." It is believed that this is the first expression of the absolute liberty of conscience in the public articles of any body of Christians. This principle of the Anglo-Dutch Baptists was imported into England. It was three years after this memorable declaration had been made in Amsterdam that a tract appeared in London with the title, "Religious Peace; or, a Plea for Liberty of Conscience." This was printed in 1614, and presented to King James and the English Parliament by Leonard Busher, citizen of London. Other tracts also appeared from the same source. The Baptists clearly had the honour of leading the way in the enunciation of this great truth, in which they were followed at some interval by the Independents, and then, more reluctantly still, by the Presbyterians and Episcopalians. The last two sects cannot be said to have admitted the general principle at all. They held it with so many reservations as to essentials and non-essentials—the heresies which were deadly and those which were not—as to render their theory on the subject, if they had any, practically nugatory. It was the Americanised Welshman, Roger Williams, in his tract, "The Bloudy Tenent (*i.e.*, Bloody Tenet) of Persecution for Cause of Conscience, discussed in a Conference between Truth and Peace, written in London in 1644," who asserted the principle in its fullest extent. In this he was followed by John Goodwin, the vicar of St. Stephen's, Coleman Street, whom the Presbyterians had denounced as an Arminian, Socinian, and what not. Williams carries the theory to its natural conclusion. He shows that a National Church was not instituted by Christ Jesus. The civil commonweal and the spiritual commonweal, the Church, are not inconsistent, though independent the one of the other. "Persons," he adds in his striking way, "may with less sin be forced to marry when they cannot love than to worship what they cannot believe." The civil power owes, he says, *three* things to the true Church of Christ—1, Approbation; 2, Submission; 3, Protection;—while it owes *two* things to false worshippers—1, Permission; 2, Protection. Goodwin, in the same way, went beyond the ordinary Independent theory of tolerating within limits. He seems to have seen that to tolerate orthodox sects, but not heterodox, was to give with one hand and to take away with the other. It was to set up a State censorship of religions, and virtually thus to merge the Church in the State. How far this went beyond the ideas of the age is seen from the violent abuse heaped on both these eminent men by the Presbyterian party. In a sermon preached before Parliament in 1644, Edwards attacked two classes of underminers of temple work. First, he said there were those who would allow nothing to be *jure divino* in the Church, but held that all matters of Church constitution were to be settled by mere prudence and State convenience; in other words, the Erastians. They are lectured, but let off more easily than the second sort of underminers, "such as would have a toleration of all ways of religion in this Church." Parliament is reminded that all tendency to this way of thinking is unfaithfulness to the Covenant, and is told that to set the door so wide open as to tolerate all religions would be to make London an Amsterdam, and would lead to—in fact, would certainly lead to—Amsterdamnation. Tolerationism, in fact, in the jargon of the day, was regarded as a new form of heresy in addition to the many which abounded. The Presbyterians, who had now changed places with the Prelatists, and had stepped into their prejudices, regarded toleration as something worse than a heresy; it was the mother of heresies; it was the seed-plot and nursery of them all. Arminianism, Erastianism, Socinianism, Seekerism, Popery itself, all grew out of toleration. It is a grievous fact, but one which no candid Presbyterian can shut his eyes to, that from the year 1644, in which Prelacy went down and Presbyterianism took its place, the arrogant, persecuting spirit of the old Laudian party passed into the Puritans, who now became dominant in Church and State. The proofs, as Mr. Masson remarks,[*] are so abundant collectively, they form such an ocean, that it passes comprehension how the contrary could have been asserted. From the first appearance of the Presbyterians in force after the opening of the Long Parliament, it was their anxiety to beat down the rising idea of toleration; and after the meeting of the Westminster Assembly and the publication of the *Apologetical Narration* of the Independents, the one aim of the Presbyterians was to tie Toleration round the neck of Independency, stuff the two struggling monsters into one sack, and sink them

[*] Vide Milton's Life, vol. III., 129.

to the bottom of the sea. In all the Presbyterian literature of the times, Baillie's Letters, Rutherford's and Gillespie's Tracts, the pamphlets of English Presbyterian divines in the Assembly, this antipathy to Toleration, limited or unlimited, this desire to pinion Independency and Toleration together in one common death, appears overwhelmingly.

But before we charge the Puritan party with inconsistency in claiming toleration for themselves, and then denying it to others, we should remember that their error was only that of the age. With the exception of the Baptists and Quakers, no Church had any clear ideas of the limits of civil authority. We need no further proof of this than the notorious instance of Gallio. The one example in the New Testament of an upright magistrate, who kept himself to questions within his cognisance, was twisted into an example of indifference to the interests of truth. Such a startling mistake could not have been possible, unless men had stumbled on the threshold of the passage, unless they had looked at the narrative of the Acts through the mists of mediæval ideas as to the duty of upholding truth with the sword. All that can be said in excuse for the Presbyterians is that they were no wiser than others; they saw truth through the same coloured glasses of inveterate prejudice. They claimed to be tolerated themselves because they were " of the truth ;" but to do unto others as they would be done by was to imply that there was no such thing as truth, and no infallible guide to it in the Bible. The Latitudinarians, to do them justice, saw the duty of toleration on the ground that truth is not so patent to all as the believers in verbal inspiration supposed. They were tolerant of error because they were sceptical, or partially so, as to any certainty of religious truth. Hence it is that many argue as Buckle and Lecky do, that scepticism, which, like some strong acid, is the universal solvent of all dogmas, is the most favourable condition for the growth of toleration. It might be shown, in reply, that the most sceptical age may also become the most superstitious, and in the end, and for the same reason, the most intolerant. But we need not dispute the position that generally toleration and philosophical breadth go together. The man who has learned the lesson of his own ignorance, and feels how indistinct his own grasp of truth is, must be indulgent to the errors and even the extravagances of others. There is the toleration and contempt which is all that philosophers can feel, and there is the toleration of conviction, which is the position the Christian has reached who understands Christ's words, that His kingdom is not of this world.

But the Presbyterians of 1644 had reached neither of these two stages. They had neither the breadth of Milton and Hales and Chillingworth, nor the intensity of spiritual perception of Roger Williams and George Fox. They were evangelical, it is true, but evangelical legalists of a type not uncommon in our day. Strict Sabbatarians, scribes in their view of the letter of inspiration, precisionists in their estimate of the importance of dogma, and hard disciplinarians in their notions of the family life, it was impossible for men of this type of mind to think otherwise than they did on the question of Church and State. Instinctively men of Milton's culture and breadth of view turned from them, and described old presbyter as priest writ large. They, on the other hand, retaliated on him as a Divorcer—for they actually invented the name of a new sect, in order to dub Milton as its progenitor. With the waters of strife thus let loose, it was difficult to see how there could be any toleration at all, since all sects alike were equally willing to die for their own convictions, or to put others to death for theirs. Like fishes in the same pond preying on each other, they were equally ready to slay or be slain; and there are men in this lukewarm age of the world who look back on this state of things with a half sentimental regret. It is called " earnestness," and the men of that school are supposed to be heroes or companions to those of this degenerate day. We do not care to dispute this position. All we are anxious to show is, that the ascendancy of the Puritans, in 1644, led to their rapid decline and extinction as a party. It was with them as with the Church Evangelical party of our day. Their success was their ruin. They conquered the world, and then the world conquered them. Being persecuted, we bless, being defamed, we entreat; but when the *rôle* is reversed, when the persecuted become the persecutors, the days of the growth of the Church by the increase of God are over. Church history must be written for nothing if it does not teach us this, that toleration is only an *interim* truth, a stage to something more than itself. Nothing is more shallow than the cuckoo-note of superficial religionists in our day. They would tolerate, they tell us, all religions, but only patronise one. They would deal in this way with idolatry in India, and with Romanism in Ireland. But those who repeat phrases of this kind are unconscious that they are only wearing the old cast-off clothes of a byegone age. We thank them for nothing, when they tell us that they would not persecute false religions. We should be sorry to trust them with the power, for between patronising one religion and persecuting another there are only thin partitions. Indeed, we cannot call on the State to show favour to one set of religious opinions without requiring it, more or less, to put all others under a ban.

Toleration, then, is only the transition point between the old theocratic idea of one Divine and immutable truth binding on all and everywhere, and the modern idea that truth is a light within the candle of the Lord, for which each man is alone responsible to the God of truth. The thorough sceptic and the thorough believer may each be tolerant after his kind; but the half-believer—the Christian hedged in with dogmas, and fencing in his faith with a prickly hedge of half beliefs—must, to be consistent, persecute. As a phase of religious opinion, the history of toleration is instructive. It teaches us, as we have seen, that we must go forward or backward: there is no standing still at the half-way house of toleration. The Presbyterians went back in 1644, the other sects went forward; and the consequence is that the Nonconformity of the next age ceased to be Presbyterian. The Nonconformists, after 1688, slowly worked on—very slowly, we admit—to the position which they now take up of the absolute incompatibility of any alliance at all between Church and State.

This was the only logical outcome from the theory of toleration, which was all that the seventeenth century dared to whisper. But for us to go back to that would be for a man to go back to his intellectual childhood. Toleration is now only uttered in those circles where an excuse is sought for religious inequality, and where it is hoped in this way to disarm hostility by making the privileged sect seem as little obnoxious as possible to those who are outside its pale.

We have reached that stage, then, on the road of political progress in which religion, like art and science, is left, as a rule, to fare by itself, and all that the State does is to offer it a little left-handed patronage. In the case of art, it takes the shape of an Academy, which is more obstructive than helpful to rising genius; and in the case of science, of a Royal Society, which recognises merit when all the world has already put its stamp on the great discoverer. As a rule, these Academies and Societies are only coteries, or mutual admiration clubs, where the "ancients" of art and science sit and care for the true concerns of the cause which they are organised to promote, as Olympians do for the affairs of mortals. All corporations and guilds tend to a decay of this kind. We see it in our City Companies. The institution survives the object for which it was instituted. The history of survivals has become a branch of inquiry among those who study antiquity in something more than the spirit of a mere antiquarian. This tendency is seen everywhere and at all times. An institution ceases to answer the end for which it arose; it is not, therefore, reformed or removed. On the contrary, with its proved inutility and its acknowledged obsoleteness, a certain *religio loci* gathers around it. It is not always in politics as in physiology, where an organ disappears or becomes merely rudimentary when it has ceased to discharge its proper functions. On the contrary, it survives as a tradition of a bygone age. Sir Henry Maine notices in this way the survival of monarchical institutions on into the aristocratic period of the Greek and Roman Republics. Even, he adds, where the name of the monarchical functions does not absolutely disappear, the authority of the king is " reduced to the merest shadow. He becomes a mere hereditary general, as in Lacedæmon, a mere functionary, as the King-Archon at Athens, or a mere formal hierophant, like the *Rex Sacrificulus* at Rome."* This superstitious reverence for dead forms is as strong in the modern as in the ancient world. Among no people is it so strong as among our own. Provided the fiction be kept up, the reality may be dispensed with. We saw an instance of this recently in the willingness of the House of Lords to surrender their appellate jurisdiction, on condition that the new Court of Appeal should consist of life peers and hold their session in the accustomed place. Thus, they were willing to give up the substance for the shadow, and, provided that appearances were kept up, to yield all that was essential in maintaining the right at all. When men are so ready to cheat themselves with appearances, we need not wonder that reformers play into their hands, and leave them the empty shell when the kernel of power for which it had any value has been taken away. Much of our modern Conservatism is thus

* Vide " Maine's Ancient Law," p. 10, 4th Edition.

only a reverence for extinct forms of power, and a desire to keep up institutions which, by their name if nothing else, link us with the past. The more, too, the age moves on in new directions, the stronger will this instinct become. It is precisely because ours is a democratic age, and our nation is emphatically a shop-keeping nation, that we feel this instinct so strongly; and it is the commercial class who, more than any other, yield to this fascination. Much of what is called the revival of Church life is nothing else than the outcome of this tendency. The Church is a little relic of feudalism which has come down to our modern times. The flavour of antiquarianism about it is its special charm. Its very vocabulary must be recast in harmony with this tendency. For morning and evening prayer we must speak of matins and evensong; our communions must be celebrations; and introits, antiphons, and Gregorian chants replace the psalms and hymns of our younger days. For the learned parson of Crabbe's time,

> "Who cared not much for surplice, hood, or band,
> But kindly took them as they came to hand,"

we have the niceties of amice, alb, and tunicle—not to speak of the profounder mysteries of birettas, dalmatics, and chasubles. These things were laughed at as "man millinery" thirty years ago; but the laugh is now turned the other way. To be ignorant of these things is to be behind the age—a stupid slave of pigtail prejudice and of the "irreverend" Georgian era. Much of this is mere sentimentalism; it is the mistake of taking a survival for a revival. But it is also explained by a craving, not always unhealthy, for a visible link between the Christianity of the past and that of the present age. The Anglican Church offers itself as that link. It is a corporation with unbroken succession of office-bearers from remote centuries. Provided appearances are kept up, the majority are not troubled whether the continuity is external only or internal as well. The Church is the representative society of religion in the same way as the Royal Academy is of art, or the Royal Society of pure and applied science.

No one who has to deal with the question of Disestablishment can afford to overlook such a state of feeling as we have glanced at above. What is most remarkable is, that the Church spirit, as it is called, is more active even in towns than in the country—among the younger generation of the manufacturing classes than among the landowners. It would be natural among the latter; among the former it is cultivated as a fashion or distinguishing mark from the operative class among whom they live. The Conservative and Church reaction is a form of the present struggle between capital and labour. Capitalists as a class are instinctively Conservative, and resist the encroaching democracy of trade unions and co-operative industry, so they lean to the Church as one of their natural supports against this advancing tide of democracy. Like all reactions in this country, it is not fanatical, and has little of that passionate excitement with which the upper classes in France, for instance, threw themselves into the crusade against modern ideas. The "sons of the Church" (to borrow Mr. Disraeli's phrase) are not—like the "sons of the crusaders" in France—an excitable set of reactionaries, who, if they had the power as they have the will, would plunge Europe into a civil war for the cause of Legitimacy in France and of the Temporal Power in Italy. Conservatism in this country is tinged with our Saxon common-sense. It clings to the idea of a dominant State Church because it is the Church of the governing classes. It has no wish to disturb the seventeenth-century settlement of toleration to all. What it scruples at is the consequent truth of religious equality. In this the analogy of art to the Royal Academy holds good. Provided only that the Academicians are left on their Olympian heights undisturbed, the rank and file of artists may work on as they please, and cater for the public on their own terms. In the same way, the modern Churchman bears no ill-will to the Dissenter, as such ; on the contrary, he wishes to deal with him on the *uti possidetis* principle. If the Church tolerates Dissent, why should not Dissent in return tolerate the Church ? It is true that the one is a privileged society and the other not ; but whose fault is that ? The Nonconformist has the remedy in his own hands. He has only to drop his prejudices, and come into the Church on her own terms of communion. The bigotry is all on his side : the "sweet reasonableness" all on the side of Conformity.

The answer to all this is obvious. The age cannot stand still or live on past formulas. Toleration to all was a landing-stage in the advance of society from an age of persecution to one of civil and religious equality ; but it was only a landing-stage. We have left that point behind in our progress, and must now make good our standing on the ground of the indifference of the State to all religions alike. If the Church cannot go with the age in this respect, as it is obvious she cannot, she must be left behind. A few of her brighter intellects would attempt to save her by throwing down barriers, and creating new terms of comprehension. This she indignantly refuses to consent to. The Bishop of Lincoln, not Dean Stanley, is her representative mind; and this is why pretentions like those of the Bishop are supported by the rank and file of the rural clergy, while it is only an educated minority of University men who follow the lead of the Dean of Westminster. Even organs like the *Saturday Review* rather take sides with the Bishop against the Dean on questions like the Burials Bill, and reject a compromise which would recognise the official ministry of non-Episcopal Churches.

We are brought, then, to the conclusion that the Church, in spite of her pretentions to Catholicity— nay, in consequence of it—is fast subsiding into the position of a sect. It has this disadvantage, that while dogmatically it acts as a sect, in its administration, it still claims to be a dominant sect. That these two claims are mutually exclusive it needs no logic to prove. The knot that connects it with a State recognising the equal status of all its citizens may be cut, it cannot be untied. Already we see the Church virtually subsiding into that same attitude of proud isolation to the national religion that the Royal Academy bears to art, or the Royal Society to science, or our City Companies to the artisans of our day. The same fate has overtaken it which overtakes all old corporations. The form has survived the essence, the letter of the trust has killed the spirit. If this stagnation were peculiar to the Church, we might look out to reform it; but, finding the same tendency in all chartered corporations, we set it down to a law of decay, common to all societies. It compels us to conclude that the only remedy for this isolation consists in breaking down the monopoly of State patronage, behind which this dominant and exclusive Church entrenches itself. We are driven to conclude that as Academies have done so little for art, and Societies for true science, the policy of the State is to give over this indirect form of patronage. Bounties, as Adam Smith long ago pointed out, do not foster the growth of trade. They may give it an impulse at first; but, if long continued, their effect is disastrous in the long run. Much more is this the case with religion. It lived down the age of persecution, but it was the age of protection beginning with Constantine which killed its growth. To some extent we see this, and therefore tolerate the competition of Free Churches; but we do not see the truth to its full extent, or we should call for a surrender of that charter by which one sect is given the exclusive right to represent the nation in its religious affairs. In this respect we still lag behind the rest of Europe, and are far behind our own Colonies, where, after trying concurrent endowment, the only basis recognised is that of the complete neutrality of the State in all religious affairs.

CHAPTER X.

THE CHURCH DEFENCE ARGUMENT.

THE strength of the attack can only be measured by that of the defence. There is a stage in every siege at which the engineer becomes virtually commander-in-chief. No assault is ordered till he gives the word that it is practicable—until he has calculated every contingency, and has provided that in no case is the garrison strong enough to beat off the attack. Hence it is that the cry for Disestablishment has drawn out a counter effort on the part of Church defenders. The existence of an attacking party has called out a party in defence of Establishments. Threatened institutions, it is said, live long; and the reason for this remark is this, that it is only when threatened that the reasons for the institution become apparent to many minds. The majority of mankind only reason *ex post facto;* or, as Dr. Newman once put it, they set out with their principles derived from authority, tradition, and so forth, and then proceed to find arguments to support them. Their reasons are thus preposterous, in the strict sense of the word; they put what is last first, and what is logically first is to them last. Their real reason for supporting an institution is that it exists, and whatever exists has a sufficient reason for existing. But a reason of this kind has a flavour of the old ontological school. Some argument, must be found, therefore, beyond the bare fact that it exists, and this it is which explains the rise of a Church Defence party at the time when the institution is threatened.

Another consideration must not be overlooked before we state the case on the other side. There is a *zeit geist*, or spirit of the age, which has a law of its own, like that of the winds, which we can to some extent forecast but in no sense control. This current of public opinion directs the thoughts of men to an extent they are scarcely aware of, and makes up the common-place philosophy of the majority of mankind. Till about the end of last century, it was a fixed principle everywhere that religion was an affair of State control and patronage. It was the duty of the State to uphold truth; it had a consequent right to decide what was truth. To question this was to degrade the State into a mere police institution. Even in the United States, whose constitution since the Declaration of Independence is based on the non-intervention principle in Church affairs, this was by no means the case until the Revolution era. So heartily is this non-intervention principle accepted at present, and so unhesitatingly is it maintained, that he who should deny it would find it hard to gain a hearing, and would be suspected of holding an attitude unfriendly towards popular liberty itself. "It belongs to American liberty," says Lieber, "to separate entirely from the political government the institution which has for its object the support and diffusion of religion. But, as has been well remarked, the broad line of demarcation between the opinions of to-day and those which prevailed a century ago can nowhere be more distinctly traced than precisely at this point, and the contrast that is presented deserves the more attention for the reason that it has hardly been touched upon with sufficient discrimination even by our best historians."* That in all the colonies, previous to the Revolution, there existed a connection, more or less close, between religion and the State, is a fact often repeated and sufficiently familiar. Such a connection may be established in two ways—negatively, by means of tests excluding from public office or the civil franchise the professors of a certain faith; or, positively, by means of legislation providing for religious establishments or for the support of public worship. The thirteen colonies afforded illustrations of all these modes. In all there existed religious tests; even Delaware and Pennsylvania, the most liberal of all, denied the franchise to those who did not profess faith in Jesus Christ. Throughout the Southern colonies the Church of England enjoyed a legal recognition. Into Georgia, where the social influences which operated further North hardly found a place, it was introduced by the second Royal Governor, unmindful of the principles which the wise foresight of Locke had sought to fix in the "Grand Model." South Carolina had taken the first step in the same direction before the close of the seventeenth century. In North Carolina it had found a place, though with meagre results, early in the eighteenth century. In Virginia it was coeval with the civil constitution; and in Maryland, originally founded on the principle of complete toleration, it had so far

* See some suggestive remarks in *North American Review*, Jan., 1876.

triumphed that, in the colony which Calvert had planted, the rites of the Church of Rome could no longer be celebrated. In Jersey and New York, where the Church was not established, it basked in the sunshine of an official countenance, which secured it a hardly inferior advantage. Yet all this was but an attempt to transplant into the New World institutions which, in the Old, were already smitten with decay. The Establishment remained a sickly exotic, striking no deep roots into the soil, and it almost withered away when scorched by the fervent heat of the Revolutionary epoch. In the New England States there grew up the idea of the indissoluble alliance between the spiritual and the civil order. It was not a theocracy such as Calvin attempted in Geneva, and the Puritans and Presbyterians sought to reproduce in England and Scotland; it was rather the theory, not so much of one broad and comprehensive Church, as of the concurrent endowment of all religions within certain limits. Religion and education were alike essential to the welfare of the State, and it was equally the concern of the State to see that both should flourish. When the number of Dissenters from the early faith had sufficiently increased, the law was modified so as to allow each separate congregation to claim its proportion of the ecclesiastical tax for the support of a clergyman of its own persuasion. It contemplated no exclusive privilege.

Even the Revolution did not at once bring in the new principle of the necessary separation of Church and State. On the contrary, in every one of the new constitutions framed under the Declaration of Independence, with the single exception of New York, some connection of Church and State was expressly recognised. The Baptists, it is true, had consistently and all along protested against this State support to religion, and the year before the first blood of the Revolution was shed at Lexington no less than eighteen members of a Baptist church were imprisoned in Northampton gaol for refusing to pay ministerial rates. So little disposed were the leaders of the Revolution to accept modern ideas on the subject, that John Adams declared that "a change in the solar system might be expected as soon as a change in the ecclesiastical system of Massachusetts." The remark of Judge Story is to the same effect: "That it yet remained a problem to be solved in human affairs whether any free government can be permanent where the public worship of God and the support of religion constitute no part of the policy or duty of the State."

The silent revolution which passed over American society on the subject of the connection of Church and State was owing to three causes :—1. The conscientious objection of certain sects, such as the Baptist, to receive any public support or recognition. 2. The number of religious organisations widely differing in doctrine and worship, rendering it difficult to decide which of these bodies was to be the organ of the religious consciousness of the nation. But the principal element in the change was the influence of Mr. Jefferson, who succeeded in introducing into the Virginia Act of 1785 the principle that no religious tests should ever be required as a qualification for any office or public trust under the United States. The first amendment further provided that Congress shall make no law respecting an Establishment of religion, or prohibiting the free exercise thereof. Laws for the support of public worship lingered in Connecticut till 1816, and in Massachusetts till 1833, and religious tests in several States for a few years longer. But public opinion, from which all laws proceed, at length decided that the State, in its essence, was a purely political organism.

Thus it is a silent revolution in public sentiment as to the connection of Church and State has been witnessed during the past century. It has been completed in America, and only waits its completion in this country as soon as an impulse strong enough to overcome the *vis inertiæ* has been given. This impulse is coming in this country through the rise of what are called Church principles. There is a rising tide of opinion coming in from all quarters, and which is so general that we can only describe it as a mental epidemic. This spirit claims for the Church a Divine original, and desires to assert its independence of State control. It is found as much in the ultra-Protestant Kirk of Scotland as in the ultra-Clerical Church of Rome. In both cases these Churches are willing to accept endowments of the State, but it must be on their own terms. There is to be no reciprocity in the arrangement. The State may have its duties towards the true Church, but it has no corresponding rights growing out of the power of the purse or the right of the patron to lay down the terms on which the temporalities are given. What it gives is given without reserve or limitation. It is laid on bended knee on God's altar, and to touch it again is sacrilege; to require of the priest who lives by the altar submission to the civil supremacy is tyranny and oppression. The modern school of Church defenders actually go so far as to say that the State never has endowed the Church; that these endowments were the gifts of pious founders; that as private gifts they passed into the hands of a spiritual corporation known as the Church, and all that the State has ever done is to guarantee the clergy in the enjoyment of their endowments on the condition of complying with the terms of the trust. This is the new theory of the connection of Church and State which is rapidly replacing the old. It is, no doubt, set up by men who take a shrewd view of the state of affairs, and who wish to be prepared for coming events. They see that the old theory of the duty of the State maintaining Divine truth is dead. It is as dangerous to lean on it as for Israel to go down to Egypt and lean on that bruised reed Pharaoh. The State, then, no longer offering the support to the endowment principle, for which alone an Establishment is worth contending, they have looked out for a new support, and found it in the Divine character of the Church. They describe the Church as a corporation with a perpetual succession in itself, and able, therefore, to hand on its trusts and endowments from generation to generation. This is the new point of departure of the Church party. We wish to state it in their own words, and to give them all the benefit of their own view of their position.

The old school used to put the relation of endowment to establishment in this order—that the State first established the Church and then endowed it. The assumption was that the duty of the State being to maintain truth, it looked out among the sects to find which of them maintained the truth in its purest form, and then decided on entering into an alliance with that. It was a case of marriage, in which the bridegroom first selects his bride for her beauty, accomplishments, and suitability of temper; and then, having decided on making her his wife, provides for her a suitable dower becoming so high a match. Thus it is that the greater the State, the more ample the provision for the clergy —a dignified Establishment and a liberal endowment being assumed to go together. The new school of Church defenders reverse this account of the matter. They put the Establishment question altogether in the background, and lay stress only on the endowment. They deny altogether the Warburton theory of the Alliance. They say that it is a fiction to assume that the State made choice of one out of several sects as the possible bride of the State, and then proceeded to provide for her a suitable dower. Appealing to history, they say that the Church was dowered by her own sons, and that the State has done little more than to regulate and even to confiscate these endowments from time to time. Henry VIII. did so in England; the French Republic in the same way issued *assignats* on the Church lands; and so in Prussia the revenues of the Church in Silesia, Westphalia, and elsewhere, have been seized by the State. They deny that the scanty stipends now paid to the clergy in Prussia and France are of the nature of endowments. They are simply giving back to the Church what is her own, and even of that only a beggarly dole. To attach burdensome conditions to these State-paid stipends, as the Falk laws are now doing, is, we are told, only to add insult to injury.

The brigand who takes a purse, and then restores to the traveller enough to carry him on to the next inn, scarcely lays claim to much generosity; but suppose in addition he were to lay claim to be regarded as a benefactor, we should say that this was to add cant to extortion. On these grounds the Clerical party on the Continent deny that they are either endowed or established. They admit to their sorrow that they are stipendiaries of the State; but this only means that the State has confiscated their Church lands, and left them a bare pittance of their own patrimony on which to eke out existence. The Pope, as it is well known, still stands out against those terms; and as long as Peter's pence flow into the Papal treasury he is not likely to acknowledge himself to be the pensioner of the King of Italy. The Prince Bishops of Germany have long since had to come down to these terms, and to eat the bread of dependence; but how much they chafe under it the attitude taken up by the clerical party in Germany is sufficient evidence. It is the same in France; and now we see something like the same spirit beginning to show itself among the English clergy. They admit that they are established by the State—that fact it would be difficult to deny as long as bishops sit in the House of Lords—and that no other religion is officially recognised as the national religion but the Anglican. But they refuse to admit that they are endowed by the State. The endowments, they say, are the property of the Church—given in a sense, it is true, by the nation, but not by the State. Church lands, they maintain, in the majority of cases, were the gifts of pious founders. So with the buildings—they were erected in many, if not in all, cases by voluntary gifts. Their maintenance has, it is true, by the common law, been thrown on the inhabitants of the parish, and for this rates have been levied till the other day. But the abolition of rates has altered even this, and now the maintenance of the buildings falls on those only who are of choice members of the Church.

There is one point, however, which this new theory of the non-endowment of the Church by the State does not meet. We have never seen the case of the compulsory nature of tithes fairly met. Whatever may be said as to the origin of tithes as free-will offerings, there is no doubt that it is only by a figure of speech that they can be called endowments. They may more properly be described as an ancient tax, the obligation to pay which sprang out of public authority modified by practice, the limits and privileges of which were from time to time laid down by public authority, and the enforcement of which has in the last resort depended upon courts in which public authority is enthroned. The stages by which a voluntary offering like tithes became customary, then compulsory, and finally took the form in which we find them, extended from prædial to personal tithes, such as the wages of an agricultural labourer. By a constitution of Archbishop Winchelsea, for instance, it is ordained that personal tithes shall be paid of artificers and merchandisers—that is, of the gain of their commerce—and also of carpenters, smiths, masons, weavers, innkeepers, and all other workmen and hirelings, that they pay tithes of their *wages*, unless such hireling shall give something in certain to the use or for the light of the church, if the rector shall so think proper.* Here we see ecclesiastical law in the act of throwing out its net, and enclosing within its meshes even the wages of the day labourer—the bare subsistence money of the poorest class of all, even that is presumed to be titheable. Statute law, then, follows partly to confirm, partly to restrain, the harshness of ecclesiastical law. By the statute of 2 and 3 Ed. VI., cap. 13, sec. 7, the force of this law on personal tithes was limited to such as "heretofore within these forty years have accustomably used to pay such personal tithes, or of right ought to pay, other than such as be common day labourers." Hunting, hawking, angling, and fowling fell under the rules of personal tithes, as also did sea-fishing, when, unless a clear custom to the contrary could be established, the tithe of fish taken in the sea was payable to the parson of the parish where the fisherman resided. It is clear from these instances, which it would be easy to add to, that what was customary at first, became, in course of time, compulsory, and ecclesiastical law soon acquired the force of statute law. This arose from the nature of things. It is vain for one side to deplore that it was so, and for the other to deny the fact. The fact and its explanation are alike simple. All law is only the reflection of custom—in other words, the ideas of the age are given statutory force. Laws are barbarous in an age emerging from barbarism, and so in an ecclesiastical age the statute-book reflects the mind and opinions of an age saturated

* On the subject of the origin of tithes, and the growth of a customary into a statutory right to enforce the collection of tithes, whether prædial or personal, great or small, mixed tithes and tithes of agistment, see "Title Deeds of English Church," by E. Miall, Esq. Third Edition. 1872.

with ecclesiastical ideas. To complain of our forefathers for lending themselves to the support of the compulsory principle in religion is to show little historical insight into past ages. On the other hand, to deny the existence of these ideas, and to represent the wealth of the Church as the accretion of gifts bestowed by pious founders, is to show even less insight into the past. Our forefathers, in giving statutory force to ecclesiastical claims to endowment, thought they were doing God service, and would have learned with surprise that one section of the community in our day denied that they were doing God service, while another party went further still, and denied the fact altogether. They had none of those Permissive Bills, out of which one side could contract itself, as we do in our modern legislation. What we call persecution they would have described as wholesome discipline. The knife and the cautery were applied to the cancer of religious error in a way which we should dread to do. Their surgery we should call butchery; but it is absurd to deny that it was surgery because it was barbarous, and doubly absurd to deny the fact that they used the knife and the fire in a way which we now shudder to think of.

Precisely the same change in the *zeit geist* has passed over the age with regard to a compulsory provision for religion. Church defenders wince under the remark that tithes have a statutory force exactly in the same way as Church censures against heresy were enforced by the State. The statute *de heretico comburendo* was first enforced by the Church, then enacted by the State; at last it fell into disuse, and finally by 29 Charles II. it became virtually a dead letter, by being remanded entirely to the Ecclesiastical Courts, the Civil Courts refusing any longer to take cognisance of heresy, as such. This is the death-blow to the principle of persecution, the essence of persecution lying in the fact of a man enduring civil penalties for his religious opinions. It is no persecution to attach religious penalties for religious opinions; that is only the discipline which every society presumably may exercise on its own members. But when the discipline is enforced by the State, and attaches to the member in his capacity as a citizen, then we have a case of persecution. The spirit of the age condemns persecution, and no Churchman, whatever his theory of Establishment or State connection be, would imperil his own case by allowing the compulsory principle in religion to extend to forfeiture of goods and liberty, or even of civil status. We all draw the line at toleration, and persecution is an ugly word, given up to opprobrium even by State Churchmen. But the majority who repeat the cuckoo phrase toleration are unable to see its logical equivalent—the *indifference* of the State to all religious questions. We are willing to repeat, in the words of the Liturgy, that the Queen may "minister justice indifferently;" but we are unable to face the meaning of our own words. If the sovereign is to put no difference between man and man in distributing justice, she is equally bound to put an end to the remains of religious inequality which still exist among us. If this be so, then what becomes of the ascendancy which one sect still claims in the country? It seems to be admitted on all sides that it can only hold its position on some other ground than the compulsory principle, and this new ground is sought and found in the theory of the Church being an ancient corporation coeval with the State, holding property and transmitting what it received by gift and endowment in perpetual succession, in the same way as any other chartered company or private proprietor hands down his estates from generation to generation.

The new argument for the Church is this: that since it was not established or set up by the State—created, that is, and constituted as a National Church—it cannot be uncreated or disestablished. No one has stated this more clearly than Mr. Freeman. His contention is, that the ecclesiastical endowments of England have grown up bit by bit.

"In short, if we wish to argue this question on its true ground, we must put out of sight the popular notion that, at some time or other, the State determined to make a general national endowment of religion. And we must also put out of sight the other popular notion that, at some time or other, the State took certain funds from one religious body and gave them to another. Neither of these things ever happened. If there ever was a time when the State determined on a general national Establishment of religion, it must have been at the time of the conversion of the English nation to Christianity. But the conversion of England took place gradually, when there was no such thing as an English nation capable of a national act. The land was still cut up into small kingdoms, and Kent had been Christian for some generations at a time when Sussex still remained heathen. If any act which could be called a systematic establishment and endowment of the Church ever took place anywhere, it certainly took place in each particular kingdom for itself, not in England as a whole. The churches of Canterbury and Rochester undoubtedly held lands while men in Sussex still worshipped Woden. But it would be an abuse of language to apply such words as systematic establishment and endowment to the irregular process by which the ecclesiastical corporations received their possessions. The process began in the earliest times, and it has gone on ever since. And nothing was done systematically at any time. This king or that earl founded or enriched this or that church in which he felt a special interest; and from this it naturally followed that one church was much more richly endowed than another. The nearest approach to a regular general endowment is the tithe, and this is not a very near approach. The tithe can hardly be said to have been granted by the State. The state of the case rather is that the Church preached the payment of tithe as a duty, and that the State gradually came to enforce the duty by legal sanctions. But it is only by the Tithe Commutation Act that tithe has been put wholly on the same level as other property. As long as tithe could be recovered by a process in an ecclesiastical court, there was still something of its original nature hanging about it. The theory of the ecclesiastical court is that they act *pro salute animæ*, for the soul's health of the person brought before the court. The aim of their punishment is the reformation of the offender. In theory the tithe-stealer was brought before the court, not that the defrauded rector might recover his property, but that the man who had sinned by not paying his tithe might be brought to a better frame of mind. So with regard to the Church-rate, which was a payment for ecclesiastical purposes, though it was not in any strict sense Church property or property at all. Here, too, the old process was through the ecclesiastical court, with the same theoretical object, the reformation of the defaulter. In neither case did the State strictly make a grant; it rather enforced the decree of the Church by the secular arm. And as to tithe, it should also be remembered that, though the duty of paying tithe was taught very early, yet for a long time the tithe-payer had a good deal of choice as to the particular ecclesiastical body to which he would pay his tithe. Nothing was more common than an arbitrary grant of tithe to this or that religious house. In short, the ecclesiastical endowments of England have grown up, like everything else in England, bit by bit. A number of ecclesiastical corporations have been endowed at all manner of times and in all manner of ways; but there was no one particular moment when the State of England determined to endow one general religious body called the Church of England.

"And if there was no one particular moment when, as many people fancy, the State endowed the Church by a deliberate act, still less was there any moment when the State, as many people fancy, took the Church property from one religious body and gave it to another. The whole argument must assume, because the facts of history compel us to assume, the absolute identity of the Church of England after the Reformation with the Church of England before the Reformation. We are not talking theology; it is quite possible to argue, either from the Roman Catholic or from the Protestant side, that the Reformation really made so great a theological change that the religious body which existed after those changes cannot be said to be the same religious body as that which existed before them. With this theological argument, from whichever side it comes, we have nothing whatever to do. Our position is a much humbler one. It is simply that, whether the religious body did or did not so change theologically as no longer to be the same, yet, as a matter of law and history, as a matter of plain fact, there was no taking from one religious body and giving to another. We must remember that there was not in England, as some people seem to think, and as there really was in some foreign countries, some one act done at a definite time called the 'Reformation.' Under the name of the Reformation we jumble together a great number of changes spread over many years. In popular language the Reformation sometimes means the throwing off of the authority of the Pope, sometimes the suppression of the monasteries, sometimes the actual religious changes, the putting forth of the English Prayer-book and the Articles of Religion. Here are three sets of changes, all of which are undoubtedly connected as results of a general spirit of change; but, as a matter of fact, they were acts done by different people, at different times, and those who, at any stage, wrought one change had no thought that the others would follow. The final results might be that theological continuity was broken, but no act was done by which legal and historical continuity was broken. Any lawyer must know that, though Pole succeeded Cranmer and Parker succeeded Pole, yet nothing was done to break the uninterrupted succession of the Archbishopric of Canterbury as a corporation sole in the eye of the law. This is all that we mean; in the sixteenth century, as at several other times before and since, laws were made to which the holders of ecclesiastical benefices had to conform under pain of losing those benefices. As a matter of fact, the great mass of their holders did conform through all changes. There was much less than people commonly think even of taking from one person and giving to another; and the general taking from one religious body and giving to another, which many people fancy took place under Henry VIII. or Elizabeth, simply never happened at all. In this last statement we wish to be thoroughly well understood. We are not wishing in any way to undervalue the greatness either of the direct theological change or of the indirect changes of all kinds which followed on the long series of events known as the English Reformation. In a general view of history these changes cannot be rated too highly. They were changes far greater than those who made them dreamed of. But we are dealing with a dry matter of fact and of law. There was no one particular moment, called the Reformation, at which the State of England determined to take property from one Church or set of people and give it to another. As there was no systematic endowment in the sixth or seventh century, still less was there any systematic disendowment and re-endowment in the sixteenth."

Thus, according to Mr. Freeman, there was no particular moment when, as many people fancy, the State endowed the Church by a deliberate act; still less was there any moment when the State, as many people fancy, took the Church property from one body and gave it to another. Both these statements are very questionable, and it would be easy to produce a long list of Acts of Parliament directly bearing on the endowment of one particular Church, and that to the exclusion of every other. Let us glance at a few of these facts. Passing over pre-Reformation times, we open the Statute Book at the reign of the first Protestant King :—

"The first law on this subject was passed in the reign of Edward VI., in which all persons were commanded to attend their parish church and receive the sacraments upon pain of excommunication, or such other punishment as the Ecclesiastical Judge might inflict. This was followed by the Act of Uniformity of 1551, commanding all persons to resort to their parish church upon pain of censure and the forfeiture of one shilling for every offence. Next came another Act of Elizabeth,* providing that any persons above the age of sixteen, who should be absent from church for a month, or should persuade others to absent themselves from church and repair to conventicles, or should join any conventicle, should be committed to prison without bail, until they should conform, make submission, attend the service established by law, and make declaration of their conformity. If they should refuse within three months to do this, they were required to abjure and depart the realm as felons. The form of submission was as follows :—

"'I, A. B., do humbly confess and acknowledge that I have grievously offended God, in contemning Her Majesty's godly and lawful government and authority, by absenting myself from church, and from hearing Divine service, contrary to the godly laws and statutes of this realm, and in using and frequenting disordered and unlawful conventicles and assemblies, under pretence and colour of exercise of religion ; and I am heartily sorry for the same, and do acknowledge and testify in my conscience that no other person hath or ought to have any power or authority over Her Majesty ; and I do promise and protest, without any dissimulation, or any colour or means of any dispensation, that from henceforth I will, from time to time, obey and perform Her Majesty's laws and statutes, in repairing to the church, and hearing Divine service, and do my uttermost endeavour to maintain and defend the same.'

"By a singular confusion of equity, any 'recusant' either abjuring or *not* abjuring the realm equally forfeited all his goods and chattels to the State. In the following reign an Act † was passed inflicting a fine of ten pounds upon every person who should harbour others who did not attend the services of the Church. These laws were strengthened in the reign of Charles II., when an Act ‡ was passed providing that any person above the age of sixteen who should be present at a conventicle where five or more persons were assembled, should, for the first offence, be imprisoned for three months, or fined five pounds ; for the second offence, be imprisoned

---

* 35 c. 1.   † 3 Jas. I. c. 4.   ‡ 16 Car. II. c. 4.

for six months, or be fined ten pounds; and for the third offence, be transported for seven years. This Act remained in force for three years, soon after the conclusion of which another* was passed inflicting fines upon those attending conventicles and upon the preachers, and authorising the magistrates to break open any house in which there was such conventicle, and take the offenders into custody. How, notwithstanding the fearful sufferings inflicted by the execution of these laws, they utterly failed of their purpose, is known to every reader. Nonconformity grew, and conventicles were multiplied in spite of them, until, at last, the nation being weary equally of ecclesiastical and political tyranny, exiled the Stuarts, and passed the Toleration Act. For years after this, however, no Nonconformist preacher could exercise his ministry excepting under certain restrictions designed to protect the doctrines of the Church as established by Act of Parliament. The law now protects all, but gives special and characteristic facilities to the Established Church."

Take, again, the provision made for securing the edifices for public worship :—

"It was the common law that all churches should be repaired by the parishioners, and this law was not abolished until the year 1867. Any person could build a church, but it could not be used for public worship until it had been consecrated by the bishop of the diocese, with the consent of the Crown, in which it was situated, nor until a sufficient maintenance for the minister had been secured. After the Reformation, the deeds of gift of the founders were enrolled in Chancery, according to the statute of Henry VIII. (27 c. 16), passed for the enrolment of all bargains, sales, &c.

"EARLY CHURCH BUILDING ACTS.

"The first Act of Parliament dealing with church edifices was that of Charles II.† for the rebuilding of the City of London after the great fire. It is also the first Act for levying a rate for church building. It directed that thirty-nine of the old churches should be rebuilt, and that the old sites of the buildings should be sold for that purpose. Very soon followed another Act ‡ levying an imposition on the importation of coals for the rebuilding of St. Paul's and other church edifices, and directing that the number of parish churches to be rebuilt should be fifty-one. Next came an Act§ reviving and continuing the previous Act so far as the expenses connected with St. Paul's were concerned, charging so much a chaldron for that purpose upon coals delivered into London, such charge to be paid to the Archbishop of Canterbury. In the reign of William there is found a further Act|| to the same purport; and in the reign of Anne a similar Act.¶ Next came a statute of wider purpose,** entitled

---

* 22 Car. II. c. 1.   † 19 Car. II. c. 3.   ‡ 22 Car II. c. 11.   § 1 Jas. II. c. 11.
|| 8 & 9 Wm. III. c. 14.   ¶ 1 Anne, s. 2, c. 12   ** 9 Anne, c. 22.

'An Act for granting to Her Majesty several duties upon coals for building fifty new churches in and about the cities of London and Westminster and suburbs thereof,' which authorised a levy of two shillings a chaldron or ton upon coals for that purpose. Another Act* of the same reign extended the power of previous Acts, which was followed by still another.†

"ACTS OF THE GEORGES.

"Next, and very naturally, came an Act of Geo. I. for making provision for the ministers of the fifty new churches, which was directed to be done by an additional imposition upon the coal rates. Another Act of the same reign‡ not only extended the power of those that had previously been passed, but established a lottery for the further raising of money for this purpose, with specific directions as to how the lottery was to be conducted. There were two or three other Acts passed in the reign of Geo. II.; but in the reign of Geo. III. the Church Building Acts became numerous. The first is for repairing Westminster Abbey from the funds of the Treasury.§ Later, came one‖ entitled 'An Act to promote the building, repairing, or otherwise providing of churches and chapels, and of houses for the residences of ministers, and the providing of churchyards and glebes,' which simply gave facilities for private persons to endow a church with land, or goods, or chattels, the intent being as follows:—
'Likewise a sufficient number of churches and chapels for the celebration of Divine service, according to the rites and ceremonies of the United Church of England and Ireland, and of mission houses with competent glebes for the residences of ministers officiating in such churches and chapels, is necessary towards the promotion of religion and morality, and whereas the same are either wholly wanting or materially deficient in many parts of England and Ireland,' and so on. This Act did not succeed in its purpose, and, therefore, was followed by another¶ providing that the king himself, out of the Crown property, might grant lands for building or repairing any church or chapel, or house of residence for the minister.

"THE CHURCH BUILDING COMMISSION ACTS.

"Even this, however, was not deemed to be sufficient. The next year another Act was passed to give further facilities. By the 58 Geo. III. c. 45 (A.D. 1818) the Treasury was empowered to raise the sum of a million sterling for 'building, and promoting the building of additional churches in populous parishes,' which Act, at the same time, established the body termed the Church Building Commission, since merged (1856) into the Ecclesiastical Commission. The operations of this Act have been detailed in the several reports of the Church Building Commissioners, by which it appears that through the powers invested in the Commission, with the money provided by Parliament, aided by contributions from other sources, numbers of churches were built in various parts of the kingdom."

---

* 10 Anne, c. 11.   † 12 Anne, c. 17.   ‡ 5 Geo. I. c. 9.   § 6 Geo. III. c. 25.
‖ 43 Geo. III. c. 108.   ¶ 57 Geo. III. c. 115.

But we have stated enough to show the strength and the weakness of the new argument which meets the objections to a State Establishment by boldly denying the fact. The difference, it has been said, between the sceptics of the old school and the new is this—that the one denied the evidential value of the Christian miracles, the other their credibility. In early times no one denied the facts themselves; it is only in our age that they dispute not so much the inference as the original fact. Precisely so with State connection. The principle was admitted formerly, but the fact that it worked prejudicially in favour of one dominant sect was evaded. Now that there is no denying the principle that religious inequality is contrary to the spirit of the age, Church defenders turn round and dispute the fact that the Church is endowed and established by the State. They do not deny that it is endowed—that would be too preposterous; but they contend that those endowments came not from the State, but were the benefactions of pious founders. Then, again, with regard to the Establishment theory, they admit that the Church is established—*i.e.*, settled—in the enjoyment of certain favours from the State not shared in by other religious bodies; but they say these are nothing to the favours enjoyed by the mediæval Church. If the Church of our day is a privileged and, to some extent, a dominant Church, what is this to the privileges enjoyed by the Church before the Reformation? Besides, as they add, the Church pays a dear price for these favours; "Give us back our own, restore to us the monastic and other Church lands confiscated by that arch-robber of churches, Henry VIII., and we shall be only too glad to set up on our own foundation, and to forego all the favours and immunities of our State connection." As for the advantages of the connection, Establishment is an arrangement, as the zealous Churchman contends, much more favourable to the State than the Church. "We give," he says, "much more than we get. For a few paltry privileges, such as a seat for our Bishops in the House of Lords, we surrender the control of our own revenues, the making of our own laws, and, in a word, all the rights of self-government enjoyed by the Free Churches."

Clearly, there is in this argument a surrender of the principle of Establishments, and a preparation for the Church taking up new ground when it shall be finally separated from the State. The position which the Church is now taking up on these questions, resembles, in fact, that of the Royal Academy. Sir Charles Dilke, in his speech on a motion of inquiry into the management of the Royal Academy, quoted, with great justice, a remark of Westmacott, "When we wish not to be interfered with we are private; when we want anything we are public." This is the new ground taken up by the Church party in our day. When they want grants for their schools, on the denominational principle, then they set up the claim that the Church is national, and so the natural educator of the poor. But when there is a question of touching its revenues, or in any way redistributing them for purposes more truly national than the public teaching of a theology from which large masses of the people dissent, then the ground is changed, and we are told that the Church is a society holding the apostolic succession, and enjoying certain revenues in right of this tenure—that the State did not give these revenues, and has no right to confiscate them, or even to deal with them as if they were national property. The old school of High Churchmen were Erastian *pur sang*, and admitted, in the words of Bishop Horsley, that they enjoyed the temporalities of their office from the favour of the Prince. The new school set up the ecclesiastical supremacy argument, and abhor and abjure the Erastianism of a bygone generation. But we question whether they are as logical and consistent. They reject Cæsarism, and put themselves on the other horn of the dilemma, which is Clericalism. Since they are not prepared to part with the temporalities, and are at a loss to make out any other case for retaining them, they set up this new claim, that they are not public endowments but private benefactions. Instead of admitting that the State is the owner, and they only the trustees, with a beneficiary interest, they reverse the position, and claim to be owners in absolute possession as well as beneficiaries, and leave only the right to the State of interfering, as in any other case of open breach of trust.

Thus the ground taken up by the Church Defence party in our day is identical in principle with that of the Ultramontane party on the Continent. They claim the utmost independence from State control, but refuse, at the same time, to relinquish the status and dignity of an endowed Church. This was very much the ground taken up by the Free Kirk party after the Disruption of 1844. They did not recede from the position that it is the duty of the magistrate to maintain truth and provide for the emolument of its ministers, but they held that in doing this the magistrate had discharged his duty, and that the *jus circa sacra* lay entirely within the Church. The temporalities might come from what source they may, but the right to administer them was part of the self-government inherent in the Church. It was this inconsistency which tainted the whole case of the Free Kirk party, and they are coming now to see it. In one sense they were Voluntaries, in another not. They wanted all the advantages of State recognition without any of its drawbacks. They were thus open to the taunt of Lady Macbeth to her husband :—

> " What thou would'st highly,
> That would'st thou holily ; would'st not play false,
> And yet would'st wrongly win."

All but an insignificant minority of the Free Kirk party in Scotland now see this. They have come to see that it is no use to accept endowment and then rail the seal from off the bond by denouncing, as Erastianism, the only conditions on which endowment is possible. It does not need Dogberry's wisdom to see that when two are on horseback together one must sit on the saddle in front, and one on the pillion behind. We may drink to "Church and State," and not to "State and Church," as they do in Germany ; but this will not alter the fact that when Church and State are allied in modern times the State leads and the Church follows. The days have gone by when spiritual and political power claimed to be co-ordinate, and when the spiritual presumed to rule the secular. Even in Hildebrand's times this claim was fiercely resisted ; it is now so out of date that those who cling to it, as the modern Ultramontanes do, and a few antiquated Free Kirk men like Dr. Begg, simply proclaim their inability to read the signs of the times. There is only one logical *locus standi* for a National or State Church, and that is extreme and unqualified Erastianism. We are not sure, indeed, that consistent State Churchmen do not go further than Erastus even. The Hegelian law of identity between Church and State, in which the Church is only the inner side of the State, has been carried one step farther by Rothe and the Heidelberg school. It is a singular coincidence, accidental it may be, but none the less remarkable, that in Heidelberg, where Lieber, the body physician to the Elector Palatine, first broached the theory of the supremacy of the State and the subjection of the Church—which the Presbyterians of that day rejected with such abhorrence—a new form of Erastianism, still more offensive than the old, is now the current theory. According to Rothe, the old dogmatic Christianity is now as much out of date as Judaism. It has done its work and played its part. The residuum, or, as we might call it, its sublimated essence in the form of a refined code of ethics, may survive. This may be taught by State-paid teachers, and thus we come round to the "moral policeman" theory which was in fashion in this country a century ago. Of this sublimated ethics we may say in the well-known lines—

"Unless above himself he can
Exalt himself, how mean is man."

An ethical system may be taken up and taught by the State, and our religious teachers may be national schoolmasters of the doctrines of sweetness and light so dear to Church defenders of the type of Mr. Matthew Arnold; but the State will soon learn, to its surprise, that it has paid a dear price for thus evacuating the supernatural out of Christianity, and leaving a *caput mortuum* of pure ethics to be taught by State-paid functionaries. Ethics of this kind are of no more use than a water-wheel and machinery attached to it without the water power, and for this there must be a fall of some kind. No mechanical skill can overcome this original defect—unless there are two levels, and the water descends from one level to the other, water power is out of the question. It is the same with those moral forces on which the State relies to carry on the machinery of government. The spiritual element in religion must be there, or the ethical will soon come to a standstill; and this brings us to see how short-sighted is the argument of Rothe and his school. They assume the very point in question. Admitted that ethical forces are enough for the ends of a State Church, but what is to create and keep up these ethical forces? In China we see an elaborate educational hierarchy, Confucianism, which, as an ethical system set in motion by the State, and for secular ends, such as the State must approve of, is all that we can wish if we take only a mechanical view of life. But, judged by its results, its dynamical effect is *nil*. It is the old difficulty how to move the water which is to move the wheels of life. A spiritual principle somehow is needed, and as the State cannot supply this principle, we are brought back to the problem we set out with, How are we to get it? If it comes from a Divine source, if it is the water of life, clear as crystal, proceeding out of the throne of God and of the Lamb, then we have the power; it is a power which we may utilise, if we will, but cannot produce. We may fit it to our water-wheel—or, rather, our waterwheel to it—but this is all. It will turn our driving-wheel, and thus set the whole machinery of public life and duty in motion; but, having done us this good turn, it goes on its way rejoicing—past town and hamlet it flows, and it foams, it winds, or it wanders, till it loses itself at last in the ocean of God's universal love.

The last theory, then, of State connection with religion is thus at once the most logical and the most absurd. The only terms of the connection which are possible in our day are that the State shall control religion, and use it for ethical purposes only. But a religion from which the spiritual or independent element is so evacuated loses all its force—it becomes like stagnant water, and useless even for the secondary purposes for which it is wanted. We are driven, then, to reject Erastianism as much in the dress of the modern Heidelberg school as in that of the Heidelberg of the times of the Elector Palatine and his body physician Lieber, commonly known as Erastus. The compromise we have arrived at in this country, though it is less logical, is more practical than this. Here at least we leave the Church free to teach spiritual truth in her own way, and under such dogmatic forms as she thinks fit. The State does not draw these up in the first instance, or even define them. All that the Court of Appeal does is to interpret their meaning when disputes arise between contending schools of theology within the Church. This theory of the connection which stops short of extreme Erastianism leaves a certain initiative and independence to the Church. It does not confound the functions of Church and State, or merge them in some Hegelian law of identity, which is self-destructive to both. But then, on the other hand, this theory of modified Erastianism, like all compromises, does not work smoothly. The Erastian party attacks it on one side, and the Ecclesiastical on the other; while the Evangelicals of this country, who, like the Pietists of Germany, would be happy to accept a compromise midway between Romanism and Rationalism, find themselves squeezed out by both. They are between the upper and nether millstone of Cæsarism and Clericalism, and, like all men who cling to the past, they cry out feebly for help in all directions, and no help comes. They try to justify their position and strengthen it by prosecuting offenders on either side, and organise a "Prosecution Society, Limited," as it has been described, to put down these innovators. It is all in vain. The spirit of the age is too much for them. The bolder spirits on either side go in for theories, either of entire absorption of the Church in the State, as Dean Stanley and the English supporters of the Heidelberg school; or of entire separation, as the Ritualists. Others, again, seeing how impossible it is to regulate conscience at all by Acts of Uniformity, discard all attempts to do so, and openly advocate a break-up of all traditional Churches and organised systems. Between these conflicting claims of an impossible past and a visionary future, the plain man of sense, much puzzled, feels himself drifting on to Disestablishment, but by a bit-by-bit process.

Between abolition of Church-rates and Burial Bills and University Reform Bills, the ascendancy of our dominant Church is slowly melting away, like an iceberg floating down to the Gulf of Mexico. It may be some time before the end comes, but it is only a question of time, and the very attempts of the Church to defend herself only hasten on her dissolution. Nothing can be more fatal than the new-fangled claim to hold her temporalities by an indefensible right as the Church of Augustine and the Middle Ages. Held to this plea, she has no right to say that the compromise which Henry VIII. accepted and Elizabeth ratified is to be a final settlement. They asserted the Royal supremacy, but this carries everything; and now that Royal supremacy means Parliamentary control, it is impossible to say why some scheme of comprehension should not be tried which should embrace the whole nation. In vain does the Church party resist this. It lays itself, by its timid attempts at compromise, open to the taunting retort—

> "Come back, come back! and wherefore and for what—
> To idly finger some old Gordian knot?
> Too weak to sever, and too faint to cleave,
> And idly clinging to some make-believe."

Nothing can exceed the feeble and hesitating tone of the Episcopal Bench in our day. Calling for fresh restrictions on lawlessness, or the ἀνομία, as they pedantically describe it, they are unable, or afraid, to say what is the meaning of this ἀνομία. From the charges of the Bishop of London, whom we may take as a typical mind of this spirit of compromise, one would judge that the Ritualistic clergy desire lawlessness (ἀνομία) for its own sake. This kind of reasoning is as absurd as that the dog went mad to serve his private ends. It carries with it its own refutation. The lawlessness on which the Bishop of London waxes pathetic arises from a struggle for life of two opposite theories of our mode of approach to God, commonly known as the Protestant mode of justification by faith and of justification by the sacramental system. Either of these theories may be true, or both may be equally false; or, as a third supposition, such as the Broad Church school favours, both may be partial truths, approximate expressions of a great and ineffable mystery. But to charge with lawlessness the earnest Catholic who wishes to expel the Protestant heresy of salvation by faith alone, or, conversely, to complain of Protestants such as the constituency of the Church Association for retaliating in the same spirit, shows singularly little knowledge either of history or of human nature. It is the misfortune of bishops to be highly-placed and salaried functionaries of a politico-ecclesiastical system unique in Church history. Since Byzantinism there has been no such complete confusion between the secular and the spiritual, or rather subjection of the spiritual to the secular, as in the English prelacy. Elizabeth, on the whole, treated her bishops as she did her Ministers of State. She used them as instruments of statecraft, and then flung them aside when useless. But James, with more cunning and less force of character, discerned the use of the Episcopate as a kind of breakwater to the rising tide of popular liberty. It was James who accordingly gave that set to the English Episcopate which it has never lost. As a rule (for there have been honourable exceptions in all times), the Episcopate have been Conservative politicians first and theologians, *longo intervallo*, afterwards. Hence it is that their dread of change is instinctive. They are set up and highly placed as flying buttresses of our present social system, founded on feudal privileges and class distinctions. The bishops as an order represent the past, and instinctively dread anything which resembles change. Can it be wondered, then, that an earnest assertion of spiritual convictions (be they right or wrong is a question we do not here enter into) seems to these conservators of the past as lawlessness? This was precisely the tone which they took at the preaching of Wesley. To them, as to the town-clerk of Ephesus, the question of the truth or falsehood of the doctrine taught was quite secondary to the question, What are its bearings on the present settlement in Church and State? Does it unsettle men's minds, and bring in new views which tend to destroy the existing balance of the Constitution? then it is a lawlessness—something not customary—and is to be discouraged by all the secret pressure which a bishop can bring to bear on these troublers in Israel. The very same complaints uttered in our day by the Ritualists were uttered as loudly a generation ago by the Evangelicals against the insincerity and double-mindedness of the bishops, saying one thing in public and another in private. The charge is a true one; but the fault lay not so much with the men as with the false position into which they have been put— a position so humiliating, that it is not easy to see how a mind of force and originality can submit to it. Before all things else, the bishops are the ecclesiastical finials and ornaments of a feudal society. As such, they are expected to frown down innovations which might, if tolerated, make an end of the present settlement of society. The bishops are never allowed to forget that the purple, or Byzantine, livery as courtiers is more to be regarded than the lawn of their spiritual office. There is only one remedy for this most mischievous confusion between the kingdoms of Christ and of Cæsar, and till it is applied we shall continue to find bishops acting as they do. The fault lies in the institution itself, not so much in the particular men who administer it. As far as the bishops personally are concerned, they are, as a rule, men of blameless lives and high conscientiousness, but set to work a vicious system, and unable, in consequence, to see their spiritual functions in their true light. They have been so long regarded as great officers of State, that, although their functions in this respect are now purely honorary—as the offices of Lord Steward and Lord Chamberlain—they cannot get rid of that flavour of the past which clings to them. Their very dress is archaic, without being really ancient—as if they held back just half a century behind the rest of the world, without either going back to what is really primitive, or going forward to what is truly modern. This compromise with the past as to dress is only too characteristic of the episcopal attitude on all questions. They are unable to judge a theological question on its own merits; they must take its bearings on the social and political system which they are there to uphold. They never can forget that the Church, like the milk-white hind, is always in danger. It is in danger at one time from too much Protestantism, and at another from too much Romanism; but it is always in danger, and, indeed, its only safety lies in nicely poising itself between contending enemies. All these hesitations would be at an end if the bishops ceased to represent a social system, and were only set as watchmen over a spiritual Zion. But this implies a drastic remedy for an acknowledged evil, and "society" has too many interests of its own in keeping up the institution as it is on its present basis, to permit of the first step in reform by an entire release of the bishops from all attendance at Parliament. The House of Lords, with a keen instinct, discerns that one change would call for another, and the surrender of the life peerages of the bishops might bring their hereditary peerages into question. Thus it is that bit by bit Disestablishment, however desirable, and in some respects preferable, is not feasible. We must wait for some tidal wave of public opinion which shall sweep away the whole institution as it is. When it falls, it will come down with a crash in proportion to the obstinacy with which all change has been resisted.

CHAPTER XI.

THE CHURCH IN DANGER.

THE memory of man runneth not back to the time when the cry of the Church in danger has not been heard in some quarter or other. The milk-white hind of Dryden's fancy was not hunted and hounded down more fiercely by wild beasts, and still wilder men, than is the Church of our day. The cry of the Church in danger is supposed to summon to the rescue all who call themselves Churchmen; but the cry has been so often raised that its defenders are left in doubt as to the quarter whence the danger comes, and who are the class who should fly to the rescue. At the cry of fire at night we send for the brigade, at a cry of burglars for the police; but danger is such an indefinite term, that unless we send for a *posse comitatus*, and tell them their duties when they come up, we shall be unable to satisfy these alarmists on Church matters. As it is, we may find men hastening with buckets and hose when a pair of handcuffs are wanted, and bawling "Stop thief!" when "All hands to the pumps" should be the order passed round.

Before rushing to the rescue, then, let us pause and ask ourselves two questions, which, after all, only amount to one—namely, What Church is in danger, and whence does the danger come? Is it an attack from without, or is the danger one arising from disruption within?

Is the spiritual Church of Christ in danger? The answer to that is, that the only danger that it can meet with arises from the fears of its too faithless members. We do not say that there never have been fears for the true spiritual Church of Christ, for as long as the Church of Christ on earth contains such faint-hearted men and women as we know she consists of, there will be fears within as well as fightings without. But we are bound to remember the answer of the stout old sailor to a lady in a storm: "Madam, there is fear, but no danger." Sometimes the reverse is the case, and with a true sailor there may be danger, but no fear. But with the inexperienced landsman it is far more often that there is fear when there is no real danger. We do not deny that there are fears for the spiritual Church of Christ; but this is when our consciences accuse us of unfaithfulness—then we tremble as Eli did for the ark of God. But the true Church is, nevertheless, safe. She is as far beyond the reach of attack as her glorified Head. In the true sense of the word the Church is, where the vast majority of its members already are, safe beyond the flood, safe in the heavenly Jerusalem, with the innumerable company of angels and the spirits of just men made perfect.

Nor, again, is the Church which is in danger that Episcopal Church whose doctrines are contained in the Thirty-nine Articles, and whose discipline is Episcopal as contrasted with Presbyterian discipline on the one hand, and Congregational on the other. It is only the more ignorant class of Church defenders who confound attacks on the Establishment with hostility to the doctrines of the Church, and who speak of all Dissenters as men who have joined themselves, like Gebal, Ammon, and Amalek of old, to hew down all the carved work of the Temple with axes and hammers. The Church of England, as a spiritual society, is in no danger of attack from without; but it is another matter when we speak of attack from within. As a Protestant Episcopal Church she is in serious peril from those who are loudest in calling themselves Churchmen. The Anglo-Catholic party make no concealment of their intention of rooting out Protestantism; it is to them the accursed thing, and so deep is their hatred of it, that if they can root it out in no other way than by attacking the Establishment, they will not hesitate to do this. The language of the Ritualist organs is so truculent and threatening, that if they had the power as they have the will, they would sweep away those reforms which cut down the tall tree of sacerdotalism in the sixteenth century, while it left its roots in the ground, though with a band of iron and brass around it to prevent its noxious growth. That band of iron is the civil supremacy which the Ecclesiastical party never can rid themselves of but by entire disestablishment and disendowment. They are not prepared for this, and since liberty is only to be obtained by paying the price for it, they remain as they are, and compromise with their consciences by using coarse and violent language against their ecclesiastical superiors. It has come to this pass in the Church of England at present, that Cæsarism and Clericalism, or the two principles of civil supremacy or of ecclesiastical, are now contending for the mastery. Till the rise of the " Tracts for the Times" party, the former principle was unquestioned by Churchmen. Even the Laudian party and their successors, the Non-Jurors, did not raise this point. The reason may have been, that as the Royal supremacy was exerted on their behalf, so they were supporters of the Royal supremacy. The Ecclesiastical party in England was also the Erastian party—at least, during the seventeenth century.

This is one of the causes which explains the peculiar hatred felt to Erastianism by the Puritan party. It was bitter enough to have to fight an ecclesiastical battle with Prelacy without being weighed down by a contest with the civil power in addition. In our day, however, the old alliance between Cæsarism and Clericalism, which has lasted on almost from the Reformation down to the present, has been broken up. The Erastian and Ecclesiastical parties in the Church of England, now commonly known as the Broad and the High Church, view each other with suspicion and distrust. The leaders of the two parties have not yet drawn the sword, and the Bishops, as a rule, are trying to temporise and patch-up a compromise. But any far-seeing man must feel that the question which has divided the rest of Europe into two camps must come up for settlement in this country. The *Cultus Kampf* of Prussia is nothing less than the old question of civil or ecclesiastical supremacy. The *jus circa sacra*, allowed without dispute to temporal princes, has now come up for settlement since the Pope has ceased to be a temporal prince. Shrewd observers remarked that the Pope's temporal power was, to a great extent, a check to the exorbitant demands of his spiritual supremacy. As one of the petty princes of Europe, the Pope would never push a quarrel too far with his brother kings. But now all is changed. The Pope has no interest in accommodating matters with temporal rulers; his interests and theirs are now opposed. The age of concordats is over. The old alliance between the soldier and the priest has been broken up. That this is a gain in the long run to the cause of popular liberty is too obvious to call for remark. But, like all cases of gain, it has its drawbacks. In every current there is a backwater. So it is that one of the signs of advancing liberty is the rise of the Ultramontane or sacerdotal spirit everywhere in Europe. It breaks out, too, in a similar form, and is evidently subject to the same laws. One of its special characteristics is that it is willing to ally itself with popular and even democratic tendencies, in order to counteract the Erastian or Court party. We see this in Germany, where the Ultramontanes are also Particularists, and, in some cases, in alliance with the social democrats. The same tendencies are seen in Italy, and even in this country, where the Ritualists are not seldom found in league with the political Radicals and the supporters of the Liberation Society.

There is no denying, then, that the cry of the Church in danger is no longer a senseless one. In our day there is danger as well as fear; but the public, if we may judge by the tone of the press, deride their fears as if it were the too-often repeated cry of "Wolf!" of the boy in the fable. The Church has been so often in danger at every act of concession of common liberty of conscience, that it is no wonder that at last, when really threatened as an Establishment, no one believes in the danger. This is the fate which overtakes all Cassandras, particularly those who are not wise enough to see the Baconian axiom, that "a morose retention of old customs is the greatest source of innovation." The Church party have uniformly resisted all relaxation of the laws against Dissenters. They stood out against the Toleration Act, succeeded in defeating the Comprehensive Bill, and then, to bar the door, enacted a Test Act against Occasional Conformity. They were not content even with this, but in Queen Anne's reign, under a Tory Ministry, attempted to take back the toleration already conceded, and tried to close Dissenting academies, and to make it impossible for Dissenters to educate their ministers. This foolish and wicked attempt at reaction failed, as it deserved to do; but it indicates what Churchmen would have done if they had the power, as they had the will, to legislate; and it excited such a profound distrust in clerical assemblies, that the sittings of Convocation were suspended, and one of the avenues of theological rancour thus effectually stopped up for a century and a-half. The reassembling of Convocation in our day is marked by the same spirit of intolerance and inability to discern the signs of the times. The Lower House is as unable as ever to make the smallest concession on such a point as the Burials Bill, and thus it is that the State Church lies in the trough of the sea like a water-logged vessel: it can neither sink nor swim. The Ecclesiastical party, if they had their way, would save the ship by cutting it loose from State connection, and launching it out on the open sea of Voluntaryism as a highly-organised and sacerdotal sect. On the other hand, the Erastian or Broad Church party have a policy of comprehension which would save the Church as a National Establishment, but at the cost of its creeds and articles. But neither party can expel the other, or take the command of the ship. A creedless Establishment, like the National Churches of Switzerland, or organised and exclusive sects as in America, is the only programme of the future. The inexorable logic of events elsewhere lays this alternative before the English Churchman, and he is asked to take his choice. But the average Englishman does not care to be logical. He has an instinctive dread of carrying out principles to their logical conclusions. He likes to halt half way, and to take as much of two opposite theories as will not violently contradict each other. Thus he is in favour of an Established and dominant Church, but he must allow full toleration to all who dissent from it. In the same way, the bishops of our day halt between the Erastians, who would save the Establishment by sinking the Church, and the sacerdotal party, who would save the Church by sinking the Establishment. As neither the High nor the Broad School are strong enough to carry out their own policy, the reigning theory in the Episcopal circles is that of a High-Broad compromise. They are sound Churchmen on the one hand; on the other hand, they have enough of the political instinct to know where they must give way, as on the Burials Bill, and the result is that spectacle of Episcopal helplessness, which is pitiable, if it does not deserve a stronger epithet. Like a waterlogged vessel, the State Church of this country drifts helplessly along, with a disunited crew, and a prey to the waves which are ready to engulf it.

There is no denying that this time it is no false alarm that the Church is in danger. Formerly it was only the outworks which were in danger. The admission of the Roman Catholics, and then of the Jews, to Parliament, the repeal of Corporation and Test Acts, the licensing of Dissenting chapels for the celebration of marriages, the abolition of Church-rates—these were all regarded as so many symptoms of the Church being in danger. Men who enjoy a monopoly are shrewd enough to suspect danger, and will sometimes raise the alarm before they are attacked. Nor is this such a senseless policy as it seems. It is not mere stupidity to appeal to the fears and prejudices of mankind. On the contrary, knowing that the mass of mankind never can see down to the bottom of a question, and live on certain half truths which they call the wisdom of their forefathers, it is not such a bad policy as it seems to appeal to the fears of mankind. A State Church as a "National Confession of God," or as a "bulwark against Popery"—these are the wise saws which pass for philosophy among the masses. Even men who make some pretension to think on political questions do not see through the fallacy of this kind of reasoning. With the masses, therefore, the axiom that a State Church must be upheld at all cost passes current as an unquestioned truth. The old cry, the Church is in danger, does not suggest, as it ought to do, the thought that an institution so frail, and which needs so much protection and patronage, cannot have much root in itself. The true theory that the Church has been weak because leaning on an arm of flesh, and will be strong in proportion as she casts off the State or is cast off by it, is not reached all at once. Still, in the long run, mankind does reach the true view of the matter. The singular fact that the Church gathers strength exactly in proportion as she discards endowment and establishment and throws herself on the Voluntary principle, begins to impress even the unthinking. The mass of Churchmen are now in a midway position on this question. They do not discard the old theory, they do not deny the new. They simply halt between the two. They are like a garrison shut up in a citadel of privilege, and ready to summon or surrender. But they will not haul down their flag without a struggle. Nothing shows so much the abandonment of the old ground as the statement made by Church defenders that they do not dread disestablishment so much for the Church's sake as on account of the State. The Church is Divine, and can cast herself on her Divine Master; but the poor State—this is what distresses them. The argument, if it means anything, amounts to this—that the Church can do very well without the State, but the State cannot do without the Church; and, when looked into, amounts to that half Manichæan conception of the world's government which religious people can seldom quite get rid of. All that is Divine and spiritual in man is enshrined in the Church; outside this Goshen all is dark. We need not turn aside to expose the fallacy of this kind of reasoning. Its fundamental error is in assuming the very point in question: that God has tied Himself up to one order and institution of men. It amounts to the old dogma, *extra ecclesiam nulla salus.*

It is the Augustinian theory of the Divine government in its harshest, narrowest, and most external sense. Men must break the shell of this type of dogmatism, and see for themselves that it is God who has made us, and not we ourselves, and that Church and State alike are only instruments, partial and imperfect at best, for the education of the world. Until they see this, we shall find them clinging to fallacies such as we have noticed above, and raising endless alarms that the Church is in danger, because one prop after another of political support is taken away.

For Church defenders of this class we have only one wish, which is that their worst fears may be soon verified. They may learn the same mystery with regard to the Church, the mystical body of Christ, which each believer has to learn in his own experience; the flesh must be destroyed, that the spirit may be saved in the day of the Lord Jesus. It is in the break-up of all outward and visible Churches, by their disruption from within as well as their disestablishment from without, that the true spiritual Church, the bride of Christ and the hope of the world's future, will be discovered. This twofold process of disruption and dissolution, from internal schisms, from external attacks, does not distress or disappoint us. On the contrary, it leads us to see the hastening of Christ's kingdom and coming. It is a mistake to suppose that this law of dissolution is arrested as soon as we have reached the stage of separation of Church and State. There is no magic in disestablishment to arrest the law of change, as if the Free Church led a charmed life, exempt from the ordinary changes of life which affect alike all human societies, religious as well as secular. It is this idol of uniformity and fixity which clings, yea, even to the regenerate—this delusion that if one external type of religion will not resist decay, another may be found which will. This error greatly weakens the testimony of those who oppose State Churches, but show in every act of their Church life that they are stamping on Plato's pride with greater, and who oppose Establishments of one kind by setting up an Establishment of their own. Hence it is that Church defenders retort on Dissenters that they do not attack the Establishment with clean hands, and that their motive is no better than that of the fox in the fable who lost his tail. It is more candid to admit that all endowment is a *quasi* Establishment of religion, and that between the *religio licita* and the *religio civilis* there are but thin partitions. Creeds and confessions, trust deeds, colleges, and bursaries—these are the props which our popular Dissent made for itself last century. When Dissent has fully organised itself in this way, and donned a coat of mail of Saul's armour, it finds itself unable to go out against the giant of unbelief. The very students who were trained in the academies of Doddridge and Watts fell away in many cases into infidelity. Some stayed at the half-way house of Unitarianism, and of the few Abdiel-like spirits faithful among the faithless found, there was seldom any mark of originality or of spiritual power at first hand. They were feeble copyists and imitators of the Puritans of a more heroic age. The difference between the Churchmen and Dissenters of last century was well summed up by the late Mr. Jay, that the Church was asleep in the dark, and Dissent asleep in the light. Of the two, we should agree with Mr. Jay in adding that the sleep of the Church was the more excusable.

We have no right, then, to criticise and condemn endowed and established Churches unless we are prepared to cut up by the roots the principles which inevitably lead on to endowment in the first stage, and establishment in the second. If we object to "organised Christianity," *in toto*, we shall be said to be "unpractical," to entertain chimerical schemes of regenerating the world without using the right means. This text will be brought against us, " How shall they hear without a preacher, and how shall they preach except they be sent?" Now, we must clear ourselves from this charge, as if we regarded organisation as an evil, and not as a good. We would use organisation in religion, but only as means to an end. As the organisation of a plant—*stamen, calyx, pistil*, and so forth—is only to nurse the pollen which, when shed and scattered like dust on the earth, or winging its flight through the viewless air, is carrying on its mission, and continuing the life of the plant in new and endless forms; so it is with our Church organisations—they have their use, but it is a subordinate one. They are for the perfecting of the saints for the work of the ministry, for the edifying of the body of Christ, till we all come to the perfect man. The flower is for the fruit, and a plant that flowers only and does not go on to bear fruit is only half a plant. Its beauty is only an abortive birth; it has exhausted itself in the earlier stages of its being; it does not bring forth that which is fruit or enjoyment, in the strict sense of the word fruit. Much of our Church organisation is of this kind, and because it is so the testimony of the free Churches against established is so weak and wavering.

Still God fulfils Himself in many ways. The old order changeth, yielding place to new, lest one good custom should corrupt the world. Our very "century of sects," which men in Milton's day bewailed, and which we have to put up with and make the best of—even this has its good. The Presbyterian and Methodist Churches both attempted, through organisation, to defy the law of change; but have they fared better than those Churches, as the Baptist and Independent, which set up no central authority, but let churches and congregations take their own course, and make their own way to land? The "other little boats," as they have been compassionately called, of unorganised Dissent have fared no worse than the stately ships of endowed and established Churches. The lesson is this, that all organisation is only provisional, and when that which is perfect is come that which is in part shall be done away. The less organised Churches have, moreover, this advantage, that they can more easily reform and slough off the incrustation of ages. The charge of old Robinson, of Leyden, to the Pilgrim Fathers to see that God has more light yet to break out of His Word, was a thought beyond his age, and, to some extent, even beyond ours. In an age when toleration was thought a sin, and the crudest conceptions of the relation of the Old Testament to the New were held on all sides, it must have been regarded as little else than a heresy that God had more light to break out than the doctors of Lambeth and Dort could teach. Organisation is the sworn foe of discovery in all departments; it is the same in our colleges of science as in our halls of divinity; and this being so, the best Church must be the one with the fewest traditions of the past, and the lightest and most elastic constitution to adapt it to the wants of the future.

In spiritual things, moreover, order and form, however convenient, tend to repress the Divine life as much as to encourage it. It cannot be denied that the beginnings of the Divine life are often attended with extravagances, and that the spirit of the prophets should be subject to the prophets. It is right to enforce this truth, that God is the God of order, and not of confusion; but order and organisation are the second, not the first. Life is before order, and essence before form. Churches, then, have to make their choice. Where there is much form there is a low type of spiritual life. It is crushed; or, if it breaks out at all, it is among mystics and ascetics, as we find during the Middle Ages. On the other hand, where order is regarded as quite a secondary thing, and the growth of the body in love and holiness regarded as the chief thing, there a high type of spirituality is found combined with a simple and unascetic type of everyday life. We venture to say, without fear of contradiction, that the class commonly known as Evangelical Nonconformists do, on the whole, exhibit more faithfully than other endowed and established Churches what the Church was intended to be. There is a tendency to formalism, no doubt, there, as everywhere. Still the same petrifying influences are not at work in their case, or, at least, to the same extent. The exercise of free prayer is, in itself, a witness for the presence of the Abiding Comforter. Forms of prayer witness to a Holy Ghost in the past; and in so far as the Church is historical, we consider it mere prejudice to object *in toto* to forms of prayer, as some Christians do. But free prayer is a witness that the Holy Ghost is present among us; and whoever would oppose this, may be said to "quench the Spirit, and to despise prophesyings." Since edification is the great end of the Church, whatever edifies most is the best and most reasonable form of service. Now, fixed forms, especially if repeated very frequently, do certainly deaden life. On that subject there can be no question, and the best evidence to it is the craving for variety, which takes in our day the diseased form of Ritualism. But this scenic religion, with its new properties, dresses, and decorations, soon wearies us, as a play would, and the spirit is sated, but not satisfied. The remedy we cannot describe; for to be understood it must be experienced. It consists, in a word, in fresh discoveries of Christ in His Word, and fresh applications of this to our daily needs. This will raise the tone of our own spiritual life, and we shall desire in our Church fellowships to join with those who thus worship God in spirit and in truth. A Church which is growing in this way will not lay much stress on forms or ceremonies, black gowns or white. The Ritualistic controversy which is vexing the heart of our Evangelical friends of the Establishment will sound to it like the roar of some distant sea to one who is inland, far and sheltered deep from storms. The member of a free and spiritual society of this kind may be said to be like King

Arthur, when the whole Round Table is dissolved and borne away—

> "To the island valley of Avilion,
> Where falls not hail, or rain, or any snow,
> Nor ever wind blows loudly—but it lies
> Deep meadowed, happy, fair, with orchard lawns
> And bowery hollows crowned with summer sea,
> Where I will heal me of my grievous wound."

To our friends, then, of the Church Defence party, who tell us that the Church is in danger, we reply that we are glad it is so. It is possible—nay, probable—that dissolution of the State tie may lead to other changes, and this will seem the prelude to a decay as bitter as death itself. But out of that very decay there will spring a new and a better life, in which the Church will act in the world as leaven in the lump, and the Kingdom of God will come, not with observation, but by slow growth from within, as the grain of mustard seed, in which the greatest springs from the least.

CHAPTER XII.

REFORM, NOT REVOLUTION.

SINCE "Reform, not Revolution," is the plea of many excellent Christians, we are bound to show reasons why Reform is impossible, and that Revolution is the only remedy. On this subject we shall do well to attend to the distinctions of the old ceremonial law. There were two degrees of leprosy, whether in houses, in garments, or on persons; the one was malignant and contagious, the other not. Hence it was that for the former there was no remedy but the taking down of the house stone by stone. Let us apply this to the case of the English Church. Built up as she is since the Reformation on the foundations of royal supremacy, and with evils like prelacy, patronage, purchase, and, above all, the sacerdotal theory of an exclusive clerical order, worked into the very fabric itself, can we conceive of any way of reforming these evils short of entire revolution? If any one says that the Church will be the same Church after she is disendowed and disestablished, and when purged of prelacy and lay patronage and its attendant evil, the purchase system, we shall not care to dispute about names with those who cling to the word Church. Their reform amounts to our revolution. It is not improbable that a decided majority of Dissenters would conform to a Prayer-book purged of its sacramentalism, and to an Episcopacy reduced from its present status as a prelatical order to a kind of *primus inter pares* status among Presbyters. Whether the Church in England will ever be reformed in such wise as the Free Church in Ireland has been, may be doubted. In all probability the disestablished English Church would break into two, or perhaps three, hostile and rival sects. The Ecclesiastical and the Evangelical parties certainly would not hold together. It is probable that the Latitude party would also form a sect by themselves. They would probably offer themselves to the State on its own terms, to do the work of a moral police, and act as custodians of our national monuments, the cathedrals and abbeys of England; and the State might accept them, and endow them as a kind of Society of Antiquaries or College of Heralds, with a sort of secularised hierarchy like the Freemasons or the Royal Academicians. The Church of the future may, and probably will, drift into combinations of this kind; but to assert that either of these three fragments of the existing State Church could claim by any law of continuity to represent the existing State Church of our day, is more than we can in candour admit. When so thorough-going a remedy as Disestablishment is applied to an institution which is nothing if it is not a State Church, it is idle to call it a reform, and not a revolution. The Reformation revolutionised the Anglican Church of the Norman and Plantagenet period of our history. It converted it from a Pope's Church into a Crown Church, and as the supremacy was the key to the struggle, the flag around which the battle raged, when that fell the struggle was over. An old Church and order passed away, and "God, who fulfils Himself in many ways, lest one good custom should corrupt the world," allowed the old order to change, yielding place to new. The Anglican contends that it was only a reform, not a revolution. Be it so. What we desire in that case is another reform as thorough of its kind. We desire that same supremacy which was taken from the Pope and given to the Crown, to be now taken from the Crown and given to the people. Instead of the pseudo-Congregationalism of our new district churches, with their pew-rents and other imitations of the voluntary system, we should like to see Congregationalism, pure and simple, to become the rule of religion in this country. Nothing is gained by our underhand imitation of Congregationalism; like all imitations, it is the basest kind of flattery, and recoils on those who resort to it. At present we have the evils without the compensating advantages of Congregationalism. We bring in the power of the purse and other evils of plutocracy inseparable from the voluntary system, without its hearty recognition of the great truth that every congregation of believers is a Church of the living God, having fraternal relations to all other Churches, but supreme as to its internal affairs and administration. This may be an apostolic theory of church government (we think it is, but do not here discuss this), but it is at least logical and self-consistent; whereas that imitation of Congregationalism, known as the voluntary principle, in the English State Church is neither one thing nor the other. Repudiated by both, it is dying of sterility. It is unable to reproduce itself, and its chief champions, the old Evangelical party of the Church of England, can only raise the helpless cry of "Reform, not Revolution." What they would like, if we may judge by writers like Canon Ryle, is a combination of opposites as monstrous as a flying fish or a boat on wheels. They want a pure Protestant and Evangelical Church, holding all Reformation doctrine or fiction of theology known as the truths on which "Luther, Calvin, and Cranmer were agreed." This, which is the platform of the Bible and the Tract Societies, and the Evangelical Alliance, may be a true draft of apostolic doctrine or not; but it is clear to the plainest understanding that it unchurches one-half of Christendom, and leaves out in the cold, as infidels or worse, large remnants of the rest. All Roman Catholics, Unitarians, and even orthodox High Churchmen of the old type, are outside this narrow pale of the "Bible, the religion of Protestants." A growing minority, even among those who hold it, have given up the position that the Bible is an infallible book, and this disposes of the platform itself on which Evangelicals attempt to raise the frail superstructure of a National Church. A National Church for the Episcopalian subscribers to the Bible and Tract Societies—we have only to state it in this way to show that the bed is shorter than a man can stretch himself on it, and the covering narrower than that he can wrap himself in it.

The basis of a National Church of this kind is so narrow that it is worth examining into the reasons why men who are voluntaries in practice can cling to a theory of State Churches so utterly out of harmony with the age. These theories are twofold.

I. It is said that there ought to be a national confession of God.

II. It is said that we need a bulwark against the Church of Rome.

I. With regard to the argument that a State ought to have some national acknowledgment of God, the reply is to admit the major, but deny the minor, of the following syllogism :—

> "The State is bound to acknowledge God;
> To acknowledge God it must establish some religious order;
> Therefore, &c., &c."

The fallacy turns on the equivocal sense of the term "acknowledging God." Even under the Old Testament the prophets rebuked the people for preferring the ceremonial to the moral element in religion. The well-known passage—Micah vi. 6—is only one of several, all of which teach the same truth. Granted, even, that it is the duty of the State to recognise God, there are many stages between that admission and the conclusion that it is desirable to set up some national cult, with an order of men set apart for the exclusive duty of conducting that cult. It has been often urged that the universality of this idea of a national cult is an argument in its favour, for what is *quod semper, quod ubique*, and *quod ab omnibus*, must have in it the stamp of a national law or necessity of human nature. But the induction is too general, and does not meet the exceptions. True that all Oriental societies are theocratic, and that they fall to pieces as soon as the power of the priesthood is undermined. We see this in the civilisations both of Egypt and India. They owe their early growth and premature decline to the same causes.

They leaned on the power of a priesthood, and with the decline of that priesthood they faded away. Granted, also, that to some extent sacerdotal ideas and the special sanctity of a priestly caste underlay the civilisation of Greece and Rome; this would prove nothing more than that a national cult was the fittest expression of homage to a deity who was local, and who was supposed to be the tutelary patron of the State. As we see in modern saint worship, which is the exactest reproduction of the old-world Paganism, a local deity had a local shrine. It was the oracle of Delphi, the oaks of Dodona, the Venus of Paphos, the Artemis of Ephesus, the Jupiter of Ammon, and a hundred other places. The gods of the conquered places were deported with the inhabitants; the fugitive carried with him his household gods where he went. At this stage of thought a national cult suits a people. Society would not have existed at all if it had not externalised religion, and inwoven it in this way into the very fabric of society. But we remark that as ideas of a "world-order" advanced, and with it there came clearer conceptions of the ruler of this Cosmos—in other words, as men approached to Monotheism, so conceptions of a national cult, and a priestly caste to uphold it, fell into the background. In Judaism, more than anywhere else, we may see this advance marked. When the chosen race were in the rudest stage of all, slaves just escaped from Egypt, and with ideas of Magianism and priestcraft still clinging to them, the I AM was revealed to them as a tutelary Deity, going before them in a pillar of fire by night, and of cloud by day, dwelling between the cherubim, and veiled from sight by the thick curtains of the sanctuary.

In this case one tribe was set apart to exercise the priestly office, and a minute and painful ritual of sacrifice and ceremony marked that the God of Israel was as yet not fully known to His people as the Lord of the whole earth. With a local priesthood and a local sanctuary a national cult was, we admit, quite in harmony. But even in Judaism we see marks of growth and advance. The preparations for the Monotheism of the future were already made. An order of prophets was raised up, if not professedly to supersede the priests, at least to limit their functions, and reduce their supremacy. It has been remarked by the late Mr. Mill, very justly, that one of the safeguards of liberty in Israel was this order of prophets. It was owing to the prophets that Israel was preserved from sinking into a caste system of religion, as in Egypt and the East generally, and was prepared to become the herald of a higher civilisation and religion in the future. The transformation in Israel from a State-Church to a Church-State, in which the centre of gravity is shifted from the spiritual to the secular side of society, is marked, though gradual. At first the administration was hieratic, as much as in Egypt. The ruler of Israel was a priest-king, or Cohen, as in all the surrounding tribes. Then came the Shophet, or irregular military chief, assisted by an irregular and spasmodic burst of prophetism in the Roeh or Seer. Lastly, there came the Melek, or secular ruler, with a Nabi, or religious teacher, as his assessor; and as there was a succession in the kingship, so there were sons of the prophets. Under this latter administration the priesthood sank as much into the background as it did in the later times of Greece and Rome. Just as the King-Archon in Athens was the mere survival of an earlier theocratic stage of society, and so with the titular rank of Pontifex Maximus in Rome, in the same way in Israel the priesthood of later times was but the shrunk image and shadow of the earlier institution. As Ewald points out, the latest stage of the theocracy was a hierocracy, in which scribes and doctors of the law were the leaders of Israel, after prophet, priest, and king had almost, if not quite, disappeared. Rabbinism was the last and iron age of Israel. It was now nearing its decay. The things which were decaying and waxing old were ready to vanish away, and Israel, having fulfilled its predestined work as the preparation for the Gospel of Peace, passed away in a good old age, having outlived all the other civilisations of the East and West. The explanation of its very longevity lay in this, that it never surrendered its liberties to a priestly caste. There was always a balance of forces, something like what we should call in modern phrase a Constitutional system, in Israel. The first messenger of God, as Moses, who is said to have seen God face to face, was brother to the first priest, Aaron, who was ordained for God in things pertaining to men. When this apostle and high priest in one passed away with the lifetime of the two brothers, the leadership fell to a military chief and one of the sacred caste. So it continued under the Judges, and when the military leadership was fixed in one family, and the tribe of Judah became preponderant, the balance was restored by an order of prophets, raised up from time to time, and taken indifferently from all the tribes.

We argue, then, that, so far from the history of Israel, rightly interpreted, sanctioning the principle of a national cult and a priestly order of men to conduct it, it teaches the very opposite. Priestism was an accommodation on God's part to the local ideas of Deity scarcely raised above polytheism in which Israel was found in Egypt; but all the education of Israel was upward from this elementary stage. In their maturity, so far from professing a national cult, theirs was the very opposite. It was a Church-State—a kingdom of priests. Rabbinism has its faults, but they are not those of a priesthood.

The argument, then, that the past tells invariably in favour of a national recognition of religion is not worth much. It breaks down in the favourite instance. Unless we are such children in Biblical criticism as the divines of the Jacobean age, who gravely argued the question of a Levitical order presided over by a Scotch Solomon, we had better argue the question on its own merits, and not on dangerous precedents of this kind, which recoil on those who use them. Arguing, then, the question on its merits, we ask, Is the modern State bound to maintain a national worship? Do we recognise God in this way? It is childish to say that we could not acknowledge God publicly without an Archbishop of Canterbury to act as our high priest or Pontifex Maximus. So far from this, the United States officially acknowledge God through a proclamation of the President, and it is on this very account—that the act comes from a secular source, and does not flow through any ecclesiastical channel—that it is obeyed so much more cheerfully by the people. In this country, we are as afraid to bring out the old creaking machinery of a Queen's letter to the Archbishop as if it were the Coronation coach. Were a proclamation issued, and the details left to each sect and communion to observe the fast or thanksgiving in its own time and way, this would be abreast of the facts of the age. But to enforce attempts at uniformity after the principle of religious uniformity has become obsolete, is to ensure failure; and this is why, even as regards external recognition of God's moral government, we, with our State Church, are more lax than the United States without such an institution. It is a paradox, but a truth, that we, with an organisation kept up for this very object, do not attain the end in view so well as the United States with no organisation whatever. What should we say, if, with a standing army and a costly navy, we were more unprepared for war than if we kept up nothing more than a militia and a merchant marine? But so it is with regard to a national cult. Our priesthood, maintained at much cost for this, if for nothing else, fails on this very occasion, when, according to religious people whose prejudices we respect though may not agree with, we are bound as a nation to recognise God.

II. The second plea for a National Church is, that it is a bulwark against Rome. Considering that in our day the only Romeward tendencies are seen among the clergy of the National Church, it is difficult to state it seriously. We are reminded of Cicero's remark, that one augur could not look another in the face without laughing. Where is the Evangelical Churchman so simple as to believe that the bulwark theory is anything else than the cry of a few fossilised politicians, who think that the downfall of the British Constitution dates from the day of Catholic Emancipation? The men of that school are not consistent with their own sentiments. If, as a nation, we then committed apostacy—if it might then be said, "Take away her battlements, for they are not the Lord's," why are they ready to mount the breach again and die in the last ditch, as they say of themselves, in defence of one outwork after another of the old system of ascendancy? The same men who cried Ichabod over Catholic Emancipation were unwearied in denouncing the grant to Maynooth, as if the latter were not the logical and necessary sequel of the other. In the same way, they opposed the admission of the Jews to Parliament on account of its unchristianising the Legislature. Yet they seemed to forget that it had already been unchristianised, in their sense of the word, by removing the last of the Roman Catholic disabilities. In Mr. Lyle's "History of Eton College" we come upon one of these political fossils who sincerely believed in the bulwark theory. Plumptre was in his day the genial, humorous, generous, eccentric, and orthodox tutor and fellow of Eton. Popery, we are told, was his great bugbear. On the night that Catholic Emancipation was carried, he is said to have paced the cloisters all night with Mr. Briggs, a fellow of the College like-minded with himself, and he more than once declared, in after years, that the measure which he then had so deprecated was "the wickedest thing since the Crucifixion." The late Bishop of Exeter was not only the last of that school of intolerant Orange Tories of the Georgian era, but he also, in his career as a renegade from political Protestantism to the side of the reaction Romewards, shows how little this bulwark theory is to be trusted even by those who stand behind it. The same Dr. Philpotts who wrote fierce no-Popery pamphlets, and threw himself into the breach with Eldon and Sir Charles Wetherall against any, the smallest, concession of political rights to the Roman Catholics, adopted, in his old age, Church principles identical in essence with those of the Church of Rome. Nor let us be too hasty to condemn him as a turncoat. It was no transformation, but simply an evolution from one religion of authority to another. As a political Churchman, he had set up the Royal arms as supporters of the Bible and Crown. The Protestant religion, as by law established, had been his watchword, and when, as the result of Catholic Emancipation and the returning wave of Liberalism after the July revolution of 1830, the Royal support were seen to fail, he and others of his school began to look out for a fresh support for the tottering Church Establishment. They sought it in Church principles, and where they sought for it they found it. Dr. Newman, in his "Apologia," tells us the origin and rise of the "Tracts for the Times." They sprang out of the alarm and revolt of Oxford Toryism at the revolutionary measures which the Melbourne Ministry brought into Parliament—the threat of disestablishment in Ireland and the actual suppression of ten bishoprics in that country. It was out of this panic of political Churchmen that there sprang up the new school of Anglicans, who held that it was sacrilegious to touch the Episcopal office; bishops were the successors of the apostles, and consequently to strike a blow at them was to aim at the very heart of the Church, or, at least, at its historical continuity in this country. It is true that the Anglicans of our day have moved on, and left far behind the principles and professions of the earlier writers of the "Tracts for the Times." The Ritualist of our day who, in politics, is usually a Liberal, and more often indifferent, if not actually hostile, to Establishments, is as unlike as possible to the first generation of Tractarians, who, if they have any antecedents, may be said to be the direct descendants of the Non-jurors. The transformation from Orange Toryism to Anglicanism, and from that to Ritualism, is so great that, as a party, they may be said to have boxed the political compass. They are now as distinctly in favour of Roman Catholic claims as their fathers were opposed to them. A Protestant State Church is as much their abhorrence as it was the idol of the men who fiercely resisted Catholic Emancipation, and then, in disgust at the concession, threw themselves into the arms of a reaction which was, in all but the name, identical with modern Ultramontanism. The history of Churches is instructive on this subject, and should be a warning as to the dangerous and deceptive nature of all alliances of Church and State. As long as the State favours one Church and gives her an exclusive political status, we may count on her exuberant loyalty, and she will teach a doctrine of passive obedience, which is slavery thinly disguised. But let not the State reckon blindly on her loyalty when her own privileges are touched, or she may find the favoured Church break out, Absalom-like, into an unnatural rebellion against her too-indulgent lord. James II. had some reason to complain of the bad faith of the English Church, or rather of its Court divines, who had been preaching all their lives a slavish doctrine of submission to the tyranny of a Nero, and then betrayed him on the first occasion, when James did an apparently liberal thing and granted indulgence. In all probability, we should never have had the Revolution of 1688, if James II. had not been so infatuated as to attempt to force an ill-timed concession of toleration on an age not ripe for it. The people were alarmed for the cause of Protestantism, but the Church was much more alarmed for her ascendancy; and it was owing to this accidental and temporary alliance of Church and Dissent that we owe the Revolution. When the tale of bricks was doubled, then Moses appeared, as the Jewish saying runs. In the same way, when the good things of Oxford and the prizes of the Church were in danger, then the Church threw to the winds its doctrine of passive obedience. Church history is full of warnings of this kind. If it is dangerous for the Church to lean on the State for support, it is to the full as dangerous for the State to lean on the Church. Reversing the motto of "United, we stand; divided, we fall," we should say of Church and State that their union is weakness, and their separation strength. When united, the Church infects the State with the besetting fault of Churchmen—their desire to call in carnal weapons in a spiritual warfare. We see that in the case of Laud. On the other hand, the State gives a tone of secularity to the Church, and the result of the mixture of secular and spiritual is, as always must be the case, not to make the secular spiritual, but to make the spiritual secular.

It only excites a smile to hear the antiquated cry of 1827 revived in our day, that a Protestant Establishment is a bulwark against Popery. If there are any survivors of the school of Spooner and Inglis and the founders of the National Club, they must feel ashamed of the weak and childish treble into which the "big, manly voice" of fifty years ago has shrunk. The cry, though a bigoted one, was not unmeaning then. Such as it was, the Establishment, fifty years ago, was decidedly Protestant. It was Erastian and worldly, no doubt, in its tone; but its faults, such as they were, did not lie in the direction of a reaction Romewards. Dr. Newman's testimony on that point is decisive. Referring to the rise of the "Tracts for the Times," he observes, in his "Apologia"*:—"The great Reform agitation was going on around me as I wrote. The Whigs had come into power. Lord Grey had told the Bishops to set their house in order, and some of the Prelates had been insulted and threatened in the streets of London. The vital question was, How we were to keep the Church from being Liberalised? There was such apathy on the subject in some quarters, such imbecile alarm in others; the true principles of Churchmanship seemed so radically decayed; and there was such distraction in the councils of the clergy. Blomfield, the Bishop of London of the day—an active and open-hearted man—had been for years engaged in diluting the high orthodoxy of the Church by the introduction of members of the Evangelical body into places of influence and trust. He had deeply offended men who agreed in opinion with myself by an off-hand saying (as it was reported), to the effect that belief in the Apostolical Succession had gone out with the Non-jurors. 'We can count you,' he said to some of the gravest and most venerated persons of the

* *Vide* "Apologia," p. 30. Second Edition.

old school. And the Evangelical party itself, with its late successes, seemed to have lost that simplicity and unworldliness which I admired so much in Milner and Scott. It was not that I did not venerate such men as Ryder, the then Bishop of Lichfield, and others of similar sentiments who were not yet promoted out of the ranks of the clergy; but I thought little of the Evangelicals as a class. I thought that they played into the hands of the Liberals. With the Establishment thus divided and threatened, thus ignorant of its true strength, I compared that fresh vigorous power of which I was reading in the first centuries. In her triumphant zeal on behalf of that Primæval Mystery to which I had so great a devotion from my youth, I recognised the movement of my spiritual mother, *Incessu patuit Dea.*"

It is impossible to read this passage—so pathetic in its tender grace, so transparent in its truthful delineation of the state of parties in the English Church then and since—without feeling that a silent revolution has passed over that Church since the day when, as Newman himself tells us, he was taught the doctrine of the Apostolical Succession by the Rev. William James, then a Fellow of Oriel, in the course of a walk round Christ Church meadow. "I recollect," he adds, "being somewhat impatient of the subject at the time." There was some meaning in the expression that the Church of England was a bulwark against Rome forty years ago; there is none now. For better or worse—we do not discuss that point here—the spread of Church principles has rounded off the angles and smoothed down the differences between the Reformed Church of this country and the unreformed Church of Rome. If, in one sense, the Romeward tendency has been stayed in our day, it is because men are not so sensitive as they were forty years ago to the enormous differences between the Churches which accepted and those which withstood the Reformation. The abyss has been, in a measure, bridged over. Instead of a rampart against Rome, the Anglican Church has become a kind of drawbridge, across which the garrison may pass the fosse, and hold safe parley with the enemy in the gate. It is not the language of "No Popery" panic-mongers, but the serious remonstrance of the entire Episcopal Bench, with only two exceptions, that the danger cannot be concealed, and that there is an open conspiracy within the English Church to efface the Reformation. It is in vain to say that being a conspiracy, it is obviously the work of a contemptible minority for which the great mass of the English clergy are not to be held responsible. But the answer to this is, that minorities have a strange fashion of becoming majorities. Unless a movement of this kind is quickly put down, it gathers strength by indulgence, and, having made good its position within the Church, it succeeds, like the camel in the Eastern story, in ejecting the man from the tent. First the nose, then the neck, and finally the hump is thrust under the tent-door; and then, instead of the demand for toleration, the claim is set up that they are there, not by sufferance at all, but by right. Any one who will compare the balance of forces between the Anglican and the Evangelical parties, will see that the centre of gravity in the English Church has been silently, but steadily, shifting during the last twenty or thirty years. The secession of Dr. Newman marked the turning-point. Up to about

1845 we should say that the bulwark theory, though a little antiquated, was not quite obsolete. Now it is so completely out of date, that it raises a question whether senility is not carried to the point of doting insipience when some of the old Evangelical party tell us that, but for the State Church, we should have no bulwark against the encroachments of the Church of Rome. Mr. Ryle told us the other day, in language more homely than elegant, that the Church of Rome would come and "make mincemeat of Dissenters," if their best and only defence were removed. We do not know if Dissenters are reserved, like Ulysses, for the distinction of being eaten last by this Polyphemus of Rome; but this we are certain of, that, but for the sacerdotal party in the English Church, there would be no Polyphemus' den in this country at all. Rome is wise in her generation, and she knows this, and openly avows her intention to use the State Church as a stepping-stone to her old position of ascendancy. She is opposed to disestablishment or to any policy which would drive matters to extremities in this country. Her motto is, *Festina lente*. She would keep up the so-called barrier, using it all the while as a drawbridge. It will be time enough to drop the mask when the work of assimilation between new and old Catholics in this country has gone on, and when, almost without a sense of jar or a breach of continuity, the old cathedrals are restored to their former uses.

Let us not, then, be misled by phrases or use old watchwords after the meaning has long since died out of them. A State Church never was a real battlement of defence against the Church of Rome. The oracle advised Athens to pull down her stone walls and trust to wooden—the meaning of which was obvious. It was to be beforehand with the enemy, and to meet him by sea, and not allow him to land and invest the city of the violet crown. In the same way, we should urge on all who believe in Protestantism to trust in no defences foreign to the genius of a religion of liberty and free inquiry. It is doubtful if National Churches were much defence to the truth in the days of Luther and Calvin; but, at all events, they were not then violently out of harmony with the age as they are now. There were garrison Churches then, like that of Geneva, in which the magistrate and the minister of religion, between them, kept the city; and the result was a kind of theocracy foreign to the genius of the New Testament, and which soon broke down, as all attempts to galvanise the past invariably must. In our day, the garrison theory of State Churches as the bulwarks of Protestantism has signally failed. One such garrison Church has been removed in Ireland, to the general satisfaction of all but a prejudiced minority, who, with all their loud claims to be Protestant, show, by their intolerant manner, how little they understand of the real genius of the system of which they make so loud a profession. True Protestantism is nothing unless it is a spiritual system, using no other weapon than the sword of the Spirit, which is the Word of God; appealing to no other standard than the enlightened conscience; and claiming no authority beyond the willing submission of its own professed followers. Such a religion as this, so far from asking help from the State, finds itself weak and unable to go up to battle only when it is clad in this Saul's armour of establishment and endowment. I am aware of the special pleading by which the edge is taken off these remarks. First, we are asked, Do we object on principle to all or any form of endowment? If not, it is added, What can be the harm of securing this endowment under State control? and so it is in this way that order or organisation leads the way to endowment, and then in its turn endowment to establishment. This is the old sophism of the hairs in the horse-tail; or, in popular language, give an inch and take an ell. It is the fallacy of the Sorites applied to the question of the connection of Church and State. It is better to meet it at once by setting up such a pattern of a Church in which Congregationalism and the voluntary principle go hand in hand, and where there is no room for establishment because no desire for endowment. It is easier to guard against the evil in the future, than to say how to deal with it in the past. In this respect the remark of Macchiavelli is full of point, that maladies are at first difficult to trace out, but easy to apply the remedy to; whereas, after they have become inveterate, it is conversely easy to see the evil, but difficult to apply the remedy. This is the case with the English Church at present, and our only hope is that the nature of the evil will suggest the remedy, and that, seeing the bulwark of Protestantism has become a drawbridge to Rome, men may learn to distrust State Churches, and leave truth unarmoured to fight its own battles, when it will certainly be more than a match for error.

We have thus disposed of the two excuses of those who argue that we should reform the State Church and not abolish it. They tell us that a State Church is a national recognition of God, and also that it is a bulwark against Rome. We reply by an appeal to facts. Do we recognise God so much by endowing a certain clerical corporation as by national acts of righteousness, mercy, and truth? Again, What is the worth of a bulwark when it actually invites the attack of the enemy, and is rather a defence to traitors within than from the besieging army without? A theory which is thus tested by facts, and so signally breaks down, cannot be worth much, and, indeed, it remains what it always was, a mere theory—an excuse for conserving an institution when it has outlived its time. Reasons, according to that arch-sophist, Father Newman, are not so much to find out what is true, as to find arguments for maintaining what we know to be true already from other sources. Reasoning of this kind, which is *preposterous* in the strict sense of the word, is more resorted to in theology than in any other department of thought. In exact science it would be scouted at once; but the vicious method of authority has so infected theology that men are scarcely aware that they are arguing not to, but from, a foregone conclusion. On this account it is that the practical statesman has to stop and scatter a little dust on the theological hornets, and compose the strife in this way. Some day or other, the Church will be disestablished in this country, and those who spun these cobwebs of proof as to the duty of the State and the defence of a National Church to our popular Protestantism, will learn the force of the homely saying, that an ounce of mother-wit is worth a pound of clergy.

CHAPTER XIV.

THE CONSERVATIVE ARGUMENT.

"SUPPOSE the Church never to have been united to the State, where is the Christian who would not exclaim against the idea of the union were it now proposed?" This remark of Vinet points to the real difficulty of the problem of Disestablishment. Strange as it may seem, a State-Church, or a Church-State, are alike so foreign to the genius of primitive Christianity, that, finding both types in existence, men begin to argue that this after-growth of primitive times must be a normal production, as the parasite plant is of the oak. Let us regard it with the same superstitious reverence as the Druids did the mistletoe. Let us say of it in the Latin saw, *Fieri non debet, factum valet.* No one would think of setting up a State Church in this country; but no one, on the other hand, regarding the difficulties attending Disestablishment, would now think of pulling it down. This is the sententious commonplace which passes for political wisdom among the governing classes in this country. It is almost as luminous as the Hegelian law of identity, that whatever is, is. But the opinion passes current in too many circles not to engage our attention. In fact, it is the very philosophy which suits a rich and self-indulgent age, too absorbed in the pursuit of riches and the worship of art to care much for first principles. The argument, if it is worth anything, amounts to this, that we are mere trustees of the past, and not entitled to deal with our own national institutions. We are bound, in fact, to administer them as we find them. We are ready to admit that it is the part of the wise man to make the best he can of existing circumstances, to like what he has when he cannot have what he likes. None of our institutions, whether civil or military, are so perfect in theory that we should carry them on as they are if we could begin *de novo*. But the case in point is a very different one. It is an admission that a State Church is an obsolete institution, which, nevertheless, must be carried on because it is too troublesome to disturb the trust, and because questions of property are so mixed up with it, that to raise the one would disturb the settled character of the other. The *fieri non debet* argument amounts to this— either that the State has lost its power to control the Church, or that we have not a single statesman able to grapple with a question of such magnitude. In fact, an argument of this kind, which gives up the principle of an Establishment, and rests the case on the mere *vis inertiæ* of a majority of Conformists, is a most dangerous support for such an institution as the Church of England. In a letter written some few years ago to Mr. G. Mitchel, Mr. Gladstone stated his present standpoint with regard to the English State Church to be this:—"In my opinion, the Establishment of England, but not of Scotland, represents the religion of a considerable majority of the people, and that they do not seem to desire the change that you recommend. This being so, the only other question I need now ask myself is, whether the civil endowments and *status* of the Church are unfavourable to the effective maintenance and propagation of the Christian faith. If and when I am convinced that they are so, I shall adopt your conclusion, but not before." Mr. Gladstone, in this passage, rests the case of the Establishment on the support of a majority not yet brought round to the other side, with the ominous qualification, which may at any time turn the scale in the other direction, that at present the civil endowments and *status* of the Church are not unfavourable to the effective maintenance and propagation of the Christian faith. It is a complete surrender of all principle in the matter, and a direct challenge to the minority who have a conviction against State Churches to begin a crusade to convince the majority who are confessedly apathetic. If England were polled by manhood suffrage on this question, probably the immense majority would be found to be indifferent to the claims alike of Church and Dissent, although at present this neutral mass is claimed as belonging to the Church. Obviously, then, the will of majorities is a dangerous support on which to rest a State Church. It is remarkable, too, with what ease majorities are brought round to the side of the minority. It is almost as easy to dispose of them as for a few disciplined men to disperse a mere rabble. As soon as we descend from principle and argue on the *fieri non debet* principle, we quickly get on to say *factum non valet*. To men who have gone as far as this, the rest of the journey on to Disestablishment is not far to traverse. We have only to point out, in order to complete our case, that the abuses outweigh the advantages, and, further, that these abuses are inseparable from a State Church, whereas the advantages are those which any orderly and organised type of free Christianity would secure. Englishmen are never weary of proclaiming themselves to be a practical race. It is their boast that, however averse from abstract and *à priori* speculation, they are well able to deal with any question on its merits. Disembodied ideas are not to their taste; but when they take shape and touch *terra firma*, no one grasps their meaning more readily, or deals with them more determinedly, than the Englishman. With regard to such abstract questions as these—viz., whether it is the duty of the State to maintain an Establishment of religion or not—he is somewhat hazy. He looks upon these discussions as only suitable for a debating society. He leaves it to young men to debate in a discussion forum on the abstract merits of the best possible government in Church and State. What do we mean by our duty? what are we to understand by the State? is religion a mere external cult, or is it an inward conviction?—these are a few of the pitfalls which lie in the way of those who settle these points by reference solely to first principles. On this account the average Englishman is not far wrong in refusing to discuss the question of Establishments on *à priori* grounds. We should be prepared, then, to take the controversy up at the point where the practical Englishman becomes interested in it. We are going to judge the Establishment by its practical results. Franklin was in the habit of setting down the *pros* and the *cons* to any particular course of conduct like a debtor-and-creditor account in a ledger, and then to cast up the sum of the reasons for or against it. Others have done the same, and the diaries of religious people fifty years ago were made up, in a great measure, with cases of conscience calculated by these rules of mental arithmetic. The practical working of an institution is the way in which it will be judged by the great majority of men. Whatever is best administered is best; in this way they settle all questions of abstract statesmanship. In a constitution like ours, any part of the machine which does not work well, and contribute to the general welfare of the whole, is taken out and repaired. If, after it is put in again, it is still found to be no source of strength but the reverse, it is then put aside as a useless encumbrance. Not only do the judges hold their office *quamdiu se bene gesserint*, but also the judiciary itself would be reconstituted if its inefficiency as a whole became an ascertained fact. The House of Lords, for instance, as an Hereditary Chamber, does not contribute anything like its proportionate strength to the constitutional machine. As a compensation-balance to the preponderance of the Lower House, it is not up to its work; and though the majority of Conservatives are too shortsighted to see it, there would be the truest Conservatism in doing something to strengthen the House of Lords. Whether the addition of a large representative element in the shape of a life peerage would meet the necessities of the case, we need not here discuss. One thing is certain, that the constitution, like a piece of watchwork, will not put up with wheels which do not cog truly, or ratchets and pins which are not in gear. The antiquarian watchmaker may treat as a survival some piece of the machine which has been superseded by modern mechanism, and may make believe that he has put it in. But survivals which are left in only for appearance' sake, like the buttons behind a dress-coat, will not be kept up if they interfere with some useful reform. The House of Lords has, to some extent, answered this purpose in the past, and to a certain extent does so still. It is the drag-chain on the constitutional coach; but any improvement of that coach, by which the wheels could lock themselves at a touch of the driver, would at once supersede this drag-chain. This being so, it becomes the interest of all who would keep up that continuity between the past and the present which is the boast of the British Constitution, to relax no effort in order to bring every part of the machine of State into full working order, and to reform or remove it. Utility is not the final test of truth ; but ours is a world where few at best are far-sighted, and the struggle for existence is so keen that the majority must live from hand to mouth, morally as well as materially, with a few snatches of truth and philosophy provided for them in a proverbial form. Our statesmanship cannot go beyond, then, the "greatest happiness of the greatest number" principle. If any constitution answers this test of utility, we shall not inquire into its reasonableness. The eternal fitness of things will not trouble us if it fits us with things as they are. We are fain to fall back on the Latin saw, *Fieri non debet*, for which, in the light of pure reason, we must express our unmeasured contempt. *Factum valet* will hold good of any institution which works fairly well, and is not out of gear with the rest of modern society. Church Establishments will stand or fall in our day on utilitarian grounds of this kind. If, on the whole, the majority approve of them, and approve for the reasons which apparently satisfy Mr. Gladstone—that, on the whole, the Establishment is not unfavourable to the effective maintenance and propagation of the Christian faith—there will be little use in appealing to abstract principles.

The sentiment of Free Churchmen is a noble one, and might be written in letters of gold on a temple of truth. "We believe in the vitality of Christian truth, in the power of Christian character, and in the infinite energies of Christian love. If these cannot overtake the religious necessities of a country, no law will ever be able to accomplish it." But this grand sentiment, like Archimedes' lever, would move the world if we could only find a fulcrum. The Free Churchman has found a moral fulcrum in the phrase, "I believe in the vitality of Christian truth." Of course, if we can rise to this altitude, and see, as Milton did, that truth has in it an inherent vitality and power when matched single-handed against error, the question is then at an end. Our lever has moved the world. But the majority do not believe in pure truth when unbacked by power or authority of some kind. The majority must have truth, if not diluted, at least worked up in some palatable shape. It must be truth labelled as such, and packed in the sealed wrapper of some recognised Church. This being so, we are bound to meet men on their own ground, and to help them to judge of the cause by its effects. We must show them Establishments as they operate among ourselves and in our day. It will not be enough to point out that State Churches worked disadvantageously elsewhere in Europe, or formerly among ourselves. It will still be said that this is nothing to the point. Have they not reformed, and is not the State Church of our day more in harmony with the spirit of the age than it ever has been before? There is no denying this fact. So much is this the case, that Churchmen now triumphantly point to the fact, and challenge us to show the abuses which still remain unreformed. A case against Establishments would fail which relied on the corruptions of the Georgian era—the nepotism, worldliness, and unblushing avarice of bishops like those of George II.'s reign, which made that not very exemplary monarch observe, that he thought all his bishops were atheists. The answer to this is, that these were not so much the faults of the Church as of the age, and that "Other times, other manners" is a proverb as true in English as in French. We will admit the justice of this remark, and give the Church the benefit of the difference between the Georgian and the Victorian era. But, taking the Church as she exists in our day, we think that a case may be made out to show that all her increased activity is not on account of her State connection, but in spite of it. It is precisely in proportion as her *status* and privileges as an Establishment are threatened and challenged that she puts forth efforts to make good her claim to be the Church of the nation. We must have read history to very little purpose not to see that an institution often reforms on the very eve of its destruction. It is swept away at the moment when it is in the act of removing those abuses which cried loudly for reform. So it was with the old French monarchy. It fell not under the gilded hypocrisy of the Grand Monarque's reign, or the swinish sensuality of a Louis XV., but in the reign of the virtuous, amiable Louis XVI.—who, but for the fact that he was the heir of the crimes as well as the glories of his ancestors, might have gone down into history as the benevolent locksmith, as our George III. is remembered as Farmer George. Louis was of the two the better man, but how different his fate; and all this because monarchy in France attempted reform exactly a century too late. If the French, like the English, Revolution had occurred in 1689 instead of in 1789, its course might have been different. This is the reply, then, to those who argue that the Church may be saved as an Establishment through the devotion and public spirit of large numbers of its dignitaries in our day. The argument from their activity tells with fatal effect the other way. It is the result, not of State connection, but the Voluntary principle, which has led to the large expenditure of upwards of twenty-six millions on the Church and cathedrals since the year 1840—an amount, probably, twenty times as much as was spent during the century previous, before the breath of Voluntaryism had begun to stir the stagnant depths of the State Church.

Reasoning, then, on the method of concomitance, we argue that the activity of the Church varies *inversely*, not *directly*, with the amount of State support and patronage. The union is not like that of mind and body, in which the health of the mind varies directly with the soundness of the bodily organs, especially the brain. The law of concomitance shows us, in the case of the connection of Church and State, a result so invariable that we may almost describe it by the following formula: The more the Church is subsidised and supported by the State, the more her native energies languish. On the other hand, the more she is deprived of these external supports, the more she takes wing and soars, as a partridge does when the setter has fairly beaten her out of cover. It is not surprising that the Erastian press, which desires to keep religion under State control, should make use of Lord Hampton's returns to prove that so powerful and energetic a body as the Church is now seen to be must not be treated as a mere sect. But for earnest Churchmen to accept that kind of argument implies a very dim conception of where their real strength lies. Much, it is true, of this twenty-six millions was given by wealthy men who wished, in a monumental fashion, to commemorate themselves by building churches and setting up windows of stained glass in them. But still enough remains of genuine zeal to justify the statement, that the Church can work on the Voluntary system almost as energetically as any sect. If so, the inference is obvious that if she has done so much under State control, how much more might she do if set free. This return of Lord Hampton is a two-edged sword, and cuts the hand of those who wield it in favour of continuing the Church as she is as well as of those who say that her spiritual strength has departed.

We are willing to admit that the Church has remedied many abuses, and is in the fair way of purging herself from others. She is thus, as a State Church, entitled to appeal to the *cui bono* argument, and plead, as Mr. Ryle does, "What good will it do?" The retort is obvious, "What harm will it do?" If it will do Dissenters no good to disestablish the Church, may we not add it will also do the Church itself no harm to be disestablished? On this utilitarian level as much can be said on one side as on the other; and since we are arguing at present on these grounds, we may as well go on to show what are our reasons for thinking that the Church can be reformed in only one way. The inference is a fair one, that if the Bishops have done so much since they were warned by Lord Melbourne, now nearly fifty years ago, to set their house in order, they will continue to do more when released from a burdensome position. At present they are State officials, lodged in so-called palaces, and expected to keep up the state and hospitality of a country nobleman with an income which, measured by that of a peer of our day, is only genteel poverty. The Bishops, as spiritual peers, are in a thoroughly false position, and, to do them justice, they feel it. The official dress which the lay peers insist on the lords spiritual putting on when they take part in their debates is intended as a silent hint that they are there, more or less, on sufferance. It is a small but significant hint, that, like the chaplain at a nobleman's table, they are below the salt, and intended to retire after grace and when the real business of debate begins. If the Bishops, as a rule, were not raised from the class of college tutors and Greek-play-editing schoolmasters, they would resent this offensive rule of the lay peers, who dispense in everyday use with robes for themselves, but only allow the judges to sit in ermine and the bishops in lawn—the former without a vote at all, and the latter with only a consultative vote. The Bishops, in fact, are treated by the lay peers as buffers between themselves and public opinion. The peers are aware that, before reform can touch their order, it must first sweep away the Bishops; and, impressed with this danger, they rather tolerate the existence of Bishops as barons in Parliament for the sake of offering a sort of breakwater against the wave of reform which must one day rise against a Chamber of hereditary legislators like our existing House of Lords.

The argument, then, is conclusive that the Church is strong or weak in an inverse ratio to its connection with the State. But it is said we are carrying our theory too far in insisting that, if the Church grows strong exactly in proportion as it is cast off by the State, that this will continue after the separation between the two is complete. Does not the argument prove too much? Is it not like the argument for abstinence? A man has weakened his constitution by excess; he becomes temperate, and exactly in proportion as he abstains does he recover his vigour. Let him go on, then, cutting down one article of diet after another, and will it not be like the man who brought his horse down to live on a straw a day?—only, unfortunately for the success of the experiment, the horse died too soon for the theory to be verified. State support, in the same way, may enfeeble the Church's vigour; but, take it away altogether, and may she not fall away into a rabble of sects, and at last disappear altogether?

There is no saying what may not happen in the case of a Church so completely Erastianised as the English Church is. She may have lost all recuperative power, all faith in her Divine mission, and in the truth that "One is her Master, even Christ." In that case, she must infallibly perish. But, then, that is because she has long since become a dead branch of the living vine, and is only fit to be burned. But we are willing to believe better things of her than this. The zeal and activity put forth on the Voluntary principle, not by one section of the Church, but by all, show that she has not lost all her inherent vitality. She is, like Milton's lion, "part pawing to be free." Every effort which she puts forth to recover lost ground, and resume her position as the National Church, succeeds in one direction and fails in another. It succeeds in giving her an honourable position as a competitor with the Free Churches, but it fails in giving her the ascendancy she once had, and which she still sighs after. Judging by present appearances, we should say that, if there were no other forces at work to disestablish the Church, such as the attacks of Nonconformists without or the divisions of High and Low Church within her, the activity which she is now putting forth on the Voluntary principle would rack her to pieces as a State Church in a few years. She is calling, for instance, for more Bishops, and even providing for their endowment by the benefactions of her own members. The State cannot refuse to sanction this effort, but it is unable to meet these benefactions by the smallest assistance even out of ecclesiastical funds; much less is it prepared to make these new Bishops peers in Parliament. Thus at once a distinction is created between a class of Bishops who are prelates and another class who are not, and the result is, that, since the Church cannot level up, she will not be long in levelling down. In many other ways, this contrast between the Voluntary and the State-controlled action of the Church will become more marked every day. Already the missionary branch of the Church has broken loose from its fetters, and Bishops in foreign parts are consecrated, and the Church, in all its efficiency as a reproductive body, planted out without waiting for a Queen's letter. The Archbishop of Canterbury, it is true, is still tied by the Royal Supremacy, but the Colonial Bishops are not, so that the way is prepared for a complete emancipation of the Church from State control as far as her missionary work is concerned.

We are justified, then, in arguing that the maximum of internal activity is only reached when there is the minimum of State interference. We may even go one step further and say that when the last link of State connection is broken, the Church will take a new lease of life. Be this as it may, we are bound to carry on the work of disentangling our civil and ecclesiastical relations from the knot in which they were twisted during the Middle Ages. We are sure that it is for the good of the State to do so, and we believe that it will be equally for the good of the Church, although for the present those who are interested in the connection do not see it. We have thus pointed out those evils of the Church which are inseparable from State connection, and which she can never purge herself from except by Disestablishment. We have endeavoured to prove that the evils largely outweigh the advantages. We shall now, in conclusion, set down the reasons on both sides, and casting them up in the way that Franklin made us familiar with, come to a settlement which the most utilitarian mind will admit is based on a strict appeal to facts.

CHAPTER XV.

CONCLUSION AND RECAPITULATION.

OUR inquiry has thus reached the point where we are entitled to draw a conclusion. We have seen that all Church order and organisation tend to stiffen into formality; and that, having begun in the spirit, men seek, like the Galatians of old, to be made perfect by the flesh. This is the master-key to all the corruptions of later years. There are many departures from the truth, but they have all this character in common, that they set up something between Christ and the conscience, some substitute for living communion with Him who is the Fountain of Life. The earliest form of this corruption is Clericalism, or the lording it over God's heritage on the part of ecclesiastical rulers, and its later and final form is Cæsarism, the outcome and consequent of the former, when the civil power lords it over God's heritage. The one leads on to the other, and they alternately check and control each other. We have also seen that the Reformation at best very partially broke this heavy yoke. In most cases the Churches only exchanged one form of oppression for another. The so-called national type of Church has only this to be said in its excuse, that it transferred the supremacy from a foreign to a home tyrant. No inconsiderable advance, we admit, considering that the worst native tyrant is a better head of the Church than the best foreigner ; as Byron expresses this thought with regard to Miltiades, tyrant of the Chersonese—

> "A tyrant, but our masters then
> Were still at least our countrymen."

Still it was at best only an exchange of masters. It was a step in the direction of true reform ; but unless we are able to go on and complete the emancipation of the Church, we are preparing the way for a reaction Romewards.

Turning to the history of the Church of England, we see these anticipations exactly verified. We see an organised hierarchical Church constituted in the estate of Prelacy in Saxon times, and losing its local liberties and national independence at last in its subjection to the centralising despotism of the Papacy. This Papal-Cæsarism lasted some three or four centuries, from the time of the Norman kings till the Act of Supremacy of Henry VIII. Then came a change of masters, and instead of a Pope-Cæsar there was a Cæsar-Pope. This is the Establishment of the Tudor and Stuart kings, which we have to deal with to-day, and the problem is, How can we complete the Reformation of the future? A National Church, as we have seen, can only continue on these terms, that it becomes as comprehensive as the nation itself. Now, since the nation is hopelessly divided on all questions concerning the unseen world and the hereafter in general, a Church which is to embrace the nation in one form of cult must abolish dogma, abandon creeds, and dissolve into a form of Deism, resting on an ethical basis only. There are a few extreme Erastians and Broad Churchmen who are prepared to support a National Church on such terms as these; but to do the majority of earnest Christians justice, they would prefer entire Disestablishment and total Disendowment to such a compromise of principle as this. They must have a definite creed, if not a rigid and inelastic type of ritual. They would never consent to retain a National Church on the only terms on which it can exist in a free and Parliamentary-governed country like ours.

This being so, and the conditions of definiteness and comprehension being irreconcilable, there is no future for a National Church in this or any other country. It is only a question of time when the majority, who are unwilling to face the fact that they are shut in to a logical dilemma, shall begin to look at the question in its true light. They will then either decide for a National Church without dogma—like the so-called National Churches of Switzerland, which are little else than schools of unbelief—or they will decide for a dogmatic Church which, from the nature of the case, must cease to be National. We have shut our eyes long enough to this inevitable dilemma; and if we continue to do so much longer, we may have to march between Caudine Forks of a disgraceful surrender to both extremes at once. To save the Church's National character, we may surrender dogma; and then to save her dogma, when it is too late we may part with its status as an Establishment. In trying to save both, we may commit the folly of losing both, and this is what is already resulting from the unnatural alliance of the Erastian and the Ecclesiastical parties, for which the Bishops are chiefly responsible.

As wise men we are bound, then, to face this question, and adapt the existing machinery of the Church to the wants of the age. At present we have a vast accumulation of old endowments, the growth of ages; Bishops' lands, tithes commuted and converted into a rent charge, cathedral and chapter funds, all representing together a capital sum of probably more than a hundred and fifty million sterling. This vast national estate is now wastefully cultivated; if we may borrow a metaphor from much of our land tenure, it is let below its value to an unimproving tenant, who is tied down to old methods of cultivation, and which brings in much less return than it might do if otherwise distributed. It is clearly the duty of Parliament, as trustees for the nation, to break up this old farm, to let it out afresh, and get the greatest possible return for it. We have pointed out how this may be done with advantage to all parties. The present lessees of this national farm are tied by the clauses of their lease to cultivate it in only one way. The Act of Uniformity binds them to one fixed type of worship, which, however admirable in itself as a framework of devotion, is too rigid and inelastic, and certainly does not meet the needs of advanced Christians in one direction, or of the illiterate in the other. For this reason, and for others which we need not now enumerate, the majority of the nation either stands outside this National Church, or conforms from sheer indifference. The first return of life in the Church always wakens up something which is Dissent in all but name. It was so with the Evangelical Revival of the early part of this century, and so equally with the Ritualist movement of our day. Both are frowned upon by the friends of Uniformity; it seems as if life and order are incompatible in a National Church. Be this as it may, the remedy for this state of things is simple. Temporalities and spiritualities must be separated at once, and the spiritual saved by its separation from the temporal. For those who desire the name of a National Church, we would meet their case by applying these revenues to national purposes of an educational character, including sanitary and social science. We would offer facilities, as in Ireland, for a Free Episcopal Church to organise itself, and take over the existing Churches and such portion of the endowments as were not of the nature of tithe. Into the details of this we do not enter, as here we are dealing only with the principle of the question. We are not so sanguine as to suppose that Dissent would at once disappear with the Establishment, or that the cause of offence being removed in the ascendancy of one favoured Church, the other Churches would draw towards it by natural attraction of the less to the greater. But this we are sure of, we should hear less of the rivalry of Churches. To apply Burke's paradox, when all the Nonconformity had ceased, much of its morosity would disappear also. We should hear little of the Dissidence of Dissent, and what good men are sighing for in all directions would follow. We should find an interchange of pulpits, and liturgical and free forms of prayer would be used in the same building. With regard to the former we may here remark that the interchange of pulpits is illegal only in a technical sense, because the Act of Uniformity shuts the door of the State Church to all but episcopally-ordained ministers. It is the interpretation of that Act by the ablest ecclesiastical lawyers which assumes that if it is illegal on one side to admit a Nonconformist into Episcopal pulpits, it is equally illegal for the Episcopalian to enter the pulpit of his Nonconformist brother, or to use any offices but those of the Book of Common Prayer. With regard to the latter difficulty—the use of free prayer and forms interchanged—it would come of itself as soon as the straight-waistcoat of the Act of Uniformity is taken off the clergy. All must feel the deadening effect of a too rigid adherence to forms. The Liturgy itself loses its beauty when it is slavishly adhered to, as if there were a Darius-like decree that no prayer should ascend to God save in one set form of speech. Every spiritual mind must feel the numbing effect of a monotonous repetition of one set of phrases only. To do Dissenters justice, there are none more ready to admit the stately rhythm and completeness as a manual of devotion of the English Liturgy. They are ready, in most cases, to use it in some amended and modified form. What they object to is the iron yoke of uniformity; and when compelled to become Dissenters they assert themselves, as human nature is only too ready to do, by regarding all liturgical forms as a restraining of the spirit. But this narrowness in the other extreme would disappear in time, as soon as the provoking cause of it had been removed. We are not deluded with the vain expectation of a man-made millennium; but if anything would hasten on the final reunion of Christendom, it is the removal of all religious questions out of the sphere of statute law. Too long has the State unfairly weighed down religion in general, by throwing its sword into the scale of one sect against the others. But for a miserable question of endowments—which is a dubious advantage at best to any sect—Episcopalians would spring up to claim their liberties, and with them their religious autonomy. If this were conceded to them, Liberty would lead to Equality, and Equality end in Fraternity. Thus, as the Cæsaro-Papacy is the last stage of descent of hierarchical Christendom, so the goal we should aim at is a federation of Free Churches, with a maximum of internal life, and a minimum of external organisation. The last stage of the Church will thus be a return to the first, when it was only the Kingdom of God set up in men's hearts, and ruling by no other authority than that of willing allegiance, the unity of the spirit in the bond of peace, not the uniformity of the letter in the bond of discord.

We have said enough to point out the evils of existing arrangements; let us glance, in conclusion, at the existing state of the controversy and the prospects of Disestablishment in our day. There is no disguising the fact that the Conservative reaction, whatever that may mean in politics, is in religion a reality. It arises, as all reactions do, from a composition of forces. The age is in a state of transition; old beliefs are losing their hold on the mind—new beliefs have not yet taken their place. The result is that men, in a kind of despair of truth, call in Church authority as a sort of quietus to doubt. They neither entirely believe nor disbelieve. In the one case they would outgrow a dogmatic centre of authority; in the other case they would passionately overturn it. But, halting as they do between these poles of extreme belief and disbelief, they fall back on a kind of interim arrangement. No type of Church order seems to them so convenient as that of a National Church, which combines in itself so many compromises. It is at once broad and narrow; national, yet denominational; it is Protestant and Catholic; it touches Rome with one hand and Geneva with the other; its ministers are educated gentlemen, planted out all over the country, who are little centres of culture and civilisation. Moderation and the *via media* are the very genius of the institution. It unites a rigid uniformity of cult with a lax interpretation of creed and dogma. It is not surprising, therefore, that it should meet the wants of an age of transition. Men can neither do with nor without religion. If they desired religion for its own sake, they would leave it to its own native forces; for those who believe most deeply in a Divine remedy for human wants and woes are not, as a rule, impressed with the importance of Church organisation and authority. On the other hand, the average man of the world cannot dispense with religion altogether. It provides a sanction, as he thinks, for morality, a support for human laws, without which they would crumble beneath their own weight. Whether he believes in the popular doctrine of heaven and hell or not, he still inclines to the view that the teaching of future rewards and punishments under theological sanction is important in some sense as a safeguard of society. He may be a sceptic himself, but for that reason he is all the more anxious, as Hume was, to strengthen the supports of human law by sanctions which he does not himself allow. We do not, of course, imply that State Churchmen are sceptics, but we do affirm that many sceptics are inclined to a State-regulated religion. The reasons for this are so obvious that we need not recur to them. All history attests the truth of the remark. The present age, more than any other, is charged with tendencies of this kind. Science has sapped one by one our traditional beliefs. Men of the world say they have no longer either an infallible Book or an infallible Church to fall back on. All is in a state of flux; and as for that third tribunal of conscience, or the inner light, or private judgment enlightened by the Word of God, this is too vague and fluctuating a standard to guide the masses. It may suit a little sect of pietists, some close corporation of Christians, who exchange the password as they enter their Bethels; but the mass of mankind could never learn such Shibboleths as these.

This being so, men of the world ask for a moderate, sober religion, with few dogmas and mysteries kept well in the background, on which to rest their support of morality. A national religion, equidistant from superstition, or the abuse of external authority, and fanaticism, or the abuse of internal authority, is to them the happy compromise between faith and unbelief which they are in search of. A recent writer on Establishments, Mr. Harwood,* has put forth a defence of them which amounts to this—that there is nothing between the age and utter unbelief but a State-regulated Church. He describes a Free Church in a Free State as an Indifferent Church in an Ignoring State. But Churches, he adds, will not always remain indifferent, and then States cannot afford to remain ignoring. The Church —meaning thereby the organisation for religion—may

* Disestablishment; or, a Defence of the Principle of a National Church. By George Harwood, M.A. P. 368.

be broken up into a number of separate Churches, as it has been by Dissent in England and America, and these separate Churches may none of them be powerful enough to rival the State; but such a fragmentary condition cannot long continue unless they grow to disbelieve in the religion itself, and then a new religion must be on its way. Men eventually become sick of impotent isolations and paltry sectarian divisions. This is the condition into which Englishmen are getting at the present time; and when such a condition comes, they will either break quite away from religion, or will long for the dignity and unity of a great Church. Such a Church will then be revived either in connection with the State or separated from it. But a great Church cannot long remain separated from the State. Such a Church will possess property, and the State, unless it is to abdicate its position of being the supreme guardian of property, will be called upon, sooner or later, to interfere in the disputes of that Church in order to decide as to the rights of its property.

The insinuation that the sect principle is played out, and that either a National Church or utter scepticism is the only alternative before us, is the mistake which underlies this otherwise able defence of the Establishment. This thought does not come to the surface everywhere, but it is evidently in the writer's mind, and seems to suggest the grounds on which he rests his belief in a State Church. In common with many educated men (for he is only representative of a large class), he finds the sects narrow, traditional, and as much bound up by formularies and trust deeds as if they had an Act of Uniformity, and were held bound by subscription to Articles. If he does not describe himself in Mr. Matthew Arnold's phrase on the side of Culture against Anarchy, as the excesses of private judgment on religious questions is described by that caustic critic, it is evident that this thought is the animating principle of his revolt from Dissent and adhesion to a State Church. We are not concerned here in inquiring how far our popular forms of Dissent are opposed to "culture," whatever that term means. It must be admitted that culture and earnest personal religion are not always reconcilable, but that is only to repeat in other words that the wisdom of this world is often opposed to the wisdom which is from above. It is an old controversy; it existed in our Lord's day, and has come down to our own. It has been often discussed, and the question been looked at in both lights, and argued on both sides, long before Mr. Matthew Arnold borrowed from German criticism the contrast between the Hebrew and Hellenist type of mind. John Foster has an essay on "The Objection of Men of Taste to Evangelical Religion," which shows that the essayist was not insensible to the sins against good taste committed by Bible Christians, chiefly arising from their being the students of one book only. He does not forget, however, as critics of Mr. Arnold's school do, to trace the aversion of men of taste up to its spring head. He is careful to point out that the true source of this aversion arises from the fact that the estimate of the depraved moral condition of human nature is quite different in revelation and polite literature. Consequently, the Redemption by Jesus Christ, which appears with such momentous importance in the one, is, in comparison, a trifle in the other.

There is no bridging over this contrast. To the end of time there will be a "dispute between the Grecians and the Hebrews," as we may call them, on this aspect of the Gospel. It carries with it such humbling estimates of unregenerate human nature, it lays so little stress on man's attainments to recommend him to the Divine favour; it commands all men everywhere to repent in as thrilling tones even on Mar's Hill and to the *culturvolk* of the ancient world, as if it were appealing, in the speech of the men of Lycaonia, to a semi-barbarous people, scarcely above fetish worship. This is the offence of the Gospel, and it is not every day that men of culture like Pascal, Vinet, and others we could name, are content to become fools for Christ, in the sense that the apostle of culture—as we may describe Paul—was contented to be. If a man is not prepared for this sacrifice, and in this sense to take up his cross daily and follow Christ, he is not worthy of Him. The disciple must not expect to be above his Master; it is honour enough to him to be as his Master. This is why spiritual religion ever was and ever will be an aversion to those who are merely men of taste, and the question for the Christian is, not to evade this difficulty, or to stoop to some base compromise, but boldly to face it, and count it honour to suffer shame for His sake. The true Christian has never shrunk from this. He may or may not be a member of some National Church; if, as Henry Martyn, he is so, he will face the ridicule of the formalists and worldly minded of his own cloth and profession. He will belong to some sect within the State Church—an *ecclesiola in ecclesiâ*, as it has been described—in order to reconcile his higher allegiance to Christ with his conformity with the standards of an Establishment, professedly meant to include professors as well as true believers. We do not insist that a spiritual man is bound to withdraw from a Church, the genius of which is, that it is National first and only spiritual afterwards. This question we leave to the decision of each individual conscience; but we cannot abate the demands of Christ to meet the necessities of a theory of the alliance of such opposites as the Church and the world. The first martyr, Stephen, sealed this truth with his blood. He affirmed, when death stared him in the face for saying so, that all the worthies of the Old Testament had been uniformly rejected in their day, and that killing the prophets and then erecting their sepulchres would be the practice of National Churches or the religious world (the two terms connote the same idea) down to the end of time.

Thus that spiritual religion should be despised and rejected as much in our day as in the past, is only what we are bound to expect from the nature of the case. We are not, then, discouraged by the fact that evangelical religion is again passing over into the cold shade of opposition. Earnest pietists in the National Church find it a daily grief that they have to conform with Rationalists on the one hand, and Romanisers on the other. They are trying to purge the State Church of these evils, how feebly and vainly is best known to themselves. We do not wish to dishearten them, or to prophesy failure; but they must have learned very little from the teachings of history if they expect to make a National Church anything more than a reflection of the mind of the nation on religious thought. Whether the result of prosecuting Ritualists and Rationalists is worth the cost, we must leave them to find out for themselves, as they will do in the long run. But we conclude, as we set out, with the conviction that the Church and the world are not allies, but opposites in this present divided state of being, and as the result of that "original sin" which the Pelagian or carnal intellect rejects as a theological figment. We are not concerned to vindicate that truth in this place. We set out with it as the postulate on which all our reasoning on the subject is based. If it is true, it carries with it more than a mere proposition in formal theology; it colours our whole view of the Church and the world, and their relations to each other. It carries with it the admission that the carnal mind is enmity against God; that Divine mysteries are foolishness to the world; and that the psychical intellect cannot understand the things of God, because they are spiritually discerned.

In this point of view we are not in the least disheartened because the true Church—the Lamb's bride—is only a sect of "pietists," whether nominally or not, in communion with some external and National Church. That these "pietists" should fail to make their mark on the age, or to found any external organisation imposing enough to attract the world's lasting respect, is to us a small matter. Nay, more; we are ready to admit that as soon as the pietist party, as they are called in Germany, attempt to combine and form an external sect, with passwords and traditions of their own, they, too, miserably fail and break down. The history of sects, as the Churchman derisively tells us, is a record of failure;

it is endless splitting and subdividing, until, as Mr. Harwood tells us, men of the world are wearied with their divisions, and seek to find rest in the broad bosom of some Catholic Church, which has at least a national if not an œcumenical unity. This decline of the Free Churches and the growth of an Erastianised type of State-Church worship may dishearten timid Dissenters of a traditional type. It may lead them to say that the *zeit geist*, or spirit of the age, has gone against them, and in stress of weather they may make for port or the open haven of Conformity. Be it so; it is not for us to judge our brother or condemn him. But the more believing course is to keep the sea in all weathers, and to trust that when the danger is greatest the Master will be with us, and that He will rebuke the winds and still the waves.

As for success, it is nowhere the promise of the Church; she is promised preservation amid all perils, and in the end a full deliverance. Meanwhile, without courting defeat, Christians are to go on unconcerned from one failure to another in the attempt to settle the relations between the Church and the world. At one time the world persecutes the Church, and anon she patronises it. This is the sum of Church history for six centuries. Then the parts are reversed, and the Church, as the founder of a new society, creates a world, which in the Middle Ages is alternately the rival and the submissive slave of the Church. This carries us on to the age of the Reformation. Here there is another turn of the tables, and National Churches, that invention of the Reformation, as Vinet calls it, spring into existence. Their type is uniformly Erastian; the world rules the

Church, lest the Church should, as in the days of the Papacy, again rule over the world. To use Queen Elizabeth's expressive metaphor—the State sits on the saddle in front, and the Church on the pillion behind. It is this arrangement which so charms writers like Mr. Harwood, and we suppose satisfies their spiritual instincts. If this be so, we can only say they are easily pleased; but their ideal of the Church is scarcely that of earnest Christians of any denomination, and, least of all, of earnest Churchmen within the Establishment. There only remains the last experiment, which never has been fairly tried except in America, and only there during the last sixty or seventy years. The Pilgrim Fathers took over with them traditions of State Churchmanship, which lingered on down to the Revolution, and have only died out slowly in the light of stern necessity. It is too soon, then, to dogmatise as to the future of Christendom, but we may be certain of one thing, that the Establishment principle has no future. How long it may last where its roots in the shape of endowment have struck down so deep in the soil as with us, it is impossible to say. But its final extinction is only a question of time.

Thus it is, that, whether we like it or not, we must look to the sect principle of individualism as the platform of the Church of the future. That it will fail to subdue the world and remove the natural enmity of the carnal mind, we are ready to admit. No spiritual man is so foolish as to suppose that the sect principle is to succeed where that of Catholic unity has failed. But its failure in this latter case will be traced to its true source. We shall not lay the blame, as Churchmen now do, on the State, and say that if properly supported and endowed by the world, we should be able to convert the world. We should know at once our strength and our weakness, and it is as much to know the one as the other. At present, under the alliance theory, it is the old Jewish story of the lame man on the back of the blind man trying to steal the apples, and as they were partners in the crime, so in the punishment. In the future, politicians and Churchmen will be responsible only for their own failures, and since we are prepared to expect the sect principle to fail, we shall feel no disappointment when it does so. But its failure will at last bring on the end when Churches and States, alike carnal and corrupt through the inherent and ineradicable corruption of human nature, shall give up their delegated authority. Then a kingdom will be set up in which the existing distinctions of temporal and spiritual shall disappear. Then cometh the end, when He shall have put down all rule and all authority and power, for He must reign until He hath put all enemies under His feet. Thus Cæsarism and Clericalism are only phases of a moon which is gibbous, and not yet full. Partly lost in the earth's shadow, she does not shine as yet in the full light of her true sun. But when moving out of shadow she comes in full opposition to the sun, these Erastian and Ecclesiastical shadows, which are of the earth, earthy, shall disappear, and she shall be seen full-orbed, and, like the Bride in the Song of Songs, "looking forth as the morning, fair as the moon, clear as the sun, and terrible as an army with banners."

www.ingramcontent.com/pod-product-compliance
Lightning Source LLC
Chambersburg PA
CBHW031249250426
43672CB00029BA/1392